# THE ESSENTIAL
# KLEZMER

# THE ESSENTIAL
# KLEZMER

A Music Lover's Guide to Jewish Roots and
Soul Music, from the Old World to the Jazz Age
to the Downtown Avant-Garde

## by SETH ROGOVOY

Algonquin Books of Chapel Hill    2000

Published by
Algonquin Books of Chapel Hill
Post Office Box 2225
Chapel Hill, North Carolina 27515-2225

a division of
Workman Publishing
708 Broadway
New York, New York 10003

Library of Congress Cataloging-in-Publication Data

Rogovoy, Seth, 1960–
    The essential klezmer : a music lover's guide to Jewish soul music, from
    the Old World to the Jazz Age to the downtown avant garde / by Seth
    Rogovoy.
        p.   cm.
    Includes discography (p. ), bibliographical reference (p. ), and index.
    ISBN 1-56512-244-5
    1. Klezmer music—History and criticism.   I. Title.
ML3528.8 .R64   2000
781.62'924—dc21                                            00-020837


10   9   8   7   6   5   4   3   2   1
First Edition

# Dedication

*This book is dedicated to my grandfather, Baruch Lazar Peretz (1908–1981), of blessed memory, whose singing instilled in me a love for the sound of the* khazones, *and to my grandmother, Rose Schiff Peretz, whose strength of will has been a tremendous inspiration and whose love has been the greatest gift.*

*This book is also for Anna and Willie, their great-grandchildren, coiners of the term* real klezmer. *They know it when they hear it.*

# Contents

## ACKNOWLEDGMENTS

This is my first book, and therefore it feels only right to credit everyone who helped me along the way in my career as a writer. I've been fortunate to work with the best of editors, including Tom Bleezarde at the *Williams Alumni Review,* Jon Garelick at the *Boston Phoenix,* Seth Lipsky and Jonathan Rosen at the *Forward,* Mark Moss at *Sing Out!* magazine, David Holzel at *Moment* magazine, and Laurie Muchnick at *Newsday.*

For over a dozen years I've been a music critic and columnist at the *Berkshire Eagle* in Pittsfield, Massachusetts, one of the best small newspapers in America, in large part due to editors such as Nada Samuels, David Scribner, Charles Bonenti, Clarence Fanto, and Lesley Ann Beck. I owe my deepest gratitude to Jeffrey Borak, who gets the lion's share of the credit for getting me started writing about music and keeping me going through good times and bad, and to Randall Howe, a friend first and foremost, but also a great editor.

One of the best things about writing this book has been enjoying the friendship and support of so many of the musicians who made it all happen in the first place. I am especially indebted to Alan Bern, Hankus Netsky, Lev Liberman, and Michael Alpert for their incredible generosity in opening up their hearts, minds, and archives to me. Thanks also to Frank London, Alicia Svigals, Andy Statman, Henry Sapoznik, Gary Lucas, David Krakauer, Ben Goldberg, David Licht, Lorin Sklamberg, Pete Rushefsky, Stuart Brotman, Itzhak Perlman, David Buchbinder, Joel Rubin, Matt Darriau, Merlin Shepherd, Sherry Mayrent, Eve Sicular, Yosl Kurland, Bob Gluck, Jeff Baker, my dad's friend Eddie Fleishman (who played with the greats, including Naftule Brandwein and Dave Tarras), and the feisty and frustrating but eminently inspiring and lovable John Zorn. All these musicians gave freely and generously of their time and help.

Special thanks to Wolf Krakowski and Paula Parsky, for friendship and Yiddish *hekhsher* and translation. Thanks also to all the musicians of the past and present, simply for making the music, and to all the authors of liner notes—klezmer liner notes are the best!

This book is lovingly illustrated thanks in part to the following photographers and archivists: Lloyd Wolf, Clemens Kalischer, Enid Farber, and Emily Botein at the Center for Traditional Music and Dance, Neil Zagorin at the National Yiddish Book Center, and the folks at YIVO.

I owe a debt of gratitude to my hometown writing pals for their steady emotional support and encouragement throughout the entire process that saw this book through from conception to reality: Jane and Peter Smith, Darra Goldstein and Dean Crawford, Jim and Karen Shepard, Paul Park, and most especially, to Michael Gizzi, a great friend as well as a great poet.

Thanks also to Jared Polens and Jesse Milden for their ongoing interest in my work and for the long-term loans of records and CDs from their own collections, to Jamaica Kincaid for her encouragement, and to Dr. Jeffrey A. Toretsky, for being an early and enthusiastic reader of my manuscript. Other friends who made up a worldwide clipping service as well as a far-flung research and support network included Karen Karp, Harold Lepidus, Peter Stone Brown, Jeffrey Gaskill, Dianne Haas, and Aunt Marsha (she hates it when I call her that—I mean Marsha Peretz Spyros).

Living in a college town meant help was close at hand from my musicologist friends Otha Day and Jennifer Bloxam at Williams

College, as well as the research and loan staff at Sawyer Library and at the Williamstown Public Library. I also want to thank my two best teachers, Richard Ford and Larry Fuchser, whose influence on how I think, read, listen, and write went far beyond the confines of the classroom.

I had help tracking down recordings from two of the best mail-order retailers specializing in Jewish music, Tara Music in Maryland and Hatikvah in Los Angeles. Special thanks especially to Zippy Freedman and Mayer Pasternak at Tara. Also thanks to Hal March at Toonerville Trolley Records right here in Williamstown, Massachusetts.

Thanks also to all the managers, agents, publicists, and record company folk who helped out, including Kazunori Sugiyama at Tzadik Records; Brian Coleman at Braithwaite & Katz; Itzik Becher with the Klezmatics; Joan Sherman with Brave Old World; Steve Burton, Kerry Murphy, Steve Netsky, and Glenn Dicker at Rounder Records; Judith Joiner and Lisa Pardini at Green Linnet/Xenophile; Cindy Byram and Charlie Dahan at Shanachie Records; Harold Hagopian at Traditional Crossroads; Emilie Liepa at Red House Records; Randy Haecker at Sony Legacy; and Sonya Kolowrat at Rykodisc. Thanks also to my friend Michaela O'Brien at Young-Hunter Publicity.

This was the book I was destined to write, but it took Gareth Esersky, my friend and agent, to tell me so. That she found my book a home at Algonquin, where I've enjoyed the great fortune of working with editor Duncan Murrell, is all the more amazing. Thanks also to Dana Stamey, Ina Stern, and everyone else at Algonquin.

I can never thank my parents enough for their unstinting support of everything I've done throughout my life, but thanks to

Lawrence and Stella Rogovoy anyway. Thanks also to the *mekhu-tonim,* Judith and Ben Watkins, for their enthusiastic interest and support.

I owe the greatest thanks and gratitude to my wife, Karin—without whose support and encouragement I would never have even begun writing about music—and to my children, Anna and Willie, whose immediate and ongoing enthusiasm for klezmer was infectious and essential to the completion of this book. I hope you like it.

## NOTES ON USAGE AND STYLE

This book is written for the general reader, and therefore I have attempted to keep the use of technical musical terms and Yiddish words to a reasonable minimum. Given the nature of the subject, however, in some cases the use of such terms could not be avoided. Yiddish words are italicized and defined upon their first introduction in the text. For those who don't read from beginning to end, and who might therefore meet up with a strange-looking word in the middle of the book, glossaries of all Yiddish and musical terms defined in the text and used more than once are also provided in the appendix.

A note regarding Yiddish orthography: For a supposedly dead language, the spelling of Yiddish words using the English alphabet is the subject of quite lively controversy and debate. In its original state, the language uses characters from the Hebrew alphabet, but even then there are various regional differences. There are currently, however, widely accepted guidelines for the spelling of Yiddish words in English as determined by the YIVO Institute for Jewish Research, and in most cases I have tried to abide by the recommendations of experts well versed in those rules.

For Yiddish words that have "crossed over" into English, or those that might be more familiar in a nonstandard spelling, however, I have reserved the right to use the more common spellings, e.g., *Hasid/Hasidim* rather than *khusid/khsidim*. Thus, any variation from YIVO's standard Yiddish should be understood as the author's choice and bears no reflection on anyone else who lent a hand in the editing process of this manuscript.

A note regarding song titles: Until the recording era, klezmer was almost totally an oral tradition, and as such, melodies were passed down from musician to musician without titles, or with titles that merely indicated genre (e.g., "Doina") or function ("Kale Baveynens"). Once musicians began recording these traditional melodies, record labels had to give them titles, but this was mostly done in haphazard fashion, and certainly with no attempt at any consistency in spelling. When referring to a specific recording, therefore, the spelling as it appears on the particular recording being referred to is used, regardless of standard orthography. This isn't meant to perpetuate a confusing tradition, but rather to reflect accurately the music's development as well as to indicate the particular version of a recording.

# THE ESSENTIAL
# KLEZMER

# KLEZMER: A "MUSICAL HOME"

L
ike most Americans my age (I was born in 1960), I was
raised on a steady diet of popular music, beginning with
the Beatles and progressing steadily onward through
whatever the pop charts threw at me. While in my case I wound up
listening to an incredible variety of music as an adult, when I found
myself writing about jazz, rock, pop, folk, funk, country, bluegrass,
blues, experimental, and world-beat music, for the most part my favorite music remained the same stuff I was listening to when I was
sixteen. The same poster of Bob Dylan that stared down on me
from my bedroom wall as a teenager now adorns the wall opposite
from where I sit, writing these words, in my home office.

While I gained an appreciation for all kinds of music in my
work as a critic, my enthusiasms were mostly intellectual ones. I
could expound at length on the various strains of traditional and
electric blues; I had a workable familiarity with the debate over
progressive versus traditional bluegrass; some of the best reviews I
wrote were vivid descriptions of memorable jazz improvisations by
the likes of Dave Brubeck, Sonny Rollins, and Cecil Taylor. But as
much as this music provoked and challenged me—as much as I

was having fun with it—I knew I wasn't connecting with it in the same way, for example, that my friend Tom McHugh connects with Celtic music. When we stand together listening to some great Irish band at our local roots-music nightclub, he seems transported to another time and place. I go along for the ride, but only as a tourist who doesn't speak or understand the local dialect.

I finally got the chance to feel what Tom feels at shows by Irish bands like Black 47 and Solas when I saw the Klezmatics for the first time at the Knitting Factory in New York City in the spring of 1997. This legendary temple of the downtown avant-garde was packed with fans that night for a concert celebrating the release of the group's new recording, *Possessed*. But this was no mere concert. With a mix of *yeshive bokhers*, bridge-and-tunnel types, and a hefty dose of black-clad bohemians packed in tightly together, swaying, jumping, pogoing, and line-dancing to the Klezmatics' eclectic, ecstatic fusion of klezmer, jazz, rock, and reggae, it was a slivovitz 'n' rhythm–fueled affirmation of cultural pride, a middle finger raised to the demon of assimilation, a shout-out to the world that said, "Jewish is hip!"

Something was happening here, and I had to know more about it. Somehow, the coolest, funkiest music in the world—part rock, part R&B, part jazz, part pure improvisation—was being built upon a firm foundation of klezmer, the "traditional, instrumental party music of Yiddish-speaking, Eastern European Jews." For some reason, virtuosos from disparate fields like bluegrass, classical, and avant-garde music were turning to klezmer and finding in the raw material of the *doina* what was for them, as Jews, the personal, musical, and spiritual equivalent of what the twelve-bar blues is to African Americans.

I started listening to everything I could get my hands on: contemporary klezmer, classic recordings, contemporary reworkings of classic recordings. The whining-yet-laughing, self-deprecating melodies of the clarinets were the musical equivalent of the great Jewish comics: Groucho Marx, Lenny Bruce, and Woody Allen. The brassy ensembles of trumpets, trombones, and tubas talking over each other were like a noisy crowd of long-lost aunts, uncles, and cousins at a Jewish family reunion. The soulful, achy violin lines atop the pulsing, jerky, forward-lurching rhythms spoke with sensual intensity and emotional rawness—the voice of the Jewish heart, bleeding but still beating.

Even before I knew on an intellectual level what I was listening to, what I heard spoke to me on a gut level. This was precisely the opposite of how I had assimilated new styles of music in all my years as a critic. While I had learned to differentiate among reels, airs, and jigs, when push came to shove, all Celtic dance tunes "sounded the same" to me, registering on an emotional level as "Celtic dance tunes" and not much more.

With klezmer, however, melodies stood out with distinction and clarity in a way I had never found with the blues, which mostly seemed like variations on the same lament: "Oh Lord, since my baby left me I feel so down and blue." The klezmer vocabulary that mixes "laughing" and "wailing" sounds on the lead instrument, typically the clarinet or violin, was immediately and viscerally recognizable. Somehow, even though I had no background with klezmer or its core repertoire, it was as if I had some innate fluency in it, some inherent capacity to recognize and appreciate its nuances.

I spoke the language.

It was *my* music.

But my story doesn't properly begin at the Knitting Factory.

It begins a half year earlier, when David Krakauer—a founding member of the Klezmatics who at the time had recently left the group to pursue a solo career—came to town to perform. The first klezmer musician I ever interviewed, Krakauer's story would resonate with deeper meaning over the course of the following months and years.

David Krakauer told me that he only really began listening to klezmer music when he started playing it in the late eighties with the Klezmatics. Until that point, he had been a classically trained clarinetist raised on a strict diet of jazz and European art music. "I had no background at all with Jewish music," he said. "The only Jewish tune I ever heard growing up was 'Hava Nagilah.' I basically grew up listening to Schnabel playing the late Beethoven piano sonatas. Then, when I was eleven, [jazz clarinetist] Sidney Bechet."

This seemed impossible. How could you with any confidence or authority play a style of music with which you were totally unfamiliar? But, as David explained, "[a]s soon as I started to play klezmer music, I had the feeling that I knew it very well. Somehow or other there was this incredible recognition. I had to conclude that what I was hearing in the music was the sound and the inflection of my grandmother, of her very heavy, Yiddish-tinged English. So klezmer music, I realized, was Yiddish language in music, and I felt like in a certain way I had found a kind of musical home."

So, too, did I, as a listener and writer, find a "musical home" in klezmer, which brought together many disparate strands of my own background. Unlike David Krakauer, I did have some roots in Jewish music going back to my childhood. For one, I have attended synagogue throughout my life and so was exposed to Jewish prayer melodies, however watered down those might have been in the primarily Reform environment in which I was raised. More significantly, however, my maternal grandfather was a part-time *khazn*—a cantor—with whom I was very close. Around the house Grandpa was always singing great, moving prayers—the ones, I was later to learn from Andy Statman, that were at the foundation of many klezmer tunes.

Undoubtedly, klezmer reconnected me with the melodies my grandfather sang. But at the same time as klezmer was reconnecting me with my own past, it was carving out a space in the present and future of my immediate family. The David Krakauer Trio's *Klezmer Madness!* was the first klezmer CD in our house. My son, three at the time, latched onto it, and every day he would ask to hear "real klezmer"—the term he coined for the Krakauer disk. I was happy to oblige, and every time I played it Willie and his five-year-old sister, Anna, would dance and jump around. The Krakauer CD quickly made it to the top of our household listening chart, where it has pretty much remained until this day.

Then, one day, to my astonishment, I watched Willie go over to the CD player and, with no hesitation, take the Krakauer compact disk out of the jewel box, press the button to open the CD drawer, put the CD in, press the button again to close the drawer, and press the button marked PLAY.

I had never shown Willie how to use the CD player. (Indeed, I hadn't wanted to, as my audio equipment is essential to my work, and I cannot afford to have a broken CD player for more than one day.) But through sheer desire to want to hear this music—to which he had *no* connection, no background other than genetic—my son taught himself how to use the CD player. My children are exposed to a wealth of music—all the styles I listen to for my writing, plus others. Yet when I saw the innate pull that this music exerted on my children, I knew there was something extraordinarily powerful about klezmer far beyond its ability to move people on a dance floor.

After the Krakauer concert, to which my family came along, and which the kids remember to this day—it took place in a big brick church, and any time they see a big brick church in a strange town, they say, innocent of the inherent irony, "that's where we saw klezmer music"—I started listening to more klezmer, and it increasingly became the soundtrack to our daily lives. Andy Statman had something interesting to say about this when I interviewed him soon after for an article in a major metropolitan arts weekly.

In talking about why so many Jews of his and my generation were attracted to klezmer—a music that hadn't played a significant role in the lives of American Jews since before World War II—Statman said, "Like with klezmer music, certain Jewish foods have a tremendous power to activate a feeling of Jewishness among Jews, in a positive way. On one level, it just shows how ready a person's *neshama* [soul] is. Eating the slightest thing, like a bagel and chicken soup, the soul will jump for it and will do some sort of Jewish experience inside a person, because the neshama is really starving. That's another reason, I think, why things are happening now, also among the Jews. I think their souls are really starving and are in some way screaming for nourishment."

The next April, at the Klezmatics concert at the Knitting Factory, I wandered around asking people why they were there. I got many different answers, but the theme running through all of them was that something important was happening, both in terms of the music, which was breaking new ground, and in terms of the greater scene of which it was a part. Here was an entry point back into their culture or religion for twenty- and thirty-somethings who felt disconnected or even alienated from more established or

שלום

Shalom

institutionally identified Jewish practices. As the *New York Times* reported in the fall of 1997, "Jews in their twenties are flocking to Yiddish-language classes and buying klezmer CD's at the city's trendiest record stores. They are searching for usable alternatives to religious orthodoxy and Zionism as the center of Jewish identity."

The music of groups like the Klezmatics and Masada is one aspect of this new Jewish alternative. Alicia Svigals of the Klezmatics affirmed this when she told the *Times*, "The Klezmatics have made it a mission to provide a soundtrack for this new Jewish identity." By combining tradition and innovation, the klezmer revivalists offer contemporary listeners and seekers a way to be more fully themselves, as thoroughly modern people and as Jews. Klezmer offers them, like it offered David Krakauer and eventually myself, a "musical home."

As I write, we are in the midst of a creative peak of the klezmer renaissance, the cutting edge of an overall revival of *yidishkayt*, or Jewish culture. At a time of rising Jewish self-awareness among baby boomers who have been propelled by aging, parenthood, or other circumstances to explore or return to their roots, klezmer is once again fulfilling its age-old role of providing the soundtrack for key life-cycle events like weddings and bar mitzvahs. For a generation raised on music as a path to aesthetic, intellectual, and spiritual fulfillment, klezmer also provides a logical, evocative, and accessible tool toward getting in touch with one's "inner Jew." This, of course, brings the music full circle, back to its origins in the Hasidic prayer melodies that are intended as paths toward meaningful and ecstatic communion with God.

When I set out to chronicle the rebirth of this music and to tell the story of the musicians who sparked its revival, one of the first things I discovered was that the term *klezmer* itself, as applied to a specific style of music, is in fact something of a relatively recent construction. Historically speaking, there is no such thing as "klezmer music." The term *klezmer* is a Yiddish contraction of two Hebrew words: *kley*, meaning vessel, and *zemer*, meaning song. Hence *klezmer* came simply to mean instrument or musician, as in "vessel of song," and was a term applied to the itinerant folk musicians of Eastern Europe.

Thus, klezmer was a term applied to a person, not a style of music. Somewhere along the line, the term *klezmer* also began to denote the style or repertoire of music that the typical Jewish folk musician played. The Soviet-Jewish ethnomusicologist Moshe Beregovski, writing in the 1930s, is believed to have been one of the first to use the term *klezmer* in this manner, applying it to the music played by the *klezmorim*. But it really only caught on as the description of a musical genre in the American revival period that began in the late 1970s. Before then, musicians who played old Jewish dance tunes at American weddings or at vacation resorts in the Catskills simply called it "playing Jewish" or "playing the *bulgars*," a reference to a popular Jewish dance genre. A typical, mid-twentieth-century Jewish-American wedding would include cha-chas, some Glenn Miller, current popular tunes, and a section of the evening set aside for a bit of cultural nostalgia, or "playing Jewish."

When Eastern European–derived Jewish dance music was revived as a cultural and musical artifact in the late 1970s, it needed a name. It wound up being called *klezmer*, in much the same way as Irish-based folk music is called *Celtic*, a term that like *klezmer* has all kinds of connotations—musical, political, and otherwise—which musicians, especially Irish ones, occasionally oppose. There is a subtle attempt to dilute or evade an overt ethnic connection by, for example, calling the music *Celtic* rather than *Irish,* or *klezmer* rather than *Yiddish* or *Jewish.* But two of the original Yiddish-music revival bands call themselves the Klezmorim and the Klezmer Conservatory Band, and Andy Statman's first album was called *Jewish Klezmer Music.* You had the makings of a revival of *some* sort of music, and *klezmer* stuck.

As it turns out, a style that encompasses everything from the acoustic, Old World elegance of Budowitz to the big-band Yiddish swing of the Klezmer Conservatory Band to the funky, second-line rhythms of the New Orleans Klezmer Allstars to the shtetl-metal dissonance of Naftule's Dream, is fodder for plenty of Talmudic-like debate over just what constitutes klezmer. Klezmer music has been variously described as Jewish jazz, Jewish blues, Jewish blue-grass, and Jewish soul music—all are catchy and somewhat re-vealing, but they're also ultimately anachronistic and dismissive attempts to place this centuries-old, Eastern European–derived musical genre into a late-twentieth-century American context. Klezmer has also been accused of being Gypsy, Romanian, Ukrai nian, or Greek music played with a Yiddish accent. It's been mocked as "cartoon music," disdained by musicians as merely "playing Jew-ish" or even "playing out of tune." It's been lost, forgotten, swept under the carpet, abandoned, left for dead, and literally vaporized into smoke, dust, and ashes, along with the bodies of the countless numbers of Jewish musicians piled into the crematoria of Ausch-witz and other Nazi factories of death.

CURIOUSLY, AS THE calendar turns from the twentieth to the twenty-first century, we are witness to an odd, almost mind-boggling phenomenon. Musicians of all colors, stripes, and na-tionalities are playing this lost, forgotten music once again. Among those drawn to klezmer are some of the foremost classical, jazz, folk, bluegrass, and electronic musicians of our time. Perhaps most curiously, a hefty proportion of our most experimental, progressive, forward-looking composers and performers—those pushing the envelope of the downtown avant-garde and the contemporary-classical realms—are doing so from a base rooted in this quaint, ethnic dance music of the Eastern European shtetl.

At the same time, there is a grassroots movement of hundreds if not thousands of local and regional amateur and semiprofessional klezmer bands springing up all around the country and the world. An entire generation of musicians raised on rock and roll are trading in their Chuck Berry riffs for Old World *krekhtsn,* the signature bends and moans—the blue notes—of klezmer. Others are combining the two, finding common ground between the R&B backbeat and the rhythmic pulse of the bulgar, creating dynamic fusions of klezmer and New World sounds.

You've got to make your reservations months in advance to guarantee a spot at KlezKamp, the weeklong seminar and festival held every December in the Catskill Mountains region of New York, where hundreds of aspiring klezmorim gather to train and schmooze with Sid Beckerman, Hankus Netsky, members of the Klezmatics, and other leading figures of the klezmer revival. KlezKamp itself has spawned numerous offspring, including California's KlezKamp West, Montreal's KlezKanada, and western New York's Buffalo on the Roof. And am I hearing things, or as I walk across the campus in the college town where I live, do I hear klezmer blasting out of the same dorm-room windows that were blasting Steely Dan and Talking Heads twenty years ago? And what are those bits of klezmer doing buried inside the latest hits by mega-pop bands like Squirrel Nut Zippers and Ben Folds Five?

*Nu?* What gives?

Back in 1979, well before he began playing klezmer music and while he was still steeped in classical and jazz, clarinetist Krakauer first heard the great klezmer clarinetist Dave Tarras in concert. He remembers one note in particular that Tarras played that sent shivers up his spine. "That's what I love about music—one note that gives people a good feeling," he once told an interviewer.

It is the mystery of that one note that contains klezmer's secret. Perhaps it is a remnant of the music's mystical roots in the Hasidic *nigunim,* the wordless prayer melodies used to induce states of transcendent consciousness. Perhaps it is in the ornamentation adopted from the *khazones,* the shaping and bending of notes, giving them a vocal inflection that speaks of its Yiddish and cantorial roots.

That connection between instrumental and vocal music—the human voice as heard through the violin or clarinet—cannot be underestimated, and it is undoubtedly in part what people respond to, what gives the music such warmth, what makes the music "sing," "laugh," and "cry," sometimes all three simultaneously. The emotional spirit of the soloist is the identifying characteristic of klezmer at its best, and it is this aspect to which contemporary audiences and musicians are most responsive. In the face of so much historical adversity and oppression, klezmer remains the raw sound of the human spirit laughing, crying, and singing—all three, impossibly, at the same time.

Klezmer, ultimately, is a music of possibilities. Like folk and classical music, it is based on rigorous, highly stylized forms, with rules regarding tempo, meter, and mode, or where the notes fall in a particular scale. But like jazz and rock music, klezmer allows for —if not wholesale improvisation—an inordinate amount of personal expression. Klezmer, like jazz, is a performer's music, and in the hands of a true artist, there's nothing greater than the musical, mystical ecstasy conjured up by the klezmer soloist.

The conventional definition of klezmer as "the instrumental party music of Yiddish-speaking, Eastern European Jews" goes a long way toward describing where klezmer came from, but it leaves out about one hundred years of klezmer history—ignoring the fact that along with the millions of Jews who emigrated from Eastern Europe to the United States at the turn of the twentieth century, so came klezmer, which like every other aspect of Jewish culture, subsequently underwent a process of Americanization and assimilation that spurred new and creative developments in the music while also rendering it safe for American audiences. And the definition does not even begin to address what has happened since the klezmer revival of the 1970s, with "Eastern European" giving way to a whole host of other influences, American and otherwise; klezmer of the contemporary renaissance finds itself, rightly or wrongly, grouped as a subset of any one of a number of contemporary, "world-beat" fusions.

In America, klezmer has enjoyed three vital periods. The first was a result of the mass wave of immigration in the late nineteenth and early twentieth centuries, when immigrant klezmorim such as Dave Tarras and Naftule Brandwein carved their own musical niches at a time when jazz was popular, variously resisting and integrating American influences into their playing styles. The second is what we will call the revival period, which began with performers like Andy Statman and groups like the Klezmorim, Kapelye, and the Klezmer Conservatory Band, all of whom engaged in a roots-oriented exploration of traditional music. The revival fed into a third period, in which the more talented and adventurous musicians among the revivalists began adding their own musical backgrounds to that tradition, including most obviously rock, jazz, and classical influences. This period of intensive innovation is the klezmer renaissance, in which we are still happily luxuriating.

Klezmer—or neo-klezmer, as some prefer—is one of the most thrilling, vibrant, *new* styles of music currently being played. What other single genre of music could boast personalities as wide ranging as Israeli-born classical violinist Itzhak Perlman, African American clarinetist Don Byron, bluegrass-fusion pioneer Andy Statman, and downtown avant-gardnik and free-jazz maven John Zorn, all in the same basket?

By implication, this book also profiles the changing face of the listener: from the townspeople of the East European shtetls to the noblemen of the Polish court to the audiences at the prewar Yiddish theater to the leisure-suited denizens of the Catskills to contemporary college kids and black-clad hipsters with fashionable tzitzit peeking out from beneath their jackets. Increasingly, neo-klezmer speaks to an audience of Jew and Gentile alike, the former attracted to it for historical and cultural reasons, the latter purely for the music's undeniable poignancy and emotional pull, to say nothing of its wit and inventiveness.

This book is not a musicological or ethnomusicological analysis of klezmer, nor is it intended to be a social history of the music. Rather, in recognition of the simple fact that music exists on recordings for the vast majority of people, it is my aim to recount the history and development of the music with reference to the available recordings, in order to enhance the contemporary listener's enjoyment and appreciation of those recordings. The stories of many of the most significant recording artists will be told; many of the key personalities of the revival and renaissance periods will speak in their own words about how klezmer music was revived and what their particular intentions were in reconstructing and re-vivifying the music. Finally, this book includes a descriptive and critical guide to the available recordings, so that readers can make informed choices about which ones to buy and enjoy.

My own personal odyssey vis-à-vis klezmer and its concomitant spiritual element is ongoing, and while it is by no means the focus of this text, it does, I hope, inform what follows in a subtextual or contextual manner.

Which of course is just a fancy-schmantzy way of saying, in the language of m-m-m-m-my generation: KLEZMER ROCKS!

## CHAPTER 1

# OLD WORLD KLEZMER

The klezmer music we hear today, the music of the contemporary klezmer renaissance, derives its characteristic flavor and sound—indeed, its very soul—from the music played by nineteenth-century musicians of Eastern Europe. It is undoubtedly that haunting, Old World quality, combined with a fresh, contemporary outlook, to which listeners respond when hearing the music of violinist Alicia Svigals, clarinetist Margot Leverett, vocalist Lorin Sklamberg, or keyboardist Alan Bern. These university- and conservatory-trained musicians, raised on rock and roll and well versed in jazz and ethnic folk musics, have steeped themselves in the sounds of the Old World klezmorim. What comes out when they write and play is, therefore, an ecstatic fusion of old and new. Undoubtedly it is precisely that fusion that gives the music its added emotional depth, that accounts for its raw power to move the heart, the soul, and the feet, that induces an immediate sense of faraway recognition, even for those who are miles and generations and cultures apart from the shtetlekh of Galicia and Bukovina.

While the Old World klezmorim mainly entertained at weddings, there were a few other occasions for which they provided live music, such as this *siyum ha-Torah*, the dedication of a newly completed Torah scroll, in Dubrovna, Belorussia.

There is no single key that can unlock the secrets of klezmer or account for its ability to move a listener or to tug at heartstrings. But just as rock and roll fans mine the life and times of Elvis Presley in search of the singular moment when he combined country and R&B to create the ultimate popular fusion, or just as blues fans trace Robert Johnson to the fateful crossroads where he made his legendary deal with the devil, or as jazz buffs try to pin down just how Louis Armstrong developed the freedom to blow his improvised compositions, thereby inventing modern jazz as we know it, so, too, do we look to the Old World in search of, if something short of a singular key moment or musical invention, some sort of musical and cultural signposts to help illuminate the extraordinary mystery of klezmer's lasting appeal. At the very least, what we eventually learn is that today's klezmer is in many respects a retelling of the life and times of the Old World klezmorim.

WITH NO RECORDINGS to access directly and very little in the way of musical notation to go by, much of what we know of Old World klezmer is contained in the pages of nineteenth-century Yiddish literature. Fortunately for our purposes, the colorful klezmorim were favorite characters of great Yiddish writers like I. L. Peretz and Sholem Aleichem, whose works have been widely anthologized and are readily available to contemporary readers. If these writers couldn't quite record the actual *sound* of the music played by Old World musicians, at least they did leave us with rich, colorfully descriptive, well-rounded accounts of real and imagined klezmer musicians and their milieu.

Perhaps the most famous literary account of a klezmer is found in Sholem Aleichem's novella, *Stempenyu*. Based on the historical figure of Yosele Druker (1822–1879), a violinist and composer from Berdichev whose *nom de musique* was Stempenyu, Aleichem's novella includes some beautifully descriptive passages of the violinist's playing:

> He would grab his fiddle, give it a swipe with his bow—just one, no more—and already it would begin to speak. But how, do you think, it spoke? With real words, with a tongue, like a living per-

son. . . . Speaking, arguing, singing with a sob, in the Jewish manner, with a shriek, with a cry from deep within the heart, from the soul. . . . Different voices poured out all kinds of songs, all so lonely, melancholy, that they would seize your heart and tear out your soul, sap you of your health. . . . Hearts would become full, overflowed, eyes would fill with tears. People would sigh, moan, weep.

In this passage and others, Aleichem captures so much of the essence of the music as we know it—its mournful aspect, its questioning tone, its spoken quality. Aleichem's story, subtitled "A Jewish Romance," is full of romantic intrigue, reflecting the passion that swirled around the music and its players. The same combination of spirituality and sensuality that powers contemporary African American soul music appears throughout the pages of Aleichem's *Stempenyu*.

"The commotion Stempenyu caused when he'd come into a shtetl with his band, the excitement that coursed through the town, is indescribable," writes Aleichem, who goes on in the course of approximately one hundred pages to describe just that sensation and turmoil in strikingly contemporary terms. Stempenyu may well have been the first rock star, the precursor of Mick Jagger, Alice Cooper, or Marilyn Manson: "They say he was acquainted with all the witches and warlocks, and that if he even felt like stealing a girl away from her intended he could. He knew a kind of spell, and all he had to do was look at her, just a direct look at a young woman, and she would be his—heaven protect us!"

In large part, Sholem Aleichem's story is about just one of those married girls, a modest but romantically inclined fan of Stempenyu's named Rachel, who allows her heart to be stolen and betrayed by the larger-than-life figure. "Something tugged on her heart, something stroked her, but what it was, she did not fathom."

Readily available in several easy-to-find translations and anthologies, *Stempenyu*—whose very name came to be a Yiddish synonym for "talented musician"—is must reading for those seeking to know more about the world of the nineteenth-century klezmorim.

Klezmorim also appear in many Yiddish short stories. A simple, two-and-a-half page story called "A Musician's Death" by I. L. Peretz, for example, is loaded with details and revealing glimpses of the Old World klezmorim. Written in 1892, the plot finds Mikhl, the patriarch of a klezmer dynasty, lying on his deathbed, surrounded by his wife and their eight sons, who like him are all musicians. We deduce that they are penniless, as we are told that the expenses of Mikhl's funeral and burial will be covered by a charitable organization.

When we meet her, however, Mikhl's wife, Mirl, has not reconciled herself to his imminent death. She is in a rage against the world. She implores the men at the synagogue to pray for Mikhl, as is the Jewish tradition, in the hope that their prayers will be heard up above and that Mikhl's meeting with his maker can be postponed. She castigates her sons, blaming her husband's illness on their wild and irreligious ways. She admonishes them that "The *kapelye* [band of musicians] is losing its glory. There will never be a proper wedding again. No Jew will be able to enjoy a true celebration." She lambastes them for having performed at non-Jewish affairs and for having eaten *treyf,* nonkosher food, connecting their refusal to abide by the traditional dictates of their religious faith with their father's sorry fate. The sons refuse even to don their tzitzit, their ritual fringes, for just one last show of respect. She screams and hollers at them, but they just stand silently, staring at the floor, until finally Mikhl himself pleads with her to stop.

This only further incites Mirl, and she turns her attention to her dying husband, rattling some old skeletons in the closet along the way. It turns out that in fine musicianly fashion, Mikhl has his own sins for which to answer. Mirl accuses him of having long pined for another woman, to which Mikhl responds laughingly that there have been many other women, not just one. "A woman is a woman, and musicians are drawn to them the way your hand is drawn to a wound," he says. (Rock and rollers, apparently, were not the first touring musicians to enjoy the favors of groupies.) And as for his sons, he forgives them for calling him a drunk behind his back, even if he was admittedly fond of more than his fair share of slivovitz.

Finally, after much screaming, crying, and hair pulling all around, Mikhl commands his weeping sons to pick up their instruments and play. Out come three fiddles, a clarinet, a bass, and a horn—a family kapelye. And Mikhl's last command to them is to "play well," and not to "clown around at a poor wedding."

IT IS FROM this simple tale and others like it that we garner most of our understanding of the life, times, and character of the klezmorim. They were an irreverent, irreligious, and even immoral bunch—the very cliché of the dissolute musician. For all their efforts, they died without so much as a ruble to their names. They were a hereditary caste, with kapelyes sometimes consisting of members of one family, fathers and sons alike. The instruments they played included violin, clarinet, bass, and trumpet. And as much as they enjoyed playing, they only gave as much as they got—they were as likely to mess around at a poor wedding, where presumably the guests were unable to tip generously, as they were to pull out all stops at a higher-class affair where the rubles flowed freely.

# THE JEWISH PALE OF SETTLEMENT IN RUSSIA, 1835–1917

SWEDEN

St. Petersburg

Lake Pskov

Lake Llmen

Baltic Sea

Moscow.

KOVNO

VITEBSK

GERMANY    SUWALKI    VILNA

PLOCK    LOMZA

MOGILEV

KALISZ  WARSAW    GRODNO    MINSK

SEDLITS

RADOM

RUSSIA

KIELCE    LUBLIN

PIOTRKOW

VOLHYNIA    CHERNIGOV

AUSTRIA HUNGARY

Kiev.

POLTAVA

KIEV

PODOLIA

BESSARABIA

EKATERINOSLAV

KHERSON

RUMANIA    Nikolaev.

TAURIDA    Sea of Azov

Sebastopol.  Yalta    Black Sea

Throughout the nineteenth and early twentieth centuries, the Russian Tsars confined Jews to an area known as the Pale of Settlement, which included parts of present-day Poland, Lithuania, and Romania. Travel within the Pale was highly regulated.

# WESTERN AND MEDIEVAL ROOTS

The music we call klezmer is a product of the unique Jewish culture of Eastern Europe, a world created out of an improvised exile resulting from the slow exodus of Jews from Western and Central Europe, where they had lived for hundreds of years under varying degrees of tolerance and oppression. Beginning as early as the fourteenth century, Jews gradually made their way east, where, having fled successive expulsions, persecutions, inquisitions, and worse, they were halfheartedly welcomed or tolerated by Polish noblemen, Russian tsars, and other local authorities, and where they began once again to build a civilization of their own within a diaspora.

These Jews brought with them a musical tradition that can be traced back to Western and Central Europe, where small, itinerant ensembles of Jewish folk musicians were found in France, Germany, and other countries. Here they undoubtedly picked up music from the world around them: Teutonic folk melodies, troubadour songs, and church music. A typical wedding scene among wealthy Italian Jews in the late sixteenth century featured professional singers conducted by the composer Salomone Rossi, or Salomone Ebreo (Solomon the Hebrew) of Mantua. Rossi's "Wedding Ode" set an anonymous wedding poem to elaborate, Renaissance-style, split-chorus *(chori spezzati)* music, an early example of Jewish music blending with an indigenous, non-Jewish style to create something new. Along with the singers, Rossi brought an instrumental emsemble, including viols, recorders, harps, and a drum—a kind of protoklezmer ensemble. Dances were led by a dance caller, as a troupe of wedding jesters, acrobats, and jugglers entertained the onlookers. In sum, the scene is a prototype of the Eastern European wedding.

The various social, cultural, legal, and religious forces bearing down on Jewish musicians in Western and Central Europe all helped to shape what was eventually to become the kapelye of Eastern Europe. Along with trade and moneylending, music was one of the few professions permitted to Jews by medieval European authorities. Thus, in every major city in Europe there were professional bands of Jewish musicians who played for their own people as well as for non-Jews. Some Jews even became court musicians, and others wound up supplying music for church ceremonies.

An active guild of klezmorim formed in Prague in 1558, and by 1641 it had won the right for its members to play for non-Jews.

Note the proliferation of violins, or *fidls*, in this Old World *kapelye*. The horns, drum, and clarinet show the influence of Tsarist military bands on the instrumental lineup of the group.

The guild also enforced strict discipline in its ranks, requiring daily synagogue attendance and weekly studies with a rabbi. Other well-known bands were based in Fürth, Frankfort, and Berlin. These groups traveled the countryside, playing markets and fairs and at inns and saloons. These bands consisted primarily of violins and cellos or double basses, with the *tsimbl* or *hackbrett,* two variations on the hammered dulcimer, gaining increasing popularity throughout the seventeenth century. An illuminated Hebrew manuscript shows a trio of musicians—two violinists and a bassist—entertaining diners at a banquet in Alsace in about 1700.

Given all this, the lot of the Jewish musician was always precarious, as he served at the whim of two masters: the local Gentile authorities and the particular rabbinical authority of his region. In an era of little to no centralized state or Jewish religious control, the restrictions imposed on him by either one could be quite arbitrary. And as these restrictions varied from place to place depending on local rule, this posed great hardship on traveling musicians who never knew just what to expect in the next town.

Regulations varied, for example, as to the days of the week or hours of performance to which a Jewish musician was limited, as well as the number of musicians allowed in one ensemble. Even the kinds of instruments Jews could play were restricted—they were often limited to so-called soft instruments, including stringed instruments and flutes. The rabbinical authorities themselves could be ruthless toward musicians, given the Jewish tradition, dating back to the destruction of the Second Temple in Jerusalem in 70 C.E., that forbade the playing of instrumental music anywhere but at weddings and on designated holidays.

Within this highly regulated framework, the success of a particular ensemble could unintentionally spell its doom. While

Gentiles sometimes preferred Jewish musicians to Christian ones because of their reputation for greater modesty and sobriety as well as their more cosmopolitan repertoire, this preference easily provoked a backlash tinged with anti-Semitism. In Bohemia in the mid-1600s, for example, Christian musicians asked the authorities to ban Jews from playing at Christian festivities, complaining that they were unable to keep strict rhythm or time, and that they "vulgarized" or imitated Christian music "in a miserable manner."

As a result of such protests, and as part of a generally worsening climate of hostility toward Jews in general in Central Europe in the seventeenth century, further restrictions were applied to Jewish musicians. In Metz, for example, only trios were permitted—quartets for weddings—and those not properly registered as living in Metz could hire only one musician at a time. Families often had to hold their weddings outside of their immediate communities in order to sidestep these restrictions. Beginning in the 1700s in Germany, Jews were no longer free to wander the countryside and hire themselves out, but were taxed heavily and required to apply for permission to play from the local governmental authority.

## THE SUN RISES IN THE EAST

By the late seventeenth century, the balance of Jewish civilization in Europe had shifted eastward, where Jews had traded the harsh regulation of the Western European ghetto for the relative isolation and autonomy of the Eastern European shtetl. Kicked out of Spain, Portugal, and then Central Europe in succession since the 1500s, Jews found a home of sorts in what became known eventually as the Pale of Settlement, an expanse of territories to which they were restricted that now includes parts of Poland, Romania, Ukraine,

Belarus, and Lithuania, stretching from the Black to the Baltic Seas. The territory—362,000 square miles—encompassed 20 percent of European Russia, 4 percent of the entire Russian empire. At the beginning of the nineteenth century, the Jewish population in the Pale numbered approximately one million; by the turn of the twentieth century, that figure had more than quintupled to five and a half million, making it perhaps the largest contiguous Jewish settlement in history.

Jews were spread throughout the Pale, about half in small towns and cities, the other half in rural villages. Contrary to the popular image of Eastern European Jews as rural shtetl-dwellers, many Jews lived in cosmopolitan cities such as Vilna, Minsk, Odessa, Kiev, and Kishinev. While life in the east, particularly in pre-nineteenth-century Poland—a haven of sorts for Jews since the early Middle Ages—was in some ways a marginal improvement over life in the west, Jewish life in Eastern Europe was also highly restricted, with rhythms imposed both by the limits of tolerance on the part of the non-Jewish hosts and by the rigorous structure that Jewish law and tradition gave to every aspect of life.

For the klezmorim, whose presence was considered as essential as that of the bride and groom at every wedding, such a concentrated settlement of Jews provided the means to scratch out a living, however meager or modest. Although most klezmorim were full-time, professional musicians, some worked other jobs, particularly as barbers, shoemakers, and carpenters. As was traditional with most occupations in the world of the shtetl, however, the job of klezmer was passed down from father to son (no women need apply in a society that banned women in public performance) in a kind of hereditary dynasty, although to call it a dynasty belies the low rung the klezmer occupied on the social ladder.

*Yikhes,* or social status, in traditional Jewish societies was calculated through a measure combining a family's wealth and relative level of education, and klezmorim typically scored low on both accounts. Musicians rarely earned large sums, they tended to be uneducated and irreligious, and their transient lifestyle lacked the sort of stability on which the ethical foundations of traditional village life were built. Their frequent travels and freelance way of life also undoubtedly brought them into contact with a wider variety of characters than the typical shtetl dweller saw in a lifetime. We learn from contemporaneous accounts, particularly from fictional portrayals such as the Peretz story previously mentioned, that although valued for their musical services, among their fellow Jews the klezmorim were seen as little better than criminals—dissolute drunkards, gamblers, and womanizers—a status or reputation shared throughout Europe by their occasional non-Jewish musical partners, the Gypsies. As such, the klezmorim ranked near the bottom of the social order. Or, as a relative once said of a mother who consented to have her daughter marry a tailor, another occupation of relatively low status, "If she married her oldest daughter to a *tailor,* to whom would she marry her youngest daughter? A *musician?*"

In its freelance nature—permeated by an all-consuming uncertainty about the next gig, and hence, the next few rubles the klezmorim's was a life not so different from that of the contemporary musician who ekes out a living playing weddings, private parties, and the occasional pickup gigs in local bars or nightspots. Indeed, the klezmorim even played bar gigs, as the majority of taverns in western Russia where the klezmorim might play for non-Jewish customers (Jews tended not to patronize taverns) were leased and operated by Jews until 1861, when the Russian government took over the sale and distribution of liquor, which up until that point had been almost exclusively the province of Jews.

In the small town of Pitovska, as a story told by Israeli composer and folklorist Yehoiakin Stutchewsky goes, there was a sugar-processing plant owned by Potovsky, an absentee Polish nobleman. Potovsky sent a message to his local overseer to prepare for a visit to the plant by the owner and a coterie of his fellow noblemen. In the scramble to put together a welcoming party, the only musicians available to perform for the occasion were the famed klezmorim of Zaslaw.

The overseer called on Yankel the Fiddler, the leader of the Zaslaw troupe, and hired him to provide the music for the party, but only on the condition that the musicians read from sheet music. Conditions in the Pale being what they were, Yankel could not very well turn down the well-paying gig, and so he agreed to the conditions and assured the overseer that he could supply him with everything as requested.

When he told them about the upcoming gig in Pitovska, Yankel's klezmorim were all very excited, not only to be playing for such a distinguished crowd, but for the handsome fixed sum they would receive, instead of just the usual table tips. But when Yankel told them that in order to make the gig they had to read music, they were crestfallen, as none of them could read, or even owned, any music.

Yankel told them not to worry. "Go to the market and buy some music stands, and bring them to the gig along with a Bible or prayer book," he said. When they got to the party, they set up their music stands, opened their books on them, and began to play. They all kept their gazes focused on the Hebrew characters in the books in front of them. As the music played, the guests danced, and the party was a great success.

One of the guests however, an amateur pianist from Warsaw,

grew suspicious. He had heard that Jewish musicians were un-trained amateurs who played strictly by ear. When the musicians took a break, he walked over to where they were and peeked at their music. "What strange notation," he said to one of them. "Is this some sort of witchcraft?"

The musicians panicked, but without skipping a beat, Yankel took control of the situation. "Ah," he said, "you see our special kind of musical notation, known only to Jewish musicians." The nobleman looked again at the odd squiggles on the page and, not recognizing the Hebrew alphabet, merely shrugged and nodded and walked away. The moment of crisis passed, the party resumed, and the klezmorim walked away with enough rubles to get them through the lean part of the musical season.

WHILE JEWS WERE spread throughout the Pale, this didn't mean that the entire territory was an easily traversed, all-Jewish ghetto. In fact, Jews were a minority in the region, with Jewish towns and villages isolated from one another. Travel throughout the Pale was difficult and subject to various restrictions, and Jews were often obliged to pay a "Jew-toll" upon entering a city and even then were only allowed to remain within the vicinity for one day. Some musicians were able to transcend such hardship and indig-nity by attracting the sponsorship of a local or regional ruler or no-ble. Put on salary, they might even move their family and those of their fellow musicians to the nobleman's land. Other musicians were official hires of a particular Hasidic religious community, and thus were able to opt out of the life of the itinerant freelancer and enjoy a more stable existence.

A few klezmorim developed reputations over time and became celebrities of sorts, such as Stempenyu, about whom a character in

Sholem Aleichem's novella cries out, "If only God will let me have Stempenyu for my youngest daughter's wedding! Oh, Lord, oh Lord!"

In addition to gaining fame on the wedding circuit, occasionally, based on pure talent and virtuosity, a klezmer would "cross over," to use a contemporary marketing term, to the world of the concert stage, where he elevated the "folk" music to the level of "art" music, or music purely for listening. Such a musician was Gusikow. Born into a family of klezmorim in Shklow on the border of Russia and Poland in 1806, Michael Joseph Gusikow was taught the flute by his father. By 1831 a lung illness he had contracted— probably tuberculosis, which was rampant in the Old World— precluded his playing the flute, and Gusikow began playing the hackbrett, a type of hammered dulcimer.

Eventually, Gusikow came up with an instrument of his own design, the *shtroyfidl,* or straw-fiddle, a kind of folk xylophone built out of chromatically tuned wooden slabs laid out on a bed of straw. The slabs were played with small sticks, much like the tsimbl, but one of the most attractive features of the instrument was its portability. The musician only had to pack along the wooden slabs and sticks, as straw was readily available anywhere. For traveling musicians, this was no small consideration, and the straw-fiddle quickly caught on with itinerant klezmorim.

It wasn't before long that Gusikow's virtuosity on the straw-fiddle gained him renown throughout and even beyond the Pale. He played concerts in major cities such as Kiev and Odessa, and he even went as far as Vienna and Leipzig. After seeing Gusikow perform in 1836, the composer Felix Mendelssohn wrote, "He is quite a phenomenon, a famous fellow, inferior to no virtuoso in the world, both in execution and facility. He, therefore, delights me more with his instrument of wood and straw than many with their

## KLEZMER INSTRUMENTATION

**Violin, or *fidl*:** The lead instrument of the Old World kapelye, which often had more than one violin. The second, or *sekunde*, would play rhythm accompaniment. The fidl created the characteristic sound of Old World klezmer, with the voicelike bends and moans called krekhtsn, patterned after the krekhtsn of the khazn.

**Tsimbl:** A trapezoidal, hammered-dulcimer-type instrument dating back to the Middle Ages in Central Europe. Sometimes played as a solo instrument, often as part of the kapelye, playing the role of the piano, and sometimes in duet with the fidl or flute. Closely related to the cimbalom.

**Clarinet:** First introduced into Old World kapelyes in the early to mid–nineteenth century, the clarinet slowly overtook the fidl as the lead instrument of the kapelye. Like the fidl, the clarinet boasts a wide range and the ability to mimic the bends and moans of the human voice adapted from the krekhts of the khazones. But the clarinet also has a greater dynamic range, meaning it could outshout the fidl, and thus it eventually usurped the violin's place in the ensemble so completely that many New World bands didn't even have violins. C and Eb instruments were preferred by early klezmer clarinetists, as opposed to the standard Bb instrument of today.

**Trumpets, trombones:** Gained ascendance in large kapelyes as musicians returned from their courses of duty in the Russian army.

**Accordion:** A late-nineteenth-century addition to the kapelye, first as a solo instrument, then as an accompaniment.

pianofortes, just because it is such a thankless kind of instrument. . . . It is long since I so much enjoyed any concert as this, for the man is a true genius." Another reviewer wrote, "Out of wood and straw he charms forth tones of deep melancholy, of profound emotion. Out of wood and straw he knows how to produce the finest vibrations, sounds of most tender softness. How painful and tender sound his national tunes." Gusikow finally succumbed to his illness in 1837, but not before his reputation was firmly established, and his name lives on in Yiddish folk literature as one of the great folk virtuosos.

Interestingly enough, today we see mirror images of Gusikow in Giora Feidman and Itzhak Perlman, both of whom, after having established themselves as virtuosos of the classical concert stage, "crossed over" to the music of their forebears. The result in Perlman's case is the ongoing "In the Fiddler's House" project, including two best-selling CDs, a home video, and annual concert tours featuring Perlman playing with four of the top klezmer bands in the world.

Other great klezmorim whose names lived on beyond their tenure include Mordchele Rosenthal (1787–1848), who wrote tunes combining Gypsy and Hungarian motifs and led an ensemble consisting entirely of Jews disguised as Gypsies, and Aron Moyshe Kholodenko (1828–1902), who gained widespread fame as the violinist Pedotser, one of the most popular composers of the late-nineteenth-century Ukraine. Pedotser's compositions were more ambitious than the typical dance repertoire, and he was the rare klezmer composer whose tunes were actually notated. Thanks to his students, who copied down many of his compositions, Pedotser's works eventually made their way into the hands of the Soviet-Jewish ethnomusicologist Moshe Beregovski and thus have been preserved for posterity.

These celebrity musicians were rare exceptions. The vast majority of klezmorim were professionals who had to scrape by in order to survive and provide for their families. Just as was done in various Central European cities, klezmorim formed guilds in Eastern Europe, which in addition to providing social welfare benefits, helped regulate territorial distribution of the various kapelyes and adjudicated disputes between competing bands when they arose.

The main role of the Old World klezmorim—much like to-day's ordinary working musicians, whether full- or part-timers—was to play music at weddings. The importance of weddings to the small communities of Eastern Europe cannot be overstated. As in most traditional communities, weddings were the glue that bound together the town or village. By joining families to one an-other and perpetuating a community's future, weddings—even for the poorest members of the community—were opportunities for community-wide celebrations. Even in the darkest days of the shtetl, weddings provided a reason to celebrate, and everyone was invited. And, of course, there was always music.

A wedding in the shtetl wasn't a wedding without a kapelye.

These wedding gigs were more than just the klezmorim's bread and butter; playing at weddings was one of the only religiously sanctioned or rabbinically tolerated outlets for live musical performance in a culture that otherwise frowned on instrumental music. Although the klezmorim got around the religious proscription against playing instrumental music by entertaining at fairs, marketplaces, and taverns—places beyond the legislative realm of the religious authorities—for the most part weddings were the mainstay of the klezmorim's professional career.

Klezmer's happy, upbeat, frenetic quality can be traced back to its origins as a party music, and as a functional music intended for the highly codified ritualistic dancing that made up a large part of the wedding ceremony. The klezmorim's rhythms were essential elements of the *simkhe,* or religious celebration, and helped all to ful-

The Old World wedding has inspired countless artistic representations, such as the one in this oil painting by Saul Raskin called "Wedding in a Shtetl" (1956).

fill the *mitzve,* or religious duty, of making the wedding a joyous occasion for the bride and groom.

What is all too often lost in the well-intentioned discussion of klezmer as functional party or dance music, however, is its equally important function as music for listening and reflection. Weddings, then as now, were about more than just dancing, and thus wedding bands, then as now, played more than just dance music. At least a third of the Old World klezmer repertoire was music meant for listening to—poignant music that expressed and enhanced the serious religious and spiritual aspects of the event.

Thus, taken as a whole, klezmer was the sound track to an event—one that often lasted several days or even weeks—that included a broad range of activity and emotion, from the most reflective and introspective moments to the most active and extroverted. To refer to klezmer as only "party" or dance music, therefore, undercuts an essential element of the repertoire—much the same as if jazz were viewed only as a dance form, with no acknowledgment of its lyrical or reflective sides.

Each part of the wedding ritual had its own choreography, its own ritual, and its own style of music. The klezmorim led processionals of the bride's and groom's parties, greeted the arrival of the guests, entertained during the banquet, provided the rhythms for dancing, and led the guests home at the end. Working in tandem with the *badkhn*—the overall master of ceremonies, jester, folk poet—the klezmorim gave shape and structure to the entire event.

For the most part, Old World weddings were arranged affairs —marriage for love was the rare exception. Each town or region had a *shadkhn,* or matchmaker, whose job it was to suggest a likely pairing between two prospective mates. The matchup was not as much one of two individuals as it was of two families, and the criteria used by the shadkhn was mostly that of yikhes—the generally accepted impression of a family's social status, which was derived from a combination of its relative wealth and piety. Thus, a rabbi's son would not marry a tailor's daughter, but the offspring of two peddlers might be suited for each other.

In any case, the shadkhn's match was only the first step in a long, involved process that involved various negotiations over the bridal dowry and an inspection of the potential bride by the groom's female relatives. In the end, once the fathers of the prospective newlyweds came to agreement, a contract was drawn up and plans were set in motion for the wedding.

The wedding day itself often began with a *khosns tish* and a *kale bazetsns,* the Old World equivalents of a bachelor party and bridal shower, respectively. At the khosns tish, it was customary for the groom to attempt to deliver a *drash,* or a speech of religious learning. To save him from embarrassment, however, soon after he began his speech, it was drowned out by the songs and festive merrymaking of his male friends, aided by the musicians in attendance.

While the men were yucking it up at the khosns tish, the women were attending to the bride at the kale bazetsns, or the ritual seating of the bride. This ceremony marked the end of her nuptial preparations, which would have included a visit to the *mikve,* or ritual bath, with a processional led by the klezmorim. At the kale bazetsns, sometimes called the *kale baveynens,* or the bride's tears, the bride's closest female friends and relatives gathered solemnly to pay their respects. If it hadn't been done so already, the bride's hair would be braided and cut, for once married, a woman no longer grew out her hair. Instead, out of a belief that it would be immodest for a married woman to display her natural hair to anyone but her husband, for the rest of her life she would wear a kerchief or a wig over her shaven head. Those attending would "weep for her hair" along with her, in a ceremony full of obvious symbolism, egged on by the badkhn and klezmorim, who would perform bazetsnish songs, rhymed verses in Yiddish studded with quotes from the Torah, such as this one:

Lovely bride, let me sing and tell you
About the old customs.
How you shall behave and what you shall do,
Because this stool stands in the middle of the room,
The stool is in the center.

Till Wednesday you must rise early,
When you will be led to the Main (river)
And wheat and corn will be thrown at you,
To which old and young will come,
Ah, the whole community.
Ah, the whole community.

Here, you will be betrothed,
With a little gold ring.
Lovely bride, you may be sure,
That after the ceremony, it will become yours,
That after the ceremony, it will become yours;

Well then, dear bride, understand me well,
And ponder now during your greatest joy.
Realize that you will not live forever.
And you must avoid the evils of the world.
And you must avoid the evils of the world.

Interspersed between such ritual songs, the klezmorim played kale baveynens—mournful, contemplative, and expressive melodies reflecting the ambivalent, bittersweet nature of the ritual, such as the one that leads off Alicia Svigals's *Fidl,* her solo CD, or "Baveynen di Kale" on *Beregovski's Khasene,* by the Joel Rubin Jewish Music Ensemble.

As much as these weddings were happy occasions, they were also tinged with ambivalence, sadness, and even fear. Old World marriages were not the result of love affairs between sweethearts, but were the product of negotiated, contractual arrangements between families. There was little or no talk of love at this point; that would come later. The bride, perhaps still in her teens, would be leaving her family—and perhaps even her own village or shtetl— to live with her husband's family, who were most likely strangers to her and who probably looked upon her with some suspicion ("She's not good enough for my boy!").

Eventually, the kale bazetsns and the khosns tish would merge, when the groom and his party would make their way to the kale bazetsns for the *kale badekn,* or ritual veiling of the bride. The groom would approach the bride and veil her face, at which point the band would break into an upbeat dance tune in 2/4 meter, perhaps a *honga* or *onga,* and proceed to escort the guests and the wedding couple to the location where the *khupe,* or wedding canopy, was set up for the actual marriage ceremony.

The ceremony itself was solemn and did not include any music. At the end of the ceremony—in one of the only Old World, Jewish wedding traditions that survives to this day—the groom would step on a glass to shatter it, and everyone would shout, *"Mazel tov!"* At this point, the musicians would strike up a lively processional and usher the wedding party and guests to the location of the feast, which would be at a local inn or at the home of one of the wealthier inhabitants of the town.

The party itself, like contemporary weddings, was filled with various toasts, speeches and dances, and a multicourse meal. All of this was presided over by the badkhn, whose role it was to introduce and entertain the guests, keep up the general level of liveliness, and call the various ritual dances.

Among these were the *broyges tants,* or angry dance, featuring a playacted quarrel between the mothers-in-law, in which they would fight and make up. There was a lot of in-law lore attached to the Old World wedding—apparently Old World Jews openly acknowledged the ambivalent feelings between the mekhutonim, or in-laws, that is still often a part of the emotional reality of marriages. Take, for example, this verse from a Yiddish folk song, "Mekhuteneste Mayne (My In-law)":

> My inlaw, dear inlaw
> My daughter comes to you in a perikl [wig]
> And if you're going to be a vicious, evil mother-in-law
> Well . . . my daughter's no treasure either!

For the *mazeltov tants,* or congratulatory dance, the badkhn would call each female guest up in turn, and they would congratulate the bride and form a circle with her. Other ritual dances include the kosher, or *mitsve tants,* the only one in which men and women were allowed to dance together, albeit only at the opposite ends of a large handkerchief or belt grasped between them. Usually the bride was the featured dancer, and all the men took their turn *mit der kale,* or with the bride.

While the meal was being served, the klezmorim played listening music such as *tish nigunim*—slow or moderate tempo melodies often associated with prayers, as well as contemplative, rubato pieces in a vocal style, or doinas, improvisational pieces based on Romanian shepherds' laments.

The party and dancing would last well into the night, until finally the klezmorim would play a slow *gut morgn,* or "good morning," a suggestive tune meant to nudge the guests along their merry way, the Old World version of "The Party's Over." Usually a fast piece, or simply a fast version of the same piece, followed the gut morgn, in order to get everyone's feet moving out the door. The klezmorim would accompany the in-laws to their homes with an escort piece called *fihren du mekhutonim aheym,* or leading the in-laws home, which would often be a *gasn nign* (street tune) or hora.

The Old World klezmorim often teamed with the badkhonim and together they worked at weddings, in the market, and in taverns. Like the klezmorim, the badkhonim trace their roots back to Central Europe, where there are written records of well-known tunes satirizing Jewish community life composed or sung by the likes of Schlome of Prague ("the Joyous Jew") and Joseph the Son of Benjamin, both well-known badkhonim of their time.

Also called *leitzim,* a term that underlines their role as jester-like figures, these early, Central European badkhonim were as much wandering minstrels, jugglers, and acrobats as they were rhymesters and folk composers, and they were mainly employed to entertain and extemporize at weddings and for *Purimshpiels,* the irreverent and satirical masquerades staged on the holiday of Purim, which commemorates the story of Esther and the Jews' deliverance from the wicked Haman. These short-run Purim plays were in part the prototypes for what would eventually become the Yiddish theater, which in itself was an incubator for what became the mainstream Broadway musical.

The badkhonim, like the klezmorim, were anonymous folk performers who worked regionally on a freelance, for-hire basis, but in nineteenth-century Eastern Europe a few more creatively ambitious badkhonim transcended their role as local wedding poets to become full-fledged folk composers who wrote songs of social and political protest. Among the best known of these proto-typical Bob Dylans were Elyokum Zunser and Mark Warschavsky. The latter was the author of the well-known Yiddish folk song "Oifen Pripitchik (In the Little Stove)," which paints a vivid portrait of students learning the *alef-beis,* the Yiddish alphabet, in a typical Eastern European *cheder,* or one-room schoolhouse. Warschavsky (1840–1907) also wrote "Die Mezhinkeh Oisgegeben (My Youngest Daughter's Married)," which captures a father's glee at marrying off his youngest daughter:

> Louder, better!
> Make the circle bigger!
> God has exalted me,
> He has brought me joy
> Let's have fun the whole night
> I've married off my youngest daughter.
>
> Louder, joyful
> You're the queen and I'm the king,
> Oy, I myself
> Have seen, with my own eyes,
> How G-d has helped me succeed.
> I've married off my youngest daughter.

In the 1860s and 1870s, Elyokum Zunser (1836–1913) achieved widespread fame as a wedding poet, for which he garnered the nickname "Elyokum Badkhn," and also for his acute songs of social protest. "He decided to raise the level of the marriage entertainer to the dignity of a singer about his people, their life and struggles. . . . With a deep affection and regard for his suffering people, he sang of his times, pointed up the evils, satirized the guilty, stressed the good," wrote historian Ruth Rubin, in a description that could just as easily apply to one of the American folk-protest singer-songwriters of a century later.

Among Zunser's six hundred original compositions were songs recounting the bitter sweep of Jewish history, as well as songs of contemporary protest lamenting the anti-Semitic pogroms that periodically plagued his people. Zunser could be equally harsh against his own community, lambasting the *kahals,* or local Jewish councils, that acted as local draft boards and sent off young Jews to serve in the tsarist military.

Zunser's songs also addressed various political and spiritual concerns in Jewish life, ranging from the Polish Insurrection of 1863 (which forced the Jews to choose between loyalty to their everyday neighbors and the relatively benevolent Russian ruler, Alexander II), to the scourge of gambling, to the incipient Zionist movement.

The average badkhn's main role, however, was more personal — organizing the wedding festivities, keeping them moving along per ritual, and keeping the guests entertained. The skilled badkhn could evoke tears and laughter from his audience, one sometimes immediately following the other. One moment he was a satirist or parodist, and the next he was a solemn sermonizer. The badkhn also led the processionals, called the dances, and kept a lid on any extremes of emotional behavior that might spontaneously erupt during the celebration, such as fights or disputes between the mekhutonim, or in-laws. (These various duties are encapsulated in a somewhat humorous but representative suite by Kapelye on "Der Badkhin.")

In the transition from Europe to America, the badkhonim and the klezmorim took divergent paths. The old country badkhn found his theatrical skills of greater use in the thriving Yiddish theater of the Lower East Side, or in the routines of the *tummler*, the stand-up comic and social director of the Borscht Belt. Eventually, though, the badkhn would find his way back to his partnership with the klezmorim in revival-era groups such as Kapelye and Brave Old World. In the former, Henry Sapoznik would emphasize the folksy, comic improvisational aspect of the badkhn, while in Brave Old World, Michael Alpert would revive the badkhn's role as political and social commentator and satirist.

## THE MUSIC OF THE KAPELYE

The vast majority of klezmorim were anonymous professionals who, if they were lucky, were members of a kapelye with some sort of reputation beyond their own shtetl. The violinist was typically the leader of the kapelye, acting as booking agent, manager, publicist, and promoter. He got the gigs, he chose the repertoire, he called the tunes, and he conducted the ensemble. The violinist was also the instrumental star of the Old World ensemble—it was he who played the lead melodies and he who would show off his virtuosity on the more improvisational numbers, such as doinas and *fantazis*.

Later on, toward the end of the nineteenth century, the clarinet would usurp the role of the violin in the ensemble, and the clarinetists would become the leaders of the kapelye and the most identifiable stars of klezmer well into the twentieth century. Of course, what the violin and clarinet have in common, and what makes them the quintessential instruments of klezmer, are their ability to mimic the human voice. Both instruments are pitched closely to the voice, and in the hands of a skilled klezmer musician, both can produce *krekhtsn, tshoks,* and *kneytshn*—the achy, bent, and cutoff notes derived from the synagogue tradition of the khazn, or cantor, which we often hear as the "laughing" and "crying" quality of klezmer. This is the essence of klezmer ornamentation and is arguably the single most important characteristic of klezmer, both musically and in terms of its "Jewishness."

Until the late nineteenth century, violinists were most often the bandleaders, and as such, they collected the tips and fees, and, undoubtedly, they paid themselves well for all the services they rendered to the kapelye. Many kapelyes would have more than one violin, however. While the first violin would play the lead melody, a *sekunde,* or second fiddle would play rhythmic accompaniment with double-stops: fast, back-and-forth bowing that provided a percussive effect as much as a harmonic one. If there was a third fiddle in the band, which there often was, that fiddle would probably double the melody of the lead violinist one octave lower. Actual harmony-playing in klezmer is rare—more likely the melody is doubled, with individual variations in ornamentation providing harmonic differentiation.

Up to the mid–nineteenth century, in various parts of the Pale, Jews were restricted to playing "soft" instruments—stringed instruments, including violin, bass, cello, tsimbl, and wooden flutes—presumably to keep them from heralding rebellion with military-style horn blasts. It wasn't until the second half of the century, when regulations loosened under the general liberalization of Tsar

Alexander II and when Jews were released from service in the tsarist army, including military bands, that clarinets, horns, accordions, and drums, along with the martial rhythms they played, made their way into the klezmer repertoire.

In Eastern Europe, Jewish folk and instrumental music developed a strong identity of its own, borne of its particular cultural and geographical influences. The distinctive modes of the khazones, or synagogue music, blended with Oriental Jewish melodies creeping up from the Jewish community of the Ottoman Empire south of the Black Sea. Various native, non-Jewish musics, including Russian drinking songs, Romanian dances and shepherds' laments, Hungarian and Gypsy melodies, and Turkish *oud* music, also exerted their influence on the repertoire of the klezmorim and the style of music they played.

Klezmer was also strongly affected by the rise of Hasidism. A popular, mystical Jewish movement born in the forests of Poland in the mid-1700s, Hasidism's emphasis on ecstatic emotion over rote learning spread throughout the Pale. Music, dancing, and particularly singing were important tools for achieving mystical states of consciousness. Reb Nachman of Bratslav (1772–1810), a Hasidic *rebbe,* or teacher, taught that "attachment to God is primarily attained through melody." To this day, many black-clad, Hasidic rebbes in Israel, in Brooklyn, and elsewhere are amateur composers, and their wordless melodies, or nigunim, are often the raw material on which klezmorim build and improvise tunes. Some contemporary recordings by leading klezmorim contain music based entirely on these Hasidic prayer melodies, including *Nigunim* by Frank London, Lorin Sklamberg, and Uri Caine, and *Between Heaven and Earth: Music of the Jewish Mystics* by Andy Statman.

Old World klezmorim occasionally borrowed and adapted

## REPERTOIRE

The music the klezmorim played was a mix of Jewish ritual music and other melodies and dances of non-Jewish origin that made their way into the klezmer's repertoire, where it all got mixed together and eventually came out in a style we now call "klezmer."

Musicologist Walter Zev Feldman has suggested a useful taxonomy for the Old World klezmer repertoire that divides it into four categories, classifying the different genres of tunes according to both their origins and their functional differences. These four categories are (1) the core repertoire, (2) the transitional or southern repertoire, (3) the co-territorial repertoire, and (4) the cosmopolitan repertoire. Taken together, the music of these four categories constituted the sum total of the Old World klezmer's repertoire and, as such, forms the foundation for much—but certainly not all—of the klezmer music of the New World.

**1. Core repertoire:** The core repertoire is the largest and most Jewish body of klezmer tunes, consisting of two main subcategories, which are

    **a. freylekhs:** literally, "happy," these were secular dance tunes of varying tempos, often borrowing melodies from Jewish religious music, including *zmiros,* or table songs, and nigunim, or wordless, Hasidic prayer melodies. They were often played in suites of two or three different melodies, typically in 8/8 time, with the first, third, and seventh beats accented. Variants of the freylekhs included:

        • the *sher,* or scissors dance—a moderate-tempo, Russian-derived, group dance along the lines of our square dance, often in the form of a medley of short, nonreligious melodies that frequently change key;

        • the *khosidl* —a slower solo, improvised dance reminiscent of Hasidic dancing in 4/4 time, with room for instrumental improvisation;

        • the *terkisher,* a tango-like dance in 4/4 based on the Greek *syrto.*

    **b. ritual tunes:** these highly stylized, nondance tunes were part of the elaborate, Old World wedding ceremony. Some in standard meter, some not, they include such genres as the *dobranoc* ("good morning"), the mazl tov ("good luck"), and the kale bazetsn ("seating the bride"). Specific holiday tunes, particularly for Purim and Chanukah, also fall into this category. Today, outside of their original setting, these pieces often form the foundation of solo improvisations.

**2. Transitional or southern repertoire:** As the name indicates, this body of nonreligious tunes bore the influence of non-Jewish musics, particularly Romanian and Near-Eastern musics. The klezmorim would have picked them up during their travels, perhaps swapping tunes with non-Jewish musicians they met along the way. After giving the melodies a particular Jewish twist or ornamentation, they became part of the klezmer's basic repertoire, played at Jewish weddings and at non-Jewish affairs. These included

a. **dance tunes:** The majority of tunes in the transitional or southern repertoire were based on Romanian dances, including the bulgarish, the honga, the *sirba,* and the *zhok,* or *hora*—not the *hora* of contemporary vintage popular in Israeli folk dance circles, but an older dance of Moldavian origin. The immigrant American klezmorim, particularly Dave Tarras, favored this genre, especially the bulgarish, and "the bulgars" became virtually synonymous with mid-twentieth-century Jewish dance music.

b. **nondance tunes:** Primarily the doina, also of Romanian vintage, an improvised melody used to entertain wedding guests while they dined. Today it is favored by soloists for its quality of lamentation and suitability for improvisation. A doina is typically followed by a hora or freylekhs. Closely related, a fantazl.

**3. Co-territorial repertoire:** Quite simply, non-Jewish songs and dances of local origin—such as the Polish mazurka, the Ruthenian *kolomeyka* and the Ukrainian *kozachok*—that made their way into the klezmorim's repertoire. Old World klezmorim often played at non-Jewish affairs and were prized as much for their command of the local idiom as they were for "playing Jewish."

**4. Cosmopolitan repertoire:** The Old World klezmer repertoire included popular, widely established Central and Western European dances such as the quadrille, the polka, and the waltz. Jewish audiences enjoyed the latest rage in non-Jewish dances in much the same way as fare like "The Macarena" and Kool and the Gang's "Celebration" are standard fare at contemporary weddings, Jewish or not.

Hasidic melodies, turning them into dance tunes and other songs of celebration, but Hasidism's greatest influence on klezmer was simply its elevation of music and dance in everyday life, unlike the more sober outlook of the *mitnagdim,* or rationalist rabbis, who thought such things frivolous.

For the most part, the music the klezmorim played was Jewish folk music—music that was transmitted orally, without written notation, without any composer's credit, and often even without specific titles. As such, the music was in constant flux, with different players and groups constantly adding and subtracting elements according to their preferences or the preferences of their particular audiences, which included non-Jewish listeners. In America, there would eventually be several attempts to collect, notate, and codify the wedding-band repertoire, but for the most part these efforts merely captured an individual group's particular repertoire and way of playing, mistakes and all.

The klezmorim primarily performed for Jewish weddings, but they also performed for non-Jewish audiences and occasionally with non-Jewish musicians, particularly Gypsies. Consequently, their repertoire included more than just traditional Jewish wedding music. They were familiar with the indigenous folk music of their particular geographic region, and local songs and dances made their way into the klezmer repertoire, albeit given a klezmerish spin. The more traveled musicians among the klezmorim had a more global repertoire that included light classical works and dances popular throughout Europe, such as polkas, quadrilles, and waltzes. The klezmorim learned this non-Jewish repertoire not only for Gentile audiences, but for the entertainment of their Jewish listeners, too, who weren't necessarily so provincial that they only wanted to dance to Jewish melodies and rhythms.

Most of what we know directly of the music of this period comes from European and American recordings of the early twentieth century. A few of these recordings, originally released on 78 rpm records, are available on some of the better-known CD reissues, such as *Klezmer Music 1910–27: The First Recordings*; *Yikhes: Early Klezmer Recordings 1911–39*; and *Klezmer Pioneers: European and American Recordings, 1905–52*.

Perhaps the most accurate rendering of the Old World sound, however, can actually be found on any of several contemporary recordings made by performers who have taken it upon themselves to reconstruct the musical roots of these and other early recordings. The best of these "neotraditional" recordings include *Fidl*, by Alicia Svigals; *Mother Tongue: Music of the Nineteenth Century Klezmorim*, by the European group Budowitz; *Sweet Home Bukovina*, by the Chicago Klezmer Ensemble; *Beregovski's Khasene*, by the Joel Rubin Jewish Music Ensemble; and *Bessarabian Symphony: Early Jewish Instrumental Music*, by Joel Rubin and Joshua Horowitz, the latter of whom also leads Budowitz.

These all-acoustic recordings are rich repositories of the Old World repertoire and style, analogous to similar attempts at recording "early music" in the European classical genre. They are also of great interest, ultimately, in that they provide a basis from which to better understand and appreciate the development of the music that followed historically, in the American immigrant period and later in the klezmer revival and renaissance.

## CHAPTER 2

# IMMIGRATION AND CLASSIC KLEZMER

T he late nineteenth century was a time of great political upheaval across Europe, particularly in the east, and Jews of the Pale bore the brunt of the turbulence. The gradual liberalization of restrictions against Jews under Tsar Alexander II came to a halt with his assassination in 1881, and from that time a series of anti-Jewish decrees, expulsions, and violent pogroms, as well as the chaos brought about by war, revolution, and the dissolution of the Russian empire, provoked a steady wave of emigration from the region.

From across the ocean the United States, and New York in particular, beckoned with the promise of freedom and prosperity, as symbolized by the Statue of Liberty. Word of a *goldene medina,* a land of gold, awaiting all comers penetrated into the deepest parts of the Pale. As a result, from 1880 until 1924, when the doors of Ellis Island finally slammed shut, approximately two and a half million Eastern European Jews made their way to the United States.

The vast majority of these immigrants washed up on the

shores of New York City, and most of them were ushered into the half-square-mile neighborhood of New York's Lower East Side, where Jews lived in numbers that rivaled the population density of turn-of-the-century Bombay. Overcrowded tenement apartments replaced the ramshackle wooden houses of the shtetl, and busy, noisy, city streets replaced the dirt roads that spanned the countryside of the Pale.

For the musicians, this meant change aplenty. While many were still freelancers chasing after jobs, they no longer did so by traveling throughout a vast territory, but rather through a small, densely populated urban landscape, one full of new deprivations and degradations. Weddings were now held in catering halls instead of at private homes and inns. Just as the elaborate rituals of the Old World wedding determined the style and repertoire of the klezmorim, the catering hall exerted its influence on the klezmorim and the music they played. The more fortunate musicians were able to opt out of the freelance life altogether by gaining employment in house bands attached to particular catering halls, where their services were part of the overall wedding package. These musicians received a fixed hourly rate, although the tradition of tipping the musicians continued, as it does in some form or fashion to this day.

As for the ceremonial rituals that comprised the Old World wedding, these were soon abandoned by new immigrants. Even in the shtetl, some had already been chafing at the quaint religious practices of their grandparents' generation. Others, on arriving in the city, were eager to shed all aspects of immigrant culture in favor of adopting the ways and manners of their new homeland. With no more ritual seating and veiling of the bride, and no more theatrical taunting of the newlywed couple, the badkhn and the elaborate kale bazetsns and kale baveynens were no longer needed.

Indeed, we have a recorded example of how low the rituals and the badkhn fell in the estimation of the immigrant population. "Der Mesader Kedushin (The Marrying Rabbi)," a 1922 recording by Gus Goldstein and Company, is a devastating, sophisticated parody that anticipates the work of cultural satirists like Mickey Katz by some thirty years. The recording mocks the rabbi, the badkhn, the ceremony, and the klezmorim—the whole Old World constituency. As for the badkhn, his role in keeping the wedding party moving along was now often assumed by an employee of the catering hall.

Fortunately for the klezmorim, live music was still considered essential at every wedding, as it remains pretty much to this day (although some contemporary musicians complain about having been usurped by DJs). The best klezmorim were always versatile musicians, ready and able to adapt to the particular needs of their audience, and this experience held them in good stead when they came to America. At weddings they still played processionals, as guests in the catering hall moved from the room set aside for the wedding ceremony to the larger banquet hall where the meal was served and dancing took place. The more ritualized pieces, such as the kale bazetsns and kale baveynens, were, if not totally abandoned, unmoored from their specific role in accompanying the rituals to become background music.

For the most part, the musician's role was now simplified: to entertain the guests with a variety of songs appropriate for listening and dancing. Hence, more upbeat genres, the freylekhs and bulgars and shers, grew in popularity. As we have already seen, the klezmer repertoire in Eastern Europe had included songs of non-Jewish origin such as waltzes and polkas. The proportion of these and newer American dances in relation to Jewish melodies eventually grew as the newly minted Americans were exposed to a greater variety of music, including fox-trots, ragtime, and later on, big-band swing, and as the Jewish wedding musicians incorporated all of these styles into their repertoire.

The vast majority of immigrant klezmorim were, like in the old country and much like freelance musicians today, journeymen chasing after jobs in order to scratch out a decent living. Those who didn't learn to read music, didn't study at conservatory, or didn't learn to play anything but Old World music, continued to be looked down upon just as in the Old World. The same stereotypes that attached to them in the Pale continued to shadow them in the New World, and the term *klezmer* was used as an insult. They continued in large part to keep to themselves as a sort of social caste, doling out work to each other through family connections. Their speech was peppered with *klezmer-loshn,* a specialized musician's lingo responsible for such colorful words as *zhlob,* a boor or a peasant, which they used as a synonym for a Gentile. They underlined their insularity and similarity to criminal gangs with nicknames like "Old Man Finklestein" and "Grossman the *Shikker,*" or drunkard.

City life presented the klezmorim with new and different opportunities to play. Within the Jewish ghetto itself musicians were regularly employed in cafés, teahouses, wine cellars, and restaurants. Klezmorim were also in demand for parades and other gatherings, including political rallies, charity socials, and public dances. Communal organizations of Jews from a particular town or shtetl in Europe, called *landsmanshaftn,* were centers of social life, and they frequently employed klezmorim, especially those from their hometown or region.

For those with talent, ambition, and an openness to playing

new repertoire—those who styled themselves *muzikantn,* or real musicians, rather than klezmorim—other opportunities awaited. Musicians who could read music obtained jobs in vaudeville houses, movie theaters, and in the pit orchestras of the Yiddish theater. Some became recording stars, applying their talents to a grab bag of musical and cultural genres. The peak years of immigration coincided with the early growth years of the American recording industry, when New York–based record companies sought to broaden their scope beyond the "parlor songs" and all-American marching band music that comprised the bulk of their catalogs. The vast immigrant populations beckoned as valuable markets for "ethnic" recordings, nostalgic evocations of their homelands.

Klezmer, heretofore a folk genre passed down orally, became a style of commercially marketed popular music; this had a significant impact on the music itself. Songs that formerly were performed in continuous twenty-minute suites for dancing at weddings and celebrations were now sold to individual consumers in the form of 78 rpm platters containing three minutes of music per side that were played in private living rooms. As the music slowly left the firsthand world of live performance for the secondhand world of recordings, whatever wound up on those recordings—stylistic variations, mistakes, and all—became the "record" of the music, in every sense of the word.

# EARLY IMMIGRANT-ERA RECORDINGS

One of the first attempts to cater to the burgeoning immigrant Jewish population was made in April 1913, when trumpeter Abe

Elenkrig and his ensemble, the Hebrew Bulgarian Orchestra, laid down some of the earliest known klezmer tracks in America. The dozen or so sides they recorded were typical of the brassy, marching-band style that predominated at the time, both in recorded klezmer and in American music at large. The violin-led kapelyes of the Old World were usurped by bands led by clarinets and horns playing melody over a strict oompah beat propelled by precise, military-style drumming.

For ten years, from 1917 to 1927, Harry Kandel enjoyed a recording stint that produced over ninety sides on the Camden, New Jersey–based Victor label, leaving a rich legacy of classic recorded klezmer. Trained in the conservatory in Odessa on clarinet, Kandel immigrated to Philadelphia around 1906, found work in vaudeville, and played under John Philip Sousa in the Pennsylvania State Militia Band. Eventually he wound up conducting the pit band at the Arch Street Theater, a Yiddish theater in Philadelphia. As his reputation spread, Kandel was in demand on the wedding and club circuit as well as in the recording studio.

Kandel's recordings are noteworthy for their brassy ensemble arrangements for large bands, which typically included a dozen players, and for their military flavor, presumably the influence of his stint with Sousa. He took a notable stylistic turn in 1926 when, recording as Kandel's Jazz Orchestra, he modified his arrangements and instrumentation, added a saxophone section and a banjo to the ensemble, and set his melodies in what we would now call a Dixieland arrangement, as on "Jakie Jazz 'Em Up." It was one of the first attempts to consciously blend klezmer and American popular music.

Among the most notable players in Kandel's orchestra was Jacob "Jakie" Hoffman (1899–1974), who played drums and percussion, but is best remembered as a virtuoso on the xylophone, to which he transferred the stylistic function of the Old World tsimbl and straw-fiddle. The best examples of his playing can be found on the klezmer staple "Der Gasn Nign (The Street Tune)," and on "Doina and Hora." Typical of the better Yiddish musicians, Hoffman worked in other venues; he played percussion with the Philadelphia Orchestra, toured with the Boston Pops and the Ballets Russe of Monte Carlo, and accompanied silent films on piano at movie theaters in Philadelphia.

Other prominent immigrant-era recording artists included accordionist Mishka Ziganoff and cymbalist Joseph Moskowitz. Ziganoff and Moskowitz were versatile musicians who shared a wide-ranging approach to repertoire not limited to klezmer or Jewish music. Although he often performed with Jewish musicians, Ziganoff's ancestry is unclear. In any case, he played up the Gypsy connection in his music, and in addition to klezmer music he also cut sides for the Greek, Polish, Lithuanian, and Hungarian markets.

Moskowitz studied music with his father in their native Romania, and he gained enough renown to tour Europe and the United States as a child prodigy. In 1913, he opened a basement wine cellar on Rivington Street on New York's Lower East Side, where he catered to a Romanian-Jewish clientele with a repertoire heavy on music from his homeland. Moskowitz's fame grew, and he wound up giving a series of concerts at New York's Town Hall. He also made several recordings, many of which are compiled on *The Art of the Cymbalom: The Music of Joseph Moskowitz, 1916–53*, which in addition to klezmer includes Romanian dances, Ukrainian folk songs, Greek and Turkish melodies, tangos, rags, waltzes, and even some Brahms—a repertoire typical of the more worldly, cosmopolitan klezmer.

# רומינישע וואלאך

# ROMANIAN VOLACH

## By ABE SCHWARTZ

Abe Schwartz famous Violin Player accompanied by the famous Pianist his daughter Miss Schwartz

PLAYED ON COLUMBIA RECORD BY ABE SCHWARTZ

## FOR PIANO

Piano 50 cts.                    Violin or Mandolin 50 cts.

Abe Schwartz was one of the most successful of the early immigrant bandleaders. He is seen here playing violin accompanied by his daughter Sylvia on piano sometime around 1922.

Recordings by Elenkrig, Kandel, and of bands led by I. J. Hochman, Itzikl Kramtveiss, and Lt. Joseph Frankel were marked by their emphasis on ensemble playing. The introduction of a distinctive, lead solo voice was an innovation of bandleader Abe Schwartz. Between the late teens and the early forties, the Romanian-born Schwartz produced more klezmer recordings than any other bandleader. He is also remembered for his reliance on Old World repertoire, particularly Hasidic melodies, and his Dixieland-like quintet arrangements. But Schwartz, a violinist and pianist who also composed his own music, is perhaps best known for having hired and recorded a couple of virtuoso clarinetists who would go on to establish themselves as the most famous and influential klezmorim of the immigrant era, and perhaps of all time.

Schwartz's "Fihren die Mechutonim Aheim," recorded in 1923, features one continuous, melodic clarinet solo throughout the song, with simple, rhythmic and harmonic backup provided by the small ensemble. This is in stark contrast to the typically rousing, large-ensemble, all-torpedoes-launched anthems one finds on earlier recordings by Kandel's or Hochman's bands. The emergence of the star soloist from the anonymity of the klezmer ensemble is roughly analogous to (as well as contemporaneous with) the same trend in jazz, which saw innovative, virtuosic players such as Louis Armstrong and Sidney Bechet eclipse their ensembles.

# NAFTULE BRANDWEIN
# AND DAVE TARRAS

The clarinetist on Schwartz's "Fihren die Mechutonim Aheim" was Naftule Brandwein, who was born in 1889 into an already well-established klezmer dynasty in the Galician shtetl of Przemyslany. Naftule's father, Pesakh Brandwein, was a fiddler and badkhn who led a family kapelye that traveled throughout eastern Galicia. All

Naftule Brandwein, left, with fellow band member Louis Spielman, on tour with the Cherniavsky orchestra, 1928.

but two of Naftule's eleven brothers eventually immigrated to the United States. (One of the brothers who stayed behind had a son, Leopold Kozlowski, who would become a hero of the klezmer revival as the subject of a documentary film, *The Last Klezmer.*) Naftule has been variously reported to have arrived in New York in 1909 and 1913. In any case, within a few years of his arrival he established a reputation as the self-appointed "king of Jewish music."

A larger-than-life figure, Brandwein (sometimes spelled Brandwine) was noted as much for his wild behavior as for his virtuosity. He supposedly once performed dressed as Uncle Sam, strung with Christmas tree lights that nearly electrocuted him when he perspired. Foreshadowing another moody, paranoid musical genius with an affinity for mood-altering substances, he is said to have often performed with his back to the audience, Miles Davis–style, the better to hide his fingering techniques from studious onlookers. He was a daredevil behind the wheel of a car, speeding down the curvy, winding roads of the Catskills while simultaneously serenading his passengers on the clarinet. He wasn't above surprising his audiences by playing with his pants around his ankles, and at times he is said to have played with a neon sign reading NAFTULE BRANDWEIN ORCHESTRA strapped around his neck. He was clearly a showman out of time, one who would have fit in rather well on the stage at a contemporary alternative rock festival or at a downtown nightclub.

Naftule "Nifty" Brandwein's freewheeling style matched his larger-than-life antics, all of which inspired contemporary klezmorim.

Brandwein was a shikker, or a serious drinker, and the very stereotype of the Old World, unreliable lowlife: a gambler, a card-player, a womanizer, allegedly the favorite musician of Murder, Inc., the so-called Jewish Mafia. His tenure with the various bands he passed through, including Schwartz's group and Joseph Cherniavsky's Yiddish-American Jazz Band, never lasted long, due to his unreliability and the refusal of his fellow musicians to bunk with him on the road. Notwithstanding his natural gifts for improvisation, Naftule Brandwein's musical illiteracy meant no work for him in the Yiddish theater or as a musician for hire in the recording studio.

Nevertheless and in spite of himself, Brandwein was much in demand for playing parties, weddings, and hotel gigs in the Catskills until his death in 1963. The two-dozen-plus recordings he made on his own, mostly between 1922 and 1927, remain some of the most influential of the period. Brandwein's playing style matched his outsized personality. He played with great emotion, florid phrasing, and ornamentation seemingly patterned after the sound of the Old World violin. Where just a few notes would do, Brandwein played many and in quick succession, as acknowledged in a 1924 press release which boasted, "Here's speed for you! Observe the swiftness of this remarkable music, the clarity and ingeniousness of the melodies that come so rapidly from Naftule Brandwein's musicians, and you will be thrilled."

Typical of his sound are the swooping notes and birdlike trills of the introductory, free-metered phrases of "Rumenishe Doina." Brandwein continues to play fluidly over the more structured rhythmic passages of the *nokshpil* section and brings the piece to a rousing climax, maintaining a balance of vibrant wit and bittersweet longing, the very essence of a doina.

Brandwein is in some ways the spiritual godfather of the late-twentieth-century klezmer revival. His rebellious image makes him an attractive icon to the more edgy, experimental performers of the renaissance period in particular. Many of his songs have become klezmer standards; "Fun Tashlich" has been recorded by contemporary groups including the Klezmatics, Kroke, and Yid Vicious. "Naftule Spielt far dem Rebin (Naftule Plays for the Rebbe)," is typical of the many Middle Eastern–influenced tunes, this one a terkisher that Brandwein favored and that several modern bands have reworked, among them the Flying Bulgar Klezmer Band and Paradox Trio. *King of the Klezmer Clarinet* is the only reissue devoted in its entirety to Brandwein's recordings, but virtually all of the compilations of early klezmer include several tracks by him.

For bandleaders worn out by Brandwein's antics, there was another clarinetist waiting in the wings, equally gifted but the complete antithesis of Brandwein in his behavior and personal style. Klezmer is a music of dualities—bitter and sweet, happy and sad, slow and fast—and ultimately the duality represented by Dave Tarras and Naftule Brandwein echoes that in the music itself: reserve versus emotional excess, dignity versus outrageousness, studied musicality versus improvisation.

As the scion of a musical dynasty of Hasidic klezmorim, Dave Tarras's klezmer roots ran deep, back to his native shtetl of Ternovka (in Podolia, near the Ukrainian city of Uman), where he was born Dovid Tarraschuk in 1897. Tucked in between Bessarabia to the southwest and Kiev to the northeast, Podolia was strong Hasidic territory, where the Besht, or Israel Baal Shem Tov, founded his movement based in ecstatic mysticism. The Tarraschuks originated in the town of Teplik, where his father worked as a trombonist and badkhn, like his father before him. An uncle had a family kapelye that won favor with a nobleman in Teplik who so enjoyed his playing that he gave him land on which to build a house.

In typical, Old World klezmer style, Tarras studied music with

Dave Tarras with his Aunt Malka, Ternovka, USSR, 1911. The young Tarras learned to play flute, mandolin, guitar, and balalaika, pictured here, before switching to clarinet in his teens.

his father. By the time he was nine he could read and write music and play the balalaika, guitar, mandolin, and flute, the last of which was his primary instrument until his early teens, when he switched to clarinet. For a few years, Tarras played in his father's kapelye, traveling widely and performing a diverse musical repertoire for equally diverse audiences.

Tarras's career as an Old World klezmer was to be short-lived, however. In 1915, with the country at war, the eighteen-year-old clarinetist was drafted into the Tsarist army. His instrumental skills helped him avoid combat, as he wound up playing in and eventually leading a military ensemble attached to an officers corps. Thus was he able to stay out of harm's way until domestic political chaos brought about by revolution resulted in the Russian army's collapse. With the countryside beset by chaos and anti-Semitic pogroms, Tarras, like thousands of others, fled to New York City in 1921.

Tarras's introduction to America was typical. Chaos greeted him at Ellis Island, the central processing station for European immigrants, where at the height of immigration over five thousand people passed through each day. When Tarras arrived, he was ordered to hand over the bag that contained his clarinet for fumigation. The procedure destroyed his instrument. Welcome to the New World.

For Tarras, this wasn't such a tragic blow; he had other things in mind besides playing music for life in the New World, where he didn't think he was qualified to be a musician. His married sister already lived in New York, and with the aid of his brother-in-law, Tarras found work in the garment industry like the vast majority of Jewish immigrants at the time. Within a year, however, Tarras earned enough to buy a new clarinet, and through family contacts he began playing weddings in the New York area.

It wasn't long before his talent won out over his insecurity, and by 1923 he had made something of a reputation for himself. He was unusual for both his technical prowess and his deportment; just the fact that he could read music separated him from many of the old-time klezmorim who were musically illiterate. Just at the time when Joseph Cherniavsky's musicians were fed up with the drunken antics of the group's clarinetist, Naftule Brandwein, Tarras came to the attention of the bandleader, whose vaudeville-style outfit played concerts dressed alternately as Cossacks and Hasids. Soon after Tarras replaced Brandwein in the group in 1925, he had his first chance to record.

Tarras's recordings with Cherniavsky, on the Victor label, only furthered his growing reputation, and soon he received offers from other labels and bands. Columbia Records brought him together with Abe Schwartz, who had recently fired Brandwein. With the Schwartz outfit, which was very much a studio group controlled by the record label, Tarras recorded Russian, Polish, and Greek songs for those immigrant markets, in addition to traditionally Jewish material. In a short time, Dave Tarras had replaced Naftule Brandwein in fact, if not in name, as the "king of klezmer clarinet."

The introductory passage of "Yiddisher March," recorded with Cherniavsky in 1925, shows Tarras's playing infused with spirit and emotion, which, if carefully apportioned, was evocative, resonant, and filled with the sort of passion and mystique at the heart of klezmer's appeal. His lead playing on "Dem Monastrisher Rebin's Chosid'l," recorded with the Abe Schwartz Orchestra later the same year, is not only vibrant but eloquent, and fully sings the melody.

Much of Tarras's work was recorded in the service of others as an orchestra sideman or as an accompanist to a vocalist. A brief scan of his song credits shows him recording with, in addition to the Schwartz and Cherniavsky groups, Lou Lockett's Orchestra,

Moishe Oysher and Florence Weiss, Michi Michalesco, Alexander Olshanetsky Orchestra, Abe Ellstein Orchestra, the Barry Sisters, the Yiddish Swing Orchestra, Yiddish Swingtette, Boibriker Kappelle, Tantz Orchestra, and Al Glaser's Bucovina Kapelle—a veritable who's who of Yiddish popular music. Tarras would go on to record hundreds of sides, not only of Jewish music, but of Russian, Polish, and Greek tunes as well. Opportunities in radio also grew more numerous, and Tarras found himself appearing on several different stations on a variety of programs. One in particular, "Yiddish Melodies in Swing" on WHN, lasted from 1939 to 1955.

As the primary exponent of American klezmer from the twenties through the fifties, Tarras is widely credited with the growth of the bulgar as a popular style of Jewish dance tune. A minor genre of Old World klezmer rooted in Bessarabia, the bulgar came to be synonymous with American klezmer by the 1940s, to the point that the music as a whole was often merely referred to as the bulgars. Tarras composed and recorded dozens of these tunes, which he favored over the Old World core repertoire, most of which he viewed as too "simple" and audiences viewed as too "religious."

The bulgars, pretty much synonymous with freylekhs, were for the most part happy, upbeat tunes in major keys—laughing rather than crying became the distinctive ornamentation of "playing Jewish" by midcentury. The bulgars were dominated by Tarras's arching melodies that matched a steady, rhythmic pulse of two beats to the measure with a strong accent on the first beat—a foolproof formula for getting a crowd of people off their feet and onto the dance floor. That quintessential Jewish dance tune, "Hava Nagila," is an example of one of these midcentury bulgars.

In addition to recording and performing, Tarras continued to be a mainstay of the Jewish society circuit, in demand for appearances at weddings and other social events. Contemporaries of his

Clarinetist Dave Tarras, the most successful
immigrant-era Yiddish musician, in a familiar pose.

tell of bandleaders who got jobs on the promise that they could
deliver Dave Tarras, and subsequently instructed their lead clarinetists, whoever they were, to pretend they were him.

Tarras was also able to parlay his versatility and technique into
a successful career in the Yiddish theater. This was not always the
case with European-born musicians, because the music in the Yiddish theater tended to look away from Europe to a more modern
sound. The Yiddish theater was very much a part of an interna-
tionalist, secularist movement within Yiddish culture. Klezmer,
with its roots in religion and Hasidism in particular, was precisely
the sort of cultural remnant of the Old World that the Yiddish theater wanted to discard. When klezmer music did appear in the Yid-

dish theater, it was likely as not the object of derision. As such, a background in klezmer was not in Tarras's favor so much as his versatility and ability to read and learn large quantities of scored music.

The startling diversity and range of Dave Tarras's music is captured on *Yiddish-American Klezmer Music 1925–56,* aptly titled because Dave Tarras's recording career parallels the evolution of Yiddish music in America. Here is Tarras in 1925, the fleet soloist whose clarinet soars like an Old World bird over the rhythmic and chordal vamping of the Abe Schwartz Orchestra on "Dem Monastrisher Rebin's Chosid'l." Here is Tarras accompanying leading Yiddish vocalists such as Seymour Rechtzeit and Michi Michalesco, and lending some authentic yidishkayt to an otherwise Americanized bit of big-band swing on "Bridegroom Special," based on the theater song "Vos Du Vilst, Dos Vil Ikh Oykh."

"Zum Gali Gali" by the Yiddish Swingtette features Tarras on a remarkably weird bit of musical miscegenation introduced as a "Palestinian work song" (in fact it *is* a Hebrew folk song, but you'd have a hard time recognizing it from the lounge-jazz treatment it gets). The number begins with a descending chordal run out of Lennie Tristano and devolves into a kind of easy-listening blues laden with vibraphone that sounds downright psychedelic to contemporary ears—Esquivel, move over. And here, finally, is Tarras leading the Abe Ellstein Orchestra in some classic, small-band klezmer on "Die Goldene Chasene," recorded in 1945.

Dave Tarras and Naftule Brandwein were as different musically as they were personally. Tracks nine and ten on *Yikhes* offer an illustrative, ready-made, back-to-back comparison of their styles. Brandwein's playing on "Heyser Bulgar" is lively, elastic, and cantorial—the notes just seemingly pour out of his clarinet in long, wailing, emotional arpeggios. On the other hand, Tarras's playing on "A Rumenisher Nign" is much more stately and dignified, each note and phrase carefully parceled out as its own carefully punctuated statement. Tarras makes much more use of pauses and rhythmic gestures and seems more aware of, and communicative with, the other musicians—he is genuinely playing *with* the band. Brandwein, on the other hand, seems almost to ignore his band—the song starts and he is off on a tear, and for the next two-and-a-half minutes the musicians are struggling to keep up with him. This isn't to say that Tarras couldn't let loose—by the end of "A Rumenisher Nign," when the rhythm has changed to a Bessarabian honga in 2/4 time, Tarras is blowing circular riffs and curlicues of acrobatic proportions, yet always with stupendous confidence and control. It has been suggested that the striking differences in Tarras's and Brandwein's playing can be traced to their early training on flute and trumpet, respectively.

AS A POPULAR MUSIC, klezmer began a long, slow decline at the end of the 1920s. The recording industry as a whole virtually shut down during the Great Depression and took another hit with the rise of radio in the 1930s. Also, by the mid-1920s, Jewish immigration from Europe ended. No longer was there a fresh supply of greenhorns waxing nostalgic for the sounds of the Old Country. And most of those who had been in America for a while had begun the long, slow process of assimilation into the American mainstream. Along the way, they became as enamored of big-band swing, Broadway, and other popular American styles as they once were of Yiddish theater and cantorial music.

In post–World War II America, the demand for Yiddish dance music further waned. Brides wanted to hear the latest popular tunes from the hit parade at their weddings. In the 1940s and 1950s, this would have meant a cha-cha or some other Latin-derived dance tune. What little interest in Jewish music remained was confined to a few token bulgars at a party. Jewish audiences were more likely to request one of the new Israeli folk dances coming from that young nation, its new Hebrew culture edging out the old affinities of American Jews still in shock over the destruction of their Yiddish culture in the Holocaust.

Klezmer dynasties died out, as the few sons of klezmorim who didn't totally spurn their fathers' profession turned their backs on the sounds of the Old World in favor of classical music and jazz. A few old-timers continued to "play Jewish" at weddings, bar mitzvah parties, and in the Catskills, the favored vacation retreat of New York–area Jews in the first half of the twentieth century. But only a very small number, including Dave Tarras, remained performers of Yiddish music exclusively.

There were some attempts made to accommodate klezmer and American popular music, particularly jazz and swing, on the same bandstand, or even in the same song. But even the most successful of these were flukes or novelties. The klezmer-jazz exchange began in the 1920s with a genre called the Oriental fox-trot, which featured Jewish- or Middle Eastern–sounding melodies in jazzy arrangements. The most popular of these was Eddie Cantor's 1930s hit "Leena from Palestina," which was based on "Nokh a Bisl (A Little Bit More)," a popular bulgar. Another curious example of a klezmer-jazz hybrid was black bandleader and vocalist Cab Calloway's version of the Yiddish folk song "Ot Azoy," replete with cantorial vocalizing and mock Hebrew.

Some claim to hear the sound of the klezmer in the opening notes of George Gershwin's 1924 composition, "Rhapsody in Blue," which begins with a tremulous clarinet glissando similar to the klezmer's crylike krekhts (an opening echoed by Dave Tarras on "Nikolaev Bulgar," recorded in 1940). Growing up in New York in the early 1900s, Gershwin undoubtedly soaked up the sounds of the khazn and the klezmer, but he had no direct experience playing or composing Jewish music. Neither did Irving Berlin, although the Yiddish-speaking composer wrote the Tin Pan Alley ditty, "Yiddle on Your Fiddle, Play Some Ragtime" in addition to such well-known standards as "White Christmas" and "Easter Parade." In popular songwriter Harold Arlen's case, his background as the son of a khazn surfaces in his 1932 hit, "It's Only a Paper Moon," the melody of which is patterned, intentionally or not, after a section of the Kiddush, the traditional blessing sanctifying the Sabbath.

The swing era ushered in the most overt and commercially successful fusion of Yiddish and American popular music. The Andrews Sisters' recording of "Bay Mir Bistu Sheyn" began its circuitous route to the top of the pop charts in 1932. It was originally composed by Sholem Secunda for a Yiddish theater production, "I Would If I Could," to be sung by Aaron Lebedeff backed by Dave Tarras on clarinet. The popular black duo Johnny and George learned the tune on a visit to the Catskills the following summer. When they took it to the stage of Harlem's Apollo Theater the next season, the predominantly black audience greeted it with great enthusiasm.

As it happened, the Tin Pan Alley songwriting duo of Sammy Cahn and Saul Chaplin were in the audience. Cahn tracked down the song's publisher and paid fifty dollars for the rights to the tune, and in November 1937, the Andrews Sisters recorded it. Interestingly enough, Cahn wanted them to sing the song in Yiddish, and it was only against his wishes that he was convinced to pen English lyrics to the tune that would become the best-selling popular record of its time.

The colossal commercial success of this ethnic novelty record sparked a brief fad of similar attempts that saw the folk song "Di Grine Kuzine" remade as "My Little Country Cousin," as well as instant cover versions of "Bay Mir Bistu Sheyn" itself, including one sung by Martha Tilton with the Benny Goodman Orchestra. The Andrews Sisters themselves followed up "Bay Mir Bistu Sheyn" with "Joseph, Joseph," their Anglicized version of "Yossel, Yossel," originally a hit for Yiddish theater performer Nellie Casman in 1923.

Less open to dispute is trumpeter Ziggy Elman's klezmer bona fides. Harry "Ziggy Elman" Finkelman played Jewish music before joining Benny Goodman's band. Along with his klezmer style, Elman brought to Goodman's band the Yiddish tune "Der Shtiler Bulgar (The Quiet Bulgar)," which he recorded under his own name in 1938 as "Frailach in Swing." The Goodman band rerecorded it in 1939 as "And the Angels Sing," with vocals by Martha Tilton and lyrics by Johnny Mercer, and thus was a swing-band hit made out of a tune first recorded by the Abe Schwartz Orchestra in 1918.

Another musician who straddled the jazz-klezmer fence was Sam Musiker, who played saxophone in Gene Krupa's swing band. An American-born, classically trained musician, Musiker was, as his name indicates, descended from a family of klezmer musicians, and he returned to his roots when he teamed with Tarras to "play Jewish" in the mid-forties. Musiker tried to push Dave toward more commercial, Benny Goodman–style arrangements, the result of which can be heard on a few tracks on *Yiddish-American Klezmer Music* credited to "Lou Lockett's Orchestra."

In Old World fashion, Musiker's partnership with Tarras would go beyond the professional—he married Tarras's daughter, Brownie. Sam and Dave would collaborate again in the recording studio in 1956, and the resulting album, *Tanz!*, released by Epic but currently out of print, shows that Tarras remained a klezmer musician of authentic power and distinction. A drama emerges between the tracks of the LP; Musiker attempts a big-band/klezmer fusion on "Sam's Bulgar" and Middle Eastern exotica on "Der Yemenite Tanz," while Tarras sticks firmly to his guns on traditional-style numbers such as "The Roumanian Fantasy" and "Gypsy."

By the 1960s, the rise of pop music and rock and roll had all but spelled the death of klezmer, in spite of occasional novelties like Dick Dale's surf-guitar versions of "Misirlou" (1962) and "Hava Nagila" (1963). Dave Tarras and a few others, including the Epstein Brothers, found a professional refuge of sorts in Brooklyn, where a large community of World War II refugees had settled, including many followers of Hasidism. Unlike earlier immigrants, these ultraorthodox Jews were in no hurry to shed their Old World ways, and they welcomed Tarras's music with its roots in nigunim. When the rest of the Jewish world ceased to be interested in anything that reeked of shtetl nostalgia, Tarras found a home in a community that went to great lengths to replicate the Old World shtetl of his youth.

It was there in the Hasidic enclave in Brooklyn that Andy Statman would rediscover Dave Tarras in the mid-1970s, leading to one of the most remarkable mentor-protege relationships in modern music, one that would in no small part be responsible for the revival of klezmer in the last two decades of the twentieth century. Largely through the efforts of Andy Statman and Walter Zev Feldman, the former Balkan Folk Arts Center (now the Center for Traditional Music and Dance) in New York presented a series of performances by Tarras in the late 1970s and issued a new recording by him, launching a revival that culminated when Tarras received a National Heritage Award from the National Endowment for the Arts in 1984. Tarras died on 14 February 1989.

## CHAPTER 3

# REVIVAL

The revival of klezmer in the 1970s and 1980s has been variously attributed to a growth in ethnic pride among American Jews spurred by the popular success of Alex Haley's book and TV miniseries *Roots,* to a reaction against the predominance of Israeli Hebrew culture at a time of political disillusionment with the State of Israel, to a folk revival and increasing interest in world music among Jewish musicians, to a gradual spiritual awakening following the disappointments of the cultural revolution of the sixties, and, finally, to the passage of time since the horrors of the Holocaust caused American Jews to repress or ignore painful reminders of Eastern European Jewish culture.

The truth is likely to contain a bit of all of these reasons. Perhaps it is best summed up by Hankus Netsky, who as the founder and leader of the Klezmer Conservatory Band, has played no small role in the revival of klezmer music since the late seventies. "Archaic things come back," says Netsky. "The blues came back. . . . And the same thing eventually happened when our generation came of age and said, 'Wait a minute. What happened? Where's *our* folk music?'"

Or, as violinist Alicia Svigals of the Klezmatics says, "It was natural that klezmer should come back. The good stuff always does."

The story of the klezmer revival is the story of a musical trend, but it is also the story of individuals—musicians whose paths independently and somewhat serendipitously led them to uncover and rediscover the music of their parents and grandparents hidden away in basements and attics and filed away as old-fashioned sounds.

For people like Andy Statman, Michael Alpert, Lev Liberman, Hankus Netsky, Henry Sapoznik, Alan Bern, and many others, the discovery of the secret music of their parents' generation was in some way the culmination of a lifelong search: a search for an identity, and for a muse. For each of them, the balance of these elements differed. For each of these musicians, this discovery marked the beginning of a new phase in their creative lives.

## THE KLEZMORIM

By the time he was in college, Lev Liberman had already amassed an eclectic musical background. His mother was an aficionado of opera and his father a fan of folk revival groups such as the Weavers and the New Lost City Ramblers. His own early musical favorites included Prokofiev. "I walked around with Russian harmonies and sonorities in my head all the time," he says. While at Pomona College in Claremont, California, Lev got turned on to the early jazz of Cab Calloway, Sidney Bechet, and Duke Ellington's Jungle Band by watching Betty Boop cartoons. He was also exposed to the music of Kurt Weill and, as an aspiring jazz musician, learned his share of Gershwin tunes on the bandstand.

Then, in 1971, he had a "eureka moment" when he realized that all the different kinds of music he liked had a common stylistic influence. "Jewish was the common denominator between Russia, New York, the radical European stage, early film, and New Orleans jazz," he says. Intrigued by his realization, Liberman began searching for the missing link, the Jewishness, in Russian and Romanian folk music, Depression-era cartoon soundtracks, early jazz, and the compositions of Gershwin, Weill, and Prokofiev.

After graduating from Pomona, Liberman took his flute—his main instrument at the time—and moved to Berkeley, where he played rock, folk, light classics, Balkan, and Greek music with various bands. He began performing with David Skuse, a mainstay of many Bay area Balkan bands, who was also well versed in Irish, Scandinavian, Russian, and other ethnic musics.

By 1974 Lev and Dave began calling themselves the Sarajevo Folk Ensemble. The next year Liberman stumbled upon a cache of old Yiddish 78s in a closet at the Judah Magnes Museum in Oakland and set to work transcribing and rehearsing the music. He and Skuse began adding klezmer songs to their band's repertoire. They needed more musicians, obviously, and after turning them down twice, David Julian Gray signed on, bringing with him his clarinets, mandolin, violin, and assorted other Balkan instruments. Charter members Greg Carageorge and Laurie Chastain filled out the ensemble on bass and fiddle, respectively, and the group began playing on the street and at weddings and parties.

Their initial efforts to play the music in the Jewish community and at weddings met with resistance. Audiences weren't primed to welcome what they still heard as embarrassing music reminiscent of Old World oppression. But when the group took its music outside the Jewish world, it received a positive response. "We'd play public venues where the audience didn't come with a lot of cultural baggage, and it worked great," says Liberman.

The group made its official debut as the Klezmorim in a series of concerts by different ethnic bands at the North Berkeley branch of the Berkeley Public Library in April 1976—the first public performances of a klezmer revival band. They soon found a home in the local folk scene, and the venerable Freight and Salvage coffeehouse in Berkeley became the band's unofficial headquarters. "It was there we developed our audience and our repertoire, learned how to put on a show, and got discovered," says Liberman. The popular success of those shows led to the release of the group's first album the next year. *East Side Wedding* was the first recording of the klezmer revival—what Liberman would refer to with undue modesty as "the first eggshell-chirpings of the klezmer renaissance"—and the first of several recordings by the Klezmorim, who would continue through various personnel changes over the next decade to perform around the world, paving the way for the full-fledged revival that was to follow. By 1984, when the Klezmorim played a headlining show at Carnegie Hall, no one could doubt that the klezmer revival was in full swing.

The Klezmorim's instrumentation and approach went through several changes over the years. They occasionally augmented the instrumental repertoire with vocals on Yiddish folk and theater tunes, but for the most part the Klezmorim remained a players' band. On its first album, the group was a small ensemble—basically a quartet, featuring flute, clarinet, violin, bass, and a few Balkan instruments —and the flavor and repertoire was very Balkan. With the group's second album, *Streets of Gold,* recorded in 1978, the lineup expanded to eleven musicians, with Liberman moving from flute to saxophone, and with a full horn section playing a repertoire almost entirely Yiddish. At one time or another the group's instrumentation included dumbek, lauto, brass whistle, peckhorn, baraban, and something called a Marxophone, which Lev Liberman describes as "an obsolete hammered dulcimer for nonmusicians."

As the first group to record, the Klezmorim didn't have the same advantages as the later groups, who had easy access to reissues of old 78s and new field recordings from Eastern Europe. Such recordings trickled to the group through the slowly developing network of klezmer revivalists and from record collector and musicologist Martin Schwartz, a professor at the University of California at Berkeley who became a mentor to the group. Nor could the members of the Klezmorim draw upon the wave of scholarship that came later as older klezmorim were discovered and their arrangements documented.

The Klezmorim, one of the pioneer revival-era groups, are remembered as much for their theatrical stage shows as for their jazzy, horn-fueled arrangements. They are pictured here at the Great American Music Hall in San Francisco in 1978. (l to r: Kevin Linscott, Lev Liberman, Stuart Brotman, David Julian Gray, John Raskin, Brian Wishnefsky)

As Liberman puts it, "It was lonely for those first several years. Musically, we were almost entirely on our own. . . . I was reading a lot at the time about the history of jazz, wistfully wishing that we had a scene like the old jazzers had in New Orleans or Kansas City, or the beboppers on 52nd Street. Club dates every night followed by jam sessions and cutting contests 'til dawn. I wanted the intensity, the stimulation, the challenge. I wanted to hear lots of different players finding their own voices in klezmer music."

Given the group's isolation, it is remarkable that the early recordings are as good as they are. As one of the earliest and best known of the first wave of klezmer revival bands, the Klezmorim laid down the parameters for the new klezmorim and played a large role in building expectations among audiences and critics. They were among the first new players to take klezmer out of the folk and Jewish ghettoes and onto stages at theaters, concert halls, jazz clubs, and on radio and TV. This meant that the group's wide-ranging approach to the repertory, which included Old World melodies, such as "Baym Rebns Sude" and "Heyser Bulgar," as well as Greek and Turkish tunes, jazz numbers, and theater tunes, all got lumped together as "klezmer music."

In performance, the group also emphasized the music's zany quality, what Liberman called "the rollicking, vodka-soaked sound of a steam calliope gone mad." Two of the groups' early members were refugees from the San Francisco street theater scene, per-forming as Professor Gizmo the One-Man Band and Hairy James the Trumpet-Playing Gorilla. In 1983–84, the group teamed with the Flying Karamazov Brothers, adding juggling and tumbling to an already vaudevillian-flavored stage act. The musicians wore fezzes and tossed rubber chickens into the crowd. The drummer used plastic Halloween bones as drumsticks. Concerts included mock socialist rallies, Holy Roller revivalist meetings, and Kabuki dramas. They ran onstage and played in midair, held long notes until they turned blue, and used their horns as swords and oars and telescopes. Their shows were crazy, antic affairs, and much to Liberman's chagrin, this is what many recall most strongly about the Klezmorim.

The Klezmorim were more than a klezmer band; they were a theatrical act, and a very effective and entertaining one at that. "I would have liked the music to have succeeded strictly on its own merits, but it would not have happened without the show," says Liberman. Hence, they painted in broad strokes in order to communicate with an audience that was just returning to the music for the first time in years.

But this isn't to dismiss the band artistically. Over the course of the group's dozen or so years, its multifaceted approach paralleled and even anticipated the development of klezmer in the revival period, from the traditionalism of "Medyatsiner Waltz," to the cross-cultural fusion of "Thalassa," to the more experimental fusions of jazz and world music. Unfortunately, little of the group's more experimental or creative work from the late 1980s ever made it onto any officially released recordings.

BY THE TIME the group recorded *Notes from Underground* in 1984, Liberman was fully indulging his love of early jazz with Oriental fox-trots like "Egyptian Ella" and "Yiddisher Charleston" alongside a pretty straightforward version of Duke Ellington's "The Mooche." A version of Sidney Bechet's "Song of the Medina" anticipates by almost fifteen years David Krakauer's klezmer tribute to the seminal jazz clarinetist. A medley of "Betty Boop" and "Gangsters in Toyland" forever fixes the adjective *zany* to the group's identity, and "Stambul" is pure Middle Eastern kitsch.

On *Jazz Babies,* recorded live in concert in Amsterdam in 1986, dance tempos are kept impossibly fast for comic effect ("Kishin-ever" and "Circus Sirba"), and the repertoire includes straight-ahead, vintage New Orleans jazz ("Digga Digga Doo") with no overt connection to klezmer (other than the fact that both musics were being played and recorded in the 1920s). The Amsterdam concert featured silly narrative passages ("The Supreme Jazz Baby Speaks") and an entire suite of musical vaudeville.

But the concert also featured moments of brilliant and imaginative playing. "Firen" is a stately, almost classically impressionistic arrangement of the Old World hora, "Firen di Mekhutonim Aheym," for trombone and tuba, and Ben Goldberg's acrobatic clarinet solo on "Oy Tate" shows that you don't need to be a Flying Karamazov Brother to do a flip. While Cab Calloway's "Minnie the Moocher" might seem out of place on a klezmer album, no doubt "Abi Gezunt" seemed out of place on a Cab Calloway session when he first recorded it back in 1939.

Among the many musicians who passed through the ranks of the Klezmorim on their way to other groups were Stuart Brotman, Ben Goldberg, and Kenny Wolleson. Brotman was a member of David Lindley's Bay area world-folk band Kaleidoscope, and was a cofounder of the Ellis Island Band, before performing with the Klezmorim. He played on *Streets of Gold* and produced *Metropolis* in 1981—the only klezmer album ever to have been nominated for a Grammy Award. Brotman would later resurface in klezmer as a founding member of Brave Old World. Clarinetist Ben Goldberg and percussionist Kenny Wolleson, who played with the Klezmorim in its last few years, would go on to form the experimental, groundbreaking New Klezmer Trio. It is impossible to overestimate the influence that the Klezmorim would ultimately have on modern klezmer music.

# ANDY STATMAN

When Andy Statman began playing klezmer music in the mid-seventies, he already had a reputation as one of the world's leading mandolin players in bluegrass music, that fusion of old-time country harmonies and fast, flashy picking. He was also a Nashville sessionman in high demand for country and rock sessions, recording with the likes of Bob Dylan, Doug Sahm (of Sir Douglas Quintet fame), and David Bromberg. He was best known for his creative efforts in modern or progressive bluegrass, working with Vassar Clements, Peter Rowan, and his mentor and duet partner, David Grisman, to blend jazz and other modern influences with the high-lonesome sounds pioneered by Bill Monroe.

Today Andy Statman lives in the Midwood section of Brooklyn, in a deeply religious Hasidic community not far from where he grew up in Jackson Heights, Queens. The twenty-minute cab ride from Queens to Brooklyn took many years and many detours, but in the end Statman wound up close to where he began: living in a Jewish community, observing the rhythms of Jewish life, listening to the sounds of the khazn and the klezmorim.

Statman remembers being exposed early on to klezmer music. "I heard klezmer as a child growing up in my house, although it wasn't even called klezmer," says Statman, who was born in 1950, and who grew up on Eighty-ninth Street near Thirty-seventh Avenue. "There wasn't even a name for it, but we used to play some of these records at family occasions and dance to them." Although his family was not observant, they sent Andy to a Talmud Torah (an afternoon Jewish school), where the rabbi taught the students to sing nigunim. "I remember me and the other students just being in a state of ecstasy singing these dance tunes." Little did young Statman know that four decades later, those very same nigunim would constitute source material for a body of sophisticated, experimental, jazz-influenced musical improvisations.

Besides klezmer, the Statman family record collection included classical music and Broadway show tunes. Andy came from a background steeped in music, Jewish and otherwise. On his mother's side were famous European cantors going back several generations, including at least one who performed outside of synagogues in concerts around Europe. Statman also had a cousin, Sammy Fain, who was a songwriter of the classic pop era and a contemporary of Cole Porter and the Gershwins, and among whose credits are "Love Is a Many-Splendored Thing" and many other standards, some of which were recorded by Duke Ellington.

But Statman also soaked in sounds coming from outside his house, including fifties rock and roll and roots music of the folk re-

Revival pioneer Andy Statman invested klezmer with a newfound spirituality.

vival. One album in particular struck his fancy—a record by the famous bluegrass duo of Earl Flatt and Lester Scruggs, a reissue of 45s they recorded in their heyday. Statman once said about the records to an interviewer, "Just straight ahead bluegrass, very passionate and beautiful. Curly Seckler was the mandolin player. He played very simple breaks, but they gave me the chills."

The sounds of bluegrass fed a young New York City boy's fantasies of life in the country. Statman would awaken early each morning to watch "Modern Farmer" on TV before leaving for school. Late at night, he pressed his ear up against the speaker of a shortwave radio, tuning in broadcasts of country and western music from around the nation. While still a teenager, he began riding the subway into Manhattan, where Greenwich Village was ground zero of the folk revival. Bill Keith, Marty Cutler, John Herald, and David Grisman could be found there, hanging out and jamming, bluegrass style. Grisman, a few years Statman's senior and also a middle-class Jew from the New York metropolitan area, became his mentor. "He was living the bluegrass life down in the Village on Thompson Street," recalls Statman. "He was playing with Red Allen, and Frank Wakefield was living with him for awhile. He had bluegrass pictures all over the house and tons of tapes of radio shows from the forties with Bill Monroe playing with Flatt and Scruggs. He'd show me some positions on the mandolin and say, 'Call me when you learn these.'"

Statman began skipping school to play bluegrass, going to festivals where Jimmy Martin or the Osborne Brothers would be singing "this hair-raising music." He became totally obsessed with bluegrass. "I just absorbed it all. I wanted to be a bluegrass musician." By the time he was seventeen, he'd learned hundreds of mandolin solos and could sound like Wakefield, Monroe, Osborne, and

McReynolds, but he also began developing his own style. Statman quickly established a reputation as a teen prodigy. He formed a band, Country Cooking, with banjoists Tony Trischka and Peter Wernick, and performed with David Bromberg, Vassar Clements, Richard Greene, and Buell Neidlinger.

Statman's talent as a bluegrass player soon outran his affection for the music, however. He didn't feel comfortable as a Nashville sessionman, nor did he feel close enough to bluegrass culture to hook up permanently with a classic bluegrass road band led by people like Jimmy Martin or Ralph Stanley. As an instrumentalist, the music wasn't satisfying him. "Emotionally, the heavier things expressed in bluegrass were done vocally and not instrumentally," he says. "Plus, I wasn't from the South."

Statman was also feeling a pull toward another style of music. Inspired by experimental jazz saxophonists Albert Ayler and John Coltrane and their work with Indian, African, and Balkan music, Statman began playing saxophone, an instrument he could "breathe into" and thereby directly express emotion. He began studying with Richard Grando, a veteran of Art Blakey's band, who was exploring the connection between music and spirituality, in particular Native American religion and the *I Ching*.

In the meantime, Statman continued playing mandolin with other like-minded progressive bluegrass musicians in a group called Breakfast Special, which included Tony Trischka from Country Cooking. The group specialized in taking traditional bluegrass, removing it from its cultural setting, and mixing it with other styles, including jazz, Hawaiian, and Jewish music. "We were breaking new ground, but the bluegrass tabloids ignored us," said Statman. "We had saxophone and drums, which were hardly used in that setting."

Around this time, with his musical partner Zev Feldman, he began studying and playing Azerbaijani and Greek music with master Armenian and Greek musicians, including Antranik Aroustamian and Perikles Halkias. Finally, Statman's generalized search led him back to his roots. "It dawned on me that if I'm looking for a spiritual path, I'm born Jewish, it was handed to me, so this is something I should explore," he said. His spiritual investigation took him to a Hasidic enclave in Brooklyn, where he began the slow process of becoming a Torah-observant Jew. Musically, he didn't have to go any farther than his parent's house, where he rummaged through their collection and found plenty of klezmer albums.

"Here I was playing with all different types of bands in New York, studying different types of ethnic music," he said. "I realized there was no one around playing traditional Jewish instrumental music. And I was getting more into it and I thought as a professional musician this was my own birthright. I would like to be able to play it as well as someone who played it in Europe a hundred years earlier."

Statman had heard that Dave Tarras was still alive and that he had recently moved to a neighborhood near Statman's own in Brooklyn. He found out where he lived, and mandolin in hand, he knocked on his door one day, introduced himself, and began playing Tarras's songs for him on mandolin. Tarras took on Statman as his protégé, passing along several of his rare, Albert-style clarinets and informally making him a kind of successor. It was a creative partnership, and along with Zev Feldman, Statman was able to get grant money to produce a new Tarras recording and a series of concerts reintroducing Tarras to a concert audience. Much to Tarras's surprise, they were sold-out affairs. Just when he thought he had been left behind and forgotten, a new generation of young musicians rediscovered him and made him their champion, in much the same way that the folk revivalists of a decade earlier scoured the Mississippi Delta for old, forgotten black bluesmen.

Equipped with Tarras's clarinets, arrangements, blessing, and support, as well as with the initial results of early musicological research, Statman and Feldman recorded their own album, *Jewish Klezmer Music*, in 1979, with bassist Marty Confurius. Although the trio format (Statman doubled on clarinet and mandolin, and Feldman played tsimbl) gave the music an Old World feel, many of the tunes were learned from American 78s recorded in the twenties by I. J. Hochman, Harry Kandel, Abe Schwartz, and Naftule Brandwein. Statman followed this recording in 1983 with *Klezmer Music*. Credited (in the style of the 1920s) to the "Andy Statman Klezmer Orchestra," the ensemble was actually a quartet, with Confurius continuing on bass, Bob Jones on guitar, and David Steinberg on French horn and trumpet. The songs on *Klezmer Music*—including "Rumanian Dance," "Ukrainer Chosid'l," "Terkisher," "Onga Bucharesti," and "Galitzianer Chusid"—provided a geographical tour of the Old World and demonstrated the influence of non-Jewish musical styles on klezmer.

The next year saw the release of *Klezmer Suite*, with the same four musicians. It continued to showcase Statman's developing style as a clarinetist in folksy arrangements, including several new compositions by Dave Tarras. Statman never abandoned mandolin, and found ways to employ his picking skills on numbers such as "Rumanian Dance," playing a lively rhythm, and "Tepliker Sher," playing lead. The meditative piece "Nigun" also hinted at Statman's growing interest in the mystical side of Judaism and the Hasidic repertoire.

But just as Statman hadn't wanted to become a modern-day version of Bill Monroe in bluegrass, he was not satisfied becoming a latter-day Dave Tarras. His spiritual quest led him deeper into klezmer, to the melodies' roots in Hasidic nigunim. For Statman, a neo-Hasid, the jazzman's improvisational approach was perfectly suited to the Hasid's meditative mysticism, and by improvising on the foundation of the nigunim, Statman found himself best able to reconcile his musical and spiritual inclinations.

"Klezmer music in itself is a music with a tremendous spirituality built into it," says Statman. "It was music by and large created to serve a particular religious function: to make a bride and groom happy at a wedding," referring to the *mitzve,* or commandment, of making joy at a simkhe. "The klezmorim of old had it in mind that they were fulfilling a particular mitzve when they were playing at these weddings."

Statman goes on. "A lot of the klezmer melodies people play are Hasidic melodies. A doina is just the tip of the iceberg. A khazn will use elements of a doina as just part of a whole thing he's singing. Same with Hasidic music. It's very deep and most of the old klezmorim, in fact, came from Hasidic families. Dave Tarras did. Naftule Brandwein, they came from Hasidic families. They were part and parcel of that whole culture and they understood what the functions of these tunes were. As the music became more and more secularized it began losing a lot of the depth and just losing a lot of what its roots were, to the point where it just became bulgars and dance tunes.

"But these guys from Europe, they knew all the different forms, the instrumental counterparts of the khazanim, or meditative Hasidic songs, the rubato songs played for various honored guests, or when people were eating. They were aware of this whole, deeper strata of the music, which really gave birth to the dance music. Not that the dance music is light. You can have the dance music, particularly the Hasidic dance music, set up to induce a trancelike state as well. But they understood what the deeper basis of this music was and where it was coming from. It came from the family of Hasidim."

The results of Statman's spiritual-musical explorations were heard on his 1997 recording, *Between Heaven and Earth: Music of the Jewish Mystics,* with the Andy Statman Quartet, followed in 1998 by *The Hidden Light.* These recordings stretched the meaning of klezmer to the breaking point, and in interviews Statman made clear he didn't consider them to be representative of the genre. These were Statman's highly personal, improvised explorations of Hasidic prayer tunes, turned into his own ecstatic compositions. While the versions that appeared on his recordings were elegant, pleasing, and accessible, in concert Statman stretched them much further, leaving more than one fan scratching his head and muttering, "Where's the klezmer?" Statman made clear that conventional klezmer was no longer of interest to him, although he continued to appear with "In the Fiddler's House," the seasonal Itzhak Perlman road show.

## KAPELYE

While Statman was jamming with Dave Tarras on his doorstep, and while Liberman's troupe was entertaining the minions in the Bay Area, Henry Sapoznik was rummaging through the stash of vintage 78s at the YIVO Institute for Jewish Research in New York, trying to recreate the history of recorded klezmer by organizing this overlooked archive. How the Brooklyn-born Sapoznik got to YIVO, ground zero for research into Old World Jewish culture, is another tale of a native New Yorker raised in an atmosphere immersed in yidishkayt, but whose path to Jewish music detoured through old-time American folk music before returning to the music of his father's generation.

Sapoznik's father, Zindel, was a cantor, and his mother, Pearl, sang Eastern European folk songs. While still a young boy studying in a Lubavitcher yeshiva, Henry embarked on the traditional route of following in his father's footsteps as a *meshoyrer,* a vocalist serving an apprenticeship in a synagogue choir. Thus, early on, he was steeped in the sounds of the *khazones*—the traditional cantorial melodies that are at the heart of klezmer.

In the 1950s, Henry was exposed to the sound of musicians "playing Jewish" in the Catskills while traveling with his father, who was hired by hotels to conduct Passover seders and services. But Henry, like many American Jewish boys raised in postwar America, wanted little to do with anything that smacked of his parents' Old Country accents. As he has said on several occasions, Beaver Cleaver was his preferred role model. Henry, calling himself "Hank," began hanging out in Greenwich Village, in Washington Square Park, and at neighborhood folk clubs, listening to old-time banjo music. By the early seventies, as a banjoist, he teamed up with mandolinist Alan Podber and fiddler Bill Garbus to form the Delaware Water Gap string band, which enjoyed a near-decade-long run through several albums and European tours.

Sapoznik was a restless student of old-timey music who frequently sought out old masters from whom to learn. Among these were Tommy Jarrell, an old-time fiddler whom Sapoznik first visited in Surry County, North Carolina, in 1973. On Henry's third

Kapelye, another revival group, combined a folk-vaudevillian approach with a high degree of Yiddish literacy. Note the banner with the group's name, in Yiddish. (l to r: Lauren Brody, Eric Berman, Henry Sapoznik, Ken Maltz, Michael Alpert)

visit to Jarrell, two years later, the bemused old-timer, ignored by his own people but worshiped by a parade of Northerners, many of them Jews, asked him bluntly, "Hank, don't your people got none of your own music?"

Hank Sapoznik took the question seriously. On his grandfather's advice, he went to YIVO's offices in New York where folklorist Barbara Kirshenblatt-Gimblett showed him the institute's overlooked and ignored stash of old 78 sound recordings—literally thousands of 78s representing a treasure trove of early-twentieth-century Yiddish popular music. Sapoznik set to work researching and cataloging the recordings. With the help of other revivalists, including Lev Liberman, Andy Statman, Zev Feldman, and Martin Schwartz, in 1980 Sapoznik produced the first reissue of klezmer 78s, *Klezmer Music: 1910–42.*

The halls at YIVO soon became crowded with other would-be klezmorim, revivalists, and musicologists searching for old-time Jewish music. Among them was Michael Alpert, who had moved to New York from Los Angeles to take a job as a community folklorist, performing Yiddish music at schools, senior centers, and old-age homes. Like Henry Sapoznik, Michael Alpert was the son of immigrants and grew up in a Yiddish-speaking household, rich in the culture of the Old World. Long before there was any talk of a musical revival, Alpert's Yiddish-speaking father was calling his music-obsessed son "klezmer-man."

A self-described folkie with a gift for foreign tongues—he majored in Slavic languages at UCLA—Alpert played violin, guitar, and accordion, and sang all sorts of ethnic folk musics, including Irish, Balkan, Serbian, Russian. In late 1976, a musician friend, Mark Simos, returned to Los Angeles from a folk conference in Philadelphia with news of an exciting development in the folk world. He had with him a tape given to him by Andy Statman and Zev Feldman, which contained a few 1920s-era klezmer tunes that Alpert instantly recognized, having heard the music on Yiddish radio broadcasts in his youth. The music was similar to some of the Balkan music played by Alpert and others in Southern California's Balkan folk scene, but it spoke a different language, one that wasn't lost on many of the players who, like Alpert and Stuart Brotman, were Jewish.

It was clear to them that this music, which Simos said they were calling "klezmer" back east, was the Jewish equivalent of the old-time Serbian and Irish music they had studied. The only difference was that this was the music of their own people. Soon Alpert, Simos, and Brotman formed a band, the Chutzpah Orchestra, to play the newly discovered Yiddish dance tunes. Occasionally the Klezmorim would come down to Los Angeles from San Francisco and jam with the Chutzpah Orchestra, one time even taking it to the streets of Fairfax, the old, inner-city Jewish neighborhood. While the band was short-lived, it laid the groundwork for much of what was to come.

Back at YIVO, Henry Sapoznik, the new point man for klezmer music, received frequent requests for klezmer bands to perform at various functions. With Alpert's arrival in New York, the pieces of a band fell into place, and in 1979 the two formed Kapelye, along with Josh Waletzky, Lauren Brody, Ken Maltz, Dan Conte, and later, Eric Berman. The core of one of the foremost bands of the klezmer revival was now in place.

With three native Yiddish speakers in its lineup—Waletzky also grew up speaking Yiddish and attending Yiddish summer camp—Kapelye exhibited a deep knowledge and appreciation for Yiddish-American culture. This would remain the band's signature—what distinguished it from the rest of the revival bands—over the course of the next decade. In addition to playing instrumental updates of classic 78s, the group incorporated Yiddish theater tunes, folk songs, and novelty numbers into its mix. Its first recording, *Future and Past,* came out in 1981; that same year, the group toured nationally in a revue called "Der Yidisher Caravan," which included Andy Statman and Henry Sapoznik's father, Zindel Sapoznik, in a program featuring klezmer, cantorial music, and Yiddish theater songs.

Kapelye went on to record and release several albums throughout the eighties and nineties, including *Levine and His Flying Machine, Chicken,* and *On the Air: Jewish-American Radio.* This last album is a brilliantly executed piece of cultural history, reconstructing the heyday of Yiddish radio broadcasts with archival material and new recordings. As always, the group's material is infused with a warm, *heymish,* or familiar, sensibility, very much like that of Yiddish music's heyday in the 1920s. The group's simple arrangements and acoustic instrumentation features the bouncy, rhythmic punch of Henry Sapoznik's banjo rubbing up against Lauren Brody's piano and Eric Berman's tuba. In addition, although Ken Maltz takes plenty of clarinet solos à la Naftule Brandwein on the group's recordings, the generous sprinkling of Yiddish vocal numbers from the folk and theater tradition infuses them with a personal touch. The recordings are lovingly and exhaustively annotated; Kapelye seems as much about cultural documentation and preservation as it is about making music, which comes as no surprise given Henry Sapoznik's key role in researching, archiving, compiling, preserving, and perpetuating klezmer music.

In addition to its recordings, Kapelye was hired to provide the sound track and appear as a Hasidic wedding band in the Hollywood film version of Chaim Potok's best-selling novel *The Chosen,* further popularizing the music. Sapoznik has noted the irony of being engaged to portray a Hasid in film, "a role I played during the major chunk of my 'Wonder Years,'" and one from which he thought he had successfully escaped. Kapelye was also the first American klezmer band to tour Europe. Over the years, such prominent Yiddish musicians as Alan Bern, Zalman Mlotek, Adrienne Cooper, and Peter Sokolow have passed through the ranks of Kapelye. Michael Alpert left the band in 1992 to devote his energies to Brave Old World, and twenty years after cofounding the band, Henry Sapoznik "retired" from the group, which was then reconstituted as an all-instrumental ensemble with Ken Maltz, Eric Berman, Peter Sokolow, and accordionist Sy Kushner.

# THE KLEZMER CONSERVATORY BAND

At about the same time that Kapelye was getting its act together in New York, Hankus Netsky, a teacher at the New England Conservatory of Music, was putting together a group in Boston that would become the Klezmer Conservatory Band. Netsky was running regular, informal klezmer jam sessions after hours at the school when someone asked him to put together a program of Jewish music. Netsky assembled various groups and ensembles, including a big band, consisting mostly of students from the conservatory, that played three swinging klezmer numbers. The band was such a hit that by the end of the show it got two offers for gigs, and thus in the winter of 1980 the Klezmer Conservatory Band was born. It continues to be one of the most perennially popular recording and performing groups in klezmer.

The creation of the Klezmer Conservatory Band wasn't entirely a lark. Netsky's grandfather and several uncles had been prominent in the Philadelphia klezmer scene in the earlier half of the century. Netsky grew up vaguely aware of their work and music and he had always harbored a deep curiosity about it. Around 1974 he began pestering his relatives to show him how to play the old tunes and taping their old 78s of Dave Tarras and Naftule Brandwein. Netsky, who majored in classical composition and began teaching at the New England Conservatory at age twenty-three, put together a book of arrangements based on their old recordings and others he found at Gratz College in Philadelphia. In 1981 the Klezmer Conservatory Band put out its first recording. *Yiddishe Renaissance* included remakes of popular Yiddish theater tunes such as "Papirosn," "Rumenye, Rumenye," and "Rozhinkes Mit Mandlen (Raisins and Almonds)," and renditions of some clas-

Saxophonist/bandleader Hankus Netsky of the Klezmer Conservatory Band working on an arrangement with pianist Alan Bern.

sic tunes from klezmer's golden era ("Beym Rebn in Palestine," "Der Heyser Bulgar"). Also featured are a poignant duet between violinist Greta Buck and Netsky on piano in a version of Solinski's "Rumenishe Fantazie," and "Yiddish Blues," a curious Yiddish ragtime novelty first recorded by Lt. Joseph Frankel's Orchestra in the 1920s.

The band followed this eclectic approach during the next two decades. The KCB, as it became known, produced albums that are a rich repository of the Yiddish music repertoire—instrumental and vocal music from the Yiddish theater and popular music tradition, labor songs, lullabies, dance tunes, songs of resistance, nigunim, movie themes, immigrant ballads, novelty numbers, holiday songs—and a gold mine of virtuoso performances.

The KCB got a big break in 1984 when Garrison Keillor's public radio variety show, *A Prairie Home Companion,* came to Boston. One of the band members got a tape over to the crew of the program, which specialized in presenting old-time and occasionally quirky American music. As chance would have it, Garrison Keillor liked what he heard and invited the group to be on the show. The KCB would return to Keillor's program several times in the next few years, and other klezmer bands, including Kapelye and the

The Klezmer Conservatory Band, circa 1997: (Back row, l to r: Robin Miller, Jeff Warschauer, Grant Smith, Gary Bohan, Javier Perez Saco, Mark Hamilton, James Guttman. Front row, l to r: Ilene Stahl, Hankus Netsky, Judy Bressler, Miriam Rabson.)

Klezmatics, would also make appearances on the show, solidly establishing a place for klezmer among Americana.

From the beginning, it was Netsky's idea that the KCB would be a revival outfit, showcasing a nostalgic brand of klezmer inspired by the American immigrant bands of the 1920s and 1930s, with a repertoire that would include Yiddish swing and theater music. As we have seen, the klezmorim in America had strong connections to the Yiddish theater and popular recordings, and the KCB recapitulated that history in the course of its concerts and recordings, alternating traditional klezmer dances with vocal numbers gleaned from Yiddish musicals and the Yiddish hit parade. "What we're about is the evolution of Yiddish music in America," says Netsky, who wears the revivalist badge with pride. "We acknowledge the entire American history of the music, and that includes the Borscht Belt, the Yiddish theater, and the American transition of the klezmer. The fact is that these guys played in big bands and that affected their music. That's all a part of what we do."

Among the charter members of the Klezmer Conservatory Band was Frank London, who would go on to help establish the Klezmatics and Hasidic New Wave and to record several albums under his own name. Trombonist David Harris went on to become cofounder of Shirim and Naftule's Dream. Clarinetist Don Byron would gain fame as the first African American to make a mark in klezmer, recording a tribute to musical parodist Mickey Katz before enjoying a career as a leading experimental-jazz improviser.

Don Byron's tenure in the KCB and his subsequent career in klezmer is a small chapter in itself. The novelty of a klezmer revival band boasting an African American clarinetist made for good copy in the general press, but fortunately, according to Hankus Netsky, this rarely got in the way of serious consideration of the band's

## GIORA FEIDMAN

In a funny way, one of the musicians most responsible for the revival of interest in and popularity of klezmer since the 1970s—especially in Europe—has actually played little or no direct role in what we commonly refer to as the "klezmer revival." This is because the "revival" itself was very much a communal movement centered around a core of American players and groups, many with backgrounds in American and Eastern European folk music and jazz. They swapped repertory tapes, jammed together, taught each other licks, formed groups promiscuously, and moved between them like so many baseball free agents (except without the signing bonuses). They were all part of one, large, klezmer-revival family.

But even as Andy Statman and Henry Sapoznik and Lev Liberman and Hankus Netsky were just beginning to play klezmer, clarinetist Giora Feidman was championing the folk melodies of Eastern Europe from his perch on the classical concert stage. Born in 1936 in Buenos Aires, Giora Feidman joined the Israeli Philharmonic at age twenty. In Israel, Feidman was shocked to discover the almost total lack of interest in Yiddish music among his colleagues. As the descendant of several generations of klezmorim with roots in Bessarabia—the Mississippi Delta of klezmer—he took it upon himself to introduce Yiddish repertoire into the classical mainstream in performance and recording.

Predating by at least a decade the major classical-to-klezmer crossover project by world-renowned violinist Itzhak Perlman, by the early eighties Feidman had gained an international following. His 1981 appearance at New

music. Byron was a classically trained musician who grew up in New York and who, by the time he attended the New England Conservatory, had an "encyclopedic knowledge" of the classical repertoire. Like several other non-Jewish members of Netsky's original klezmer pickup band, he wound up immersing himself in the music and, in his case, remaining with the KCB for seven years.

York's Avery Fisher Hall was one of the highest profile klezmer performances up to that point. He also began a prolific recording career, producing dozens of klezmer-oriented albums with titles such as *Klezmer Celebration, Viva El Klezmer, Klassic Klezmer,* and *The Magic of Klezmer.* In 1984 he played the role of the clarinetist in Peter Zadek's controversial and critically acclaimed Berlin production of Joshua Sobol's Holocaust play, *Ghetto,* which rocked the conscience of German audiences who were in the midst of a long, morally exhausting effort of coming to terms with the crimes of the not so-distant German past. As the only character to survive at the end of the drama, the role made Feidman into a kind of heroic national symbol to Germans, the living embodiment of post-Holocaust Jewry's survival.

Despite Feidman's success in popularizing klezmer, he remained apart from the revival proper. As we have seen, the klezmer revival in America was informed by a folk-roots aesthetic, whereas Feidman's musical approach remained closely rooted to the classical concert stage. Even when he was playing freylekhs and marches, or investigating the Yiddish overtones of Leonard Bernstein's *West Side Story* music, or George Gershwin's Yiddish affinities, or providing "authentic" background music for Steven Spielberg's *Schindler's List,* his arrangements were always couched in the properly starched cadences and fussy dynamics of the classical concert hall. This was in sharp contrast to the folk-, jazz-, or popular based aesthetic assumed by the vast majority of the klezmer revival groups. In this way, Feidman—one of the true pioneers of the klezmer revival and, at least in Europe, perhaps the most popular "cultural celebrity" associated with klezmer—remains just a sidebar to the main narrative of the klezmer revival.

While in the KCB, Byron became enamored of the work of Mickey Katz, a midcentury clarinetist who is best known as a comedian and musical parodist. Byron was drawn to Katz as much for his musicianship as for the unique place he held in postwar American-Jewish culture. His interest in Katz begins to show up on the band's third album, 1985's *A Touch of Klez,* which includes

Clarinetist Don Byron, seen here with Hankus Netsky, was a member of the Klezmer Conservatory Band for seven years. After recording a tribute to musical comedian Mickey Katz, Byron went on to carve out a career as a leading avant-garde jazz musician.

Katz's wedding medley, "Mazeltov Dances," and his "Tsatske Kazatske (Toy Break-Dance)." From that point on, Katz material continued to be included in the band's repertoire, even after Byron left the group in 1987.

After leaving the KCB, Byron continued to play klezmer on his own, delving further into the mystique of Mickey Katz, and not without provoking some bit of controversy by doing so. A musical comedian popular in the 1950s for his Yiddish-inflected musical parodies—in Katz's hands, such all-American fare as "Home on the Range" became "Haim Afen Range" and "April in Portugal" became "Pesach in Portugal"—Katz is variously seen as a brilliantly acerbic social critic disguised as a Borscht Belt comedian, or as an embarrassing purveyor of shtick. Byron believed the former—that Katz's blatant send-ups of the assimilationist streak in postwar American Jewry, to say nothing of his Spike Jones–influenced musical pastiches, were brilliantly inventive social satires—and in 1993 he recorded a tribute album, *Don Byron Plays the Music of Mickey Katz.* The cover photo's ersatz, space-age typography, lounge-lizard furniture, and dreadlocked clarinetist holding a rubber chicken by the neck made a strong statement of ironic cultural appropriation, continued in Byron's own compositions, "Prologue" and "Epilogue," which sampled recordings of Katz's comedy routines atop Byron's avant-garde-tinged classical composition. But in January 1994, a Sunday *New York Times Magazine* profile raised some ugly questions about the propriety of Byron's appropriation of Katz's material. The interview also showed Byron chafing against his identity as the "black guy who does klezmer." By mid-decade Byron had put his klezmer days behind him in favor of an idiosyncratic, avant-garde style he calls "bug music."

THE INITIAL SUCCESS of the Klezmorim, Kapelye, the Andy Statman Klezmer Orchestra, and the Klezmer Conservatory Band inspired growing interest in klezmer, both in the United States and abroad. Several record labels responded with a wave of reissues of vintage Yiddish recordings from early in the century. Other bands followed quickly. Clarinetist Stewart Mennin, a member of the Chutzpah Orchestra, founded the New Shtetl Band in Albuquerque, New Mexico. After a visit to campus by the Klezmorim, a group of students at the University of California at Santa Cruz, including Ben Goldberg, Dan Seamans, and Kaila Flexer, formed Hotzeplotz. Yale Strom formed the group Zmiros, which he used as a vehicle to record and perform material he discovered on several trips to Eastern Europe, where he documented the repertoire of musicians who had played with klezmorim.

The revival also started a mad scramble to locate older musicians with firsthand experience playing Yiddish dance tunes. Andy Statman's relationship with Dave Tarras was just the beginning. Michael Alpert cultivated musical friendships with Bronya Sakina, Ben Bazyler, and Leon Schwartz. Henry Sapoznik befriended Sid Beckerman, the son of immigrant-era clarinetist Shloimke Beckerman, and teamed with Sid, Howie Leess, and Peter Sokolow (a younger musician with vast experience playing with musicians of the postwar generation) in a group called Klezmer Plus. The Epstein Brothers—Max, Willie, and Julie—were pulled out of semi-retirement in Florida and collaborated with several revivalists, among them Joel Rubin, who made several recordings with them. The colorful Epsteins were also the subject of a popular documentary film, *A Tickle in the Heart*. And Ray Musiker, a third-generation klezmer whose family came from Minsk, was recorded leading a group called the New York Klezmer Ensemble, which included Ray's son, Lee.

Like other folk music revivals, the klezmer revival became a grassroots affair. Amateur musicians gathered together to learn the old tunes from the vintage and new recordings. With the support of local communities and the increased demand for the music to be performed at weddings and bar mitzvah parties, the better amateurs formed semiprofessional working bands. Some even wrote their own music and made their own recordings. By the late eighties, upward of four hundred aspiring klezmorim were attending KlezKamp, the annual klezmer workshop in the Catskills, where the teachers were the leading musicians of the revival, including Michael Alpert, Hankus Netsky, and Henry Sapoznik.

As the first revival groups began touring Europe, they met with enthusiastic response, nowhere more so than in Germany. The land that once marked Jews and their culture for extermination now provided fertile ground for a rebirth of Yiddish music. In Germany, audiences were better able to understand the Yiddish lyrics of many of the songs, Yiddish being an amalgam of different languages, but especially German. The revival also began infiltrating Eastern Europe, where the music never died completely, kept alive by those few Jews who survived the purges and the Holocaust as well as by non-Jewish musicians who shared the repertoire with their fellow Jewish musicians.

Now that it was brought back to life through the reissue of vintage recordings and through the historical reconstructions of the early revival bands, the stage was set for the true rebirth of klezmer as a vital, creative musical genre—a klezmer renaissance.

## CHAPTER 4

# RENAISSANCE

The groundbreaking work of the pioneer revival bands did more than just popularize an old style of music. By defining the parameters of modern klezmer, they helped point the way toward a future for the music. Musicians brought up on jazz, rock, classical, and other genres could approach the music not only as revivalists, but also as creative partners in its ongoing development. Since its earliest days, the history of klezmer was in part the story of a give-and-take with other styles of music. Thus it was only a few years after the first bands learned the basic styles and format of the so-called traditional repertoire that they and others began experimenting. By the mid-1990s, there was a profusion of attempts to combine klezmer with everything from Jamaican ska to punk rock to heavy metal to electronica. Some were more inventive than others, and some sounded better on paper than in their finally executed form.

The best combined a strong foundation in klezmer fundamentals with virtuosity in other realms, creating a klezmer-based, new Jewish music. Nowhere was this recipe for success more apparent than in two groups: Brave Old World and the Klezmatics.

# BRAVE OLD WORLD

Brave Old World is often called the first klezmer "supergroup," and given the yikhes of the quartet's musicians, this is hardly an exaggeration. The collective résumés of Michael Alpert, Alan Bern, Kurt Bjorling, and Stuart Brotman read like a history of the klezmer revival. Michael Alpert was a founding member of Kapelye. Alan Bern also served time in that group as well as in the Klezmer Conservatory Band. In addition to his own group, the Chicago Klezmer Ensemble, Kurt Bjorling recorded and performed frequently with the Klezmatics in its early years. And Stuart Brotman, as we have seen, shows up everywhere in this story: with Michael Alpert in the Chutzpah Orchestra; with Stewart Mennin, Barry Fisher, and Ron Holmes in the Ellis Island Band; as a performing member and producer of the Klezmorim; touring the West Coast with Kapelye; and finally, with Brave Old World.

In addition, each member of Brave Old World brought musical and cultural elements to the group from outside klezmer. Brotman followed up his early experience playing Jewish wedding gigs in Los Angeles in the 1960s with crossover experience in rock, in bands such as Canned Heat and Kaleidoscope—the latter an eclectic, world-folk-rock band led by David Lindley. Alpert and Brotman were well versed in Balkan music, and Bjorling and Bern studied both classical and jazz music. Each member was also a scholar and a virtuoso of his instrument. All these individual accomplishments add up, indeed, to the makings of a super group.

Brave Old World grew out of a series of ad hoc concert dates in Berlin in 1988. But the groundwork for the group was laid earlier in the decade, when Joel Rubin—a classically trained musician who had begun playing Yiddish and Greek music—met up with

Stuart Brotman and Michael Alpert on the West Coast and the three of them began playing klezmer together informally. Along with Alan Bern and Kurt Bjorling, they all played and taught together at the annual KlezKamp workshop in its early years, and an early cassette recording credited to the Joel Rubin Klezmer Band—featuring Alpert and Brotman with a few other musicians, including Hankus Netsky—was first released as *Brave Old World* in June 1988. (This tape was reissued ten years later on CD as *Hungry Hearts*. The quartet borrowed its name from the title of Rubin's cassette, leading to some confusion about just when the group was first formed.)

In 1988, Joel Rubin brought Alan Bern to Spain to accompany him on a series of concert dates. The two toured Spain together and eventually wound up in Berlin, where Bern had already spent some time and knew the territory. They played a series of concerts at the Café Einstein—housed in a building that originally belonged to a famous German-Jewish actress and had later been used as a headquarters for the Gestapo. The initial Rubin-Bern concert dates were such a success that more followed—first in a trio format featuring Michael Alpert, who had performed at the same venue with Kapelye back in 1984, and then in a quartet with Stuart Brotman. The stage was set for the formation of a band.

Alpert, Bern, and Brotman had all been deeply involved with first-wave revival bands, and they all shared a desire to push the music beyond mere revivalism. This was the inspiration for Brave Old World: to carve out a new Jewish music deeply rooted in Yiddish tradition yet transcending it, a music that spoke to contemporary audiences as more than just mere nostalgia by engaging the intellect with the sophistication of classical concert music while honoring the heart and soul of the Old World kapelye.

For Alan Bern—a conservatory-trained musician who had spent time at Karl Berger's Creative Music Studio in Hurley, New York, a combination retreat and think tank where the most adventurous jazz players and classical avant-gardists met to explore improvisation—the artistic challenge the group faced was to inject the elements of spontaneity and surprise into the traditional music. As he put it, "to make a music . . . where audiences will be sitting in their seats and if they're thinking at all they're going to be thinking, 'what the hell could possibly happen next?'" For Bern, this meant looking for new forms for the music, rather than re-creating existing forms.

This was the difference between the klezmer revival and the klezmer renaissance. Along with groups like the Klezmatics, the Toronto-based Flying Bulgar Klezmer Band, and the New Orleans Klezmer Allstars, Brave Old World paved the way by digging even deeper into Yiddish tradition to come up with something that was both new and yet rooted even further back in time than most of the music of the revival period. Bern credits his fellow musicians' love of and commitment to traditional Yiddish music and the great value they placed on responsive ensemble playing and improvisation (as opposed to rote reproduction) for the group's "new Jewish music."

The quartet began writing original material and rearranging old tunes and released its first album, *Klezmer Music,* in 1990. While deceptively traditional sounding, Brave Old World had already begun revealing what it was setting out to accomplish. Most of the revival bands had followed the pattern established in the era of 78s by recording songs of three minutes in length; Brave Old World discarded that limitation, artificial in the CD era, and allowed its compositions room to breathe in suites and extended song forms of between five and eight minutes. It was a modern innovation that, ironically, harkened back to the music's roots in suites for dancing.

*Klezmer Music* also includes a complete badkhones featuring Ben Bazyler, an old-time musician and badkhn whom Brotman had discovered working as a barber and with whom Alpert had established one of the signature mentor-protégé relationships of the revival. The badkhones, in which the badkhn sings and declaims in alternation with the ensemble, was a form Brave Old World continued to explore in years to come. *Klezmer Music* also introduced new Yiddish texts by Michael Alpert, songs that gave the lie to Yiddish as a dead language, and used Yiddish to confront contemporary issues, such as the nuclear disaster at Chernobyl, the fall of the

With roots in the klezmer revival as well as jazz, classical, and other ethnic folk musics, the members of Brave Old World (pictured here in concert in Berlin) draw from a rich, diverse palette when creating their contemporary brand of klezmer. (l-r: Stuart Brotman, Alan Bern, Michael Alpert, Kurt Bjorling)

Berlin Wall, and the disjunction of modern technology and Old World culture.

The members of Brave Old World briefly called it quits in early 1992, only to regroup a few months later, this time with Kurt Bjorling on clarinet. Joel Rubin would go on to carve out his own distinctive niche as a producer and compiler and to develop a reputation for exhaustively researched and annotated recordings of reconstructed Old World arrangements. He also worked with the Epstein Brothers, one of the oldest surviving groups from klezmer's heyday, and organized several European festivals and concert series.

Bjorling was the perfect match for Bern, Alpert, and Brotman in Brave Old World. An ardent student of Old World klezmer (as you can hear in his work with the Chicago Klezmer Ensemble, which he founded in 1984), he also brought to the group a broad background in classical, jazz, and other ethnic musics. With Bjorling on board, Brave Old World's second album, 1994's *Beyond the Pale*, boasted a warmer, jazzier sound, one more suited to the sort of natural improvisation and creative spontaneity that Bern was eager to explore.

*Beyond the Pale* was a concept album framed by original Yiddish songs by Michael Alpert—"Berlin Overture" and "Berlin 1990"—that directly addressed the ambivalence the musicians felt about playing in Germany ("I've played here in Germany, many's the time . . . But I swear by my muse . . . That not once has it been easy to be here"). Although a group of American musicians, Brave Old World's relationship to Germany is deep-seated. Alan Bern has spent most of his time since 1987 in Berlin, where he was musical director of the Bremen State Theater and where he directed the music for Joshua Sobol's acclaimed play, *Ghetto*. Brave Old World's formative years were largely spent in Berlin, where they enjoyed critical, artistic, and financial support for their experiments—more support, according to Bern, than would have likely been possible anywhere in the United States.

Among the highlights of *Beyond the Pale* are Bern's "Big Train," a solo accordion piece that combines several traditional melodies in an evocation of a tearful farewell. While Bern's liner notes say the song was inspired by the story of a young Russian Jew being drafted into the tsar's army for his obligatory twenty-five years of service, one cannot listen to the song in its context—on an album that explores contemporary Yiddish culture in Germany—and not think of a similar historical use of trains to transfer Jewish populations.

In 1999, ten years after the group was first formed, Brave Old World released *Blood Oranges (Royte Pomerantsn)*, an album that may well be the crowning achievement of the klezmer revival and renaissance—its *Sgt. Pepper's Lonely Hearts Club Band*. *Blood Oranges* elegantly weaves together the many disparate threads of klezmer revivalism, Old World gestures tied up in gorgeous patterns of tension and release. The music pulsates with the fluid, dynamic energy of a rock band raised on Beethoven, with an instrumental lineup modeled on an Old World acoustic ensemble. Instruments talk with each other using vocabulary adopted and adapted from classic melodies, effortlessly shifting their place in the ensemble from foreground to background, giving the music an airy, three-dimensional quality.

In the role of the badkhn, Michael Alpert interweaves vocal commentary between responsive instrumental passages; popping out of his Old World–style *shpil* are New World terms like *Internet, video, CD-ROM,* and *fiber-optic.* Stuart Brotman's bass is an equal partner in the ensemble, giving it the complete feel of a classical chamber ensemble, albeit one as likely to mix jazz, Afro-Cuban, Sondheim, Kurt Weill, and neoclassical, but always with a Yiddish accent. Given the backgrounds of the four musicians in Brave Old World, *Blood Oranges* was not a surprising achievement, but it was nevertheless a magnificent one that raised the bar for all serious works of modern klezmer music.

## THE KLEZMATICS

When it came time for the Klezmatics to celebrate the release of their album *Possessed* in the spring of 1997, a simple CD-release concert wouldn't do. Instead, the group presented a multilevel, multicultural extravaganza at New York City's Knitting Factory, the temple of the downtown avant-garde. The show included overlapping performances by Circus Amok, featuring fire-breathing sword swallowers and a genuine bearded lady; Shashmaqam, an ensemble playing the traditional music of Jews from the Bukharan region of Central Asia; X-Cheerleaders, whose radical-feminist cheers you never heard in high school; and the Richard Khuzami Pan–Middle Eastern Ensemble. And at the end of the night, a colorful mix of black-clad downtown bohemians, bridge-and-tunnel socialites and adventurous, slivovitz-fueled *yeshive bokhers* all danced together to the latest Anglo-Indian bhangra beats of DJ Rekha.

In a word, it was not your typical Hadassah social. But what tied it all together—the diverse music and audience—was the Klezmatics, a sort of fire-breathing, pan-cultural, radical musical ensemble playing a global fusion firmly rooted in a traditional dance music. So when the band got around to playing "Ale Brider

Lorin Sklamberg's cantorial-style vocals are the soul of the Klezmatics.

One of the most influential musicians in contemporary klezmer and a veteran of many bands, trumpeter Frank London.

Violin virtuoso Alicia Svigals brings the sound of the Old World to the Klezmatics.

(We're All Brothers)," an old Yiddish labor anthem the group has transformed into a theme song of pan-sexual unity, the crowd became one swirling mass, dancing and singing along on the catchy chorus, which consists of the quintessential Yiddish word *"Oy!"* repeated over and over again.

It wasn't your typical klezmer concert, although by then it wasn't particularly unusual, either. Much of the credit for that goes to the Klezmatics themselves. If Brave Old World's greatest contribution was to make klezmer safe for the uptown concert stage, then the Klezmatics paved the way in the opposite direction, bringing klezmer downtown to the hippest jazz and rock clubs.

Klezmer and rock 'n' roll are obvious bedfellows; both are dance musics at their most basic. The Klezmatics understand this, and their version of klezmer combines the party music of Old World and New. They take the essentials of the old-time music— the repertoire, the ornamentation, the arrangements—and they carefully filter them through a modern sensibility attuned to rock music and its contemporary offshoots. Thus, it is not unusual for them to juice up an old-time melody, perhaps one based on a Hasidic prayer tune, with a funk undercurrent or a reggae pulse. Nor is it out of the question for a freylekh or a bulgar to bear a suspicious resemblance to Jamaican ska, or for a solo to head out into Frank Zappa territory.

The tension between tradition and innovation is undoubtedly what fuels the Klezmatics and what accounts for their popularity among all but the most closed-minded listeners. But more than a mere old versus new duality, the internal dynamic powering the Klezmatics is the creative energy of its six talented members.

The Klezmatics first came together in 1986 on New York's Lower East Side. Several members answered an ad that had been placed in the Village Voice by an elusive figure named Rob looking for musicians who wanted to play klezmer. Rob soon disappeared, but before doing so he succeeded in bringing together trumpeter/ keyboardist Frank London, a Long Island native who had recently moved back to New York from Boston, and Alicia Svigals, who at the time was burning up the Greek music scene with her fiddle in Astoria, Queens.

A few others passed in and out of the group in the first few years, including clarinetist Margot Leverett, but within a year the core of the group had stabilized around Svigals, London, Lorin Sklamberg, David Licht, and Paul Morrissett. London had found Sklamberg, newly arrived from California, playing accordion in a Balkan brass band, and David Licht, fresh from North Carolina, playing drums in the "psychobilly" band Bongwater. After the group's first bassist, Dave Lindsay, dropped out, Sklamberg brought in Morrissett—who also plays the tsimbl—from the Balkan band. Those five players have been with the band ever since. The clarinet seat has been the only one to change hands every few years, passing from Margot Leverett to Kurt Bjorling to David Krakauer to Matt Darriau.

At the time the group had formed, only Frank London had had any significant experience playing klezmer, as a charter member of the Klezmer Conservatory Band in Boston. The other musicians had wide-ranging musical backgrounds with experience in Jewish music that ranged from some to next to none. They all immersed themselves in klezmer, however, studying and transcribing vintage recordings, some of which they found in the sound archives at YIVO, where Svigals and Sklamberg wound up working.

"We started off kind of copying other people's arrangements, trying to emulate different period styles of the way klezmer was played," recalls Sklamberg, a former cantorial soloist who had some early experience with klezmer through his involvement with Jewish and Israeli folk dancing as a teenager. "Once we did that, we started making up our own arrangements."

"It took us a while to figure out what we were doing," said London. "We put out *Shvaygn=Toyt* in 1988, which was a record made in Berlin on our first European concert tour. Then, over the next two years I would say we really developed our personality and our—not our sound so much as our theoretical, our philosophical approach to the music."

That approach encompasses the band members' politics, their spirituality, and their private lives. And while it is rooted in klezmer tradition, it scoffs at any preconceived notion of authenticity.

"We don't believe in limiting ourselves to an ultimately arbitrary piece of a musical universe," said Svigals, who majored in ethnomusicology at Brown University. "We're trying to make good music, so we don't arbitrarily dismiss different musical ideas because they are not generically correct.

"We're not about authenticity. We're not about folk fetishes and fetishizing what's supposed to be a Jewish band. . . . Our only rule for ourselves is that what we end up with should be good music."

London echoes Svigals's comments. "I come with no biases about any music," he says. "It's not like I like rock and I don't like jazz, or I like bebop and I don't like swing. It's just either good music or bad music. And I'm a very opinionated person, so when I say good or bad, I'm totally relying on my own aesthetics."

*Shvaygn=Toyt* introduced the group as a band of lively, virtuoso instrumentalists and a soulful vocalist bent on reconstructing classic Yiddish folk songs and dance tunes from the repertoires of Abe Schwartz, Abe Ellstein, and Dave Tarras. The album dropped a few hints of the modernist impulses to come, most notably in the jazzy ensemble number, "Bilvovi (In My Heart)," which drew upon the resources of Frank London's experimental brass ensemble, Les Miserables Brass Band, which accompanied the Klezmatics to Berlin to perform at the Heimatklange Festival and to record the album.

The Klezmatics cement their identity on *Rhythm + Jews*. The rousing opening track, a rendition of Naftule Brandwein's "Fun Tashlikh," underlines the song's Middle Eastern and Celtic overtones and features an extended, almost psychedelic, nignlike chant by Lorin Sklamberg. That number and the Hasidic anthem, "Shnirele Perele," have both become signature tunes. Also recorded in Berlin in late 1990, the album features several other Brandwein-derived tunes as showcases for clarinetist David Krakauer, who had joined the band. Alicia Svigals, too, steps out notably on "Violin Doyna," a showcase for her hypnotic, Gypsy-fueled fiddling. In general, arrangements are more spirited and freewheeling on the album, with bassist Paul Morrissett and drummer David Licht more willing to drive the band with a rock-derived rhythmic punch.

The group's unique sound and approach came to full fruition on its third album, 1995's *Jews with Horns*. A mix of original compositions and traditional tunes reworked Klezmatics style, the album opens with the raucous, frenetic signature tune, "Man in a Hat," featuring vocal pyrotechnics and verbal punning by Lorin Sklamberg, with backup vocals by Canadian folk-pop group Moxy Fruvous. "Fisherlid" follows, a traditional-sounding, Middle Eastern–inflected slow dance, laced with gauzy electric guitar courtesy of Marc Ribot, with lyrics by famed Yiddish poet Aliza

Greenblatt, who was Woody Guthrie's mother-in-law. A New Orleans second-line-style drum break energizes "Khsidim Tants," a traditional Hasidic dance tune. Party songs like "Simkhes-Toyre" appear side by side with meditative, delicate, mystical explorations of tone and melody such as "Romanian Fantasy," which boasts Svigals's achy-breaky cry on violin.

*Jews with Horns* was followed in 1997 by *Possessed,* perhaps the group's supreme accomplishment. By this point, the musicians had grown more confident of their own abilities as composers, and the balance had shifted from the mostly juiced-up remakes of old-style repertoire on previous albums to vibrant original melodies and experimental arrangements. Standouts here include the ode to the mystical joys of cannabis, "Mizmor Shir Lehanef," a Frank London original with lyrics by contemporary Yiddish poet/scholar Michael Wex, and "Lomir Heybn Dem Bekher," another all-group anthem of political solidarity with the oppressed, composed by Svigals with lyrics adapted from Yiddish poets I. J. Schwartz and A. Reisen.

*Possessed* also includes a terrific suite of songs and instrumentals written for Pulitzer prize–winning playwright Tony Kushner's adaptation of S. An-ski's classic Yiddish drama, *The Dybbuk.* Kushner and the Klezmatics share a queer sensibility in their art, their politics and their private lives—two members of the group are gay. As far back as the group's first album—whose title, *Shvaygn=Toyt,* was a Yiddish translation of the ACT-UP slogan, SILENCE=DEATH —singer Lorin Sklamberg has been mischievously giving masculine pronouns in love songs a cheeky, ironic twist. "We politically come from the same place," says Sklamberg about the group's creative partnership with Kushner. "And it's important to collaborate with other people who share your view of humanity, and we're lucky we can do that."

Especially in concert, the Klezmatics come across as a rock band that plays klezmer, although the instrumentation is almost entirely acoustic (only Paul Morrissett's bass and Frank London's keyboard, which he only plays occasionally, are electric). No doubt this rock-star quality in part accounts for the group's popular following, especially among younger klezmer fans. Indeed, the experience of seeing the Klezmatics perform in a rock club is unforgettable. The group's secret weapon is its killer rhythm section of David Licht and Paul Morrissett. Although Licht is studious about traditional Yiddish drumming, he also draws on his ample experience playing funk, rock, jazz, and other music to give the Klezmatics the extra oomph that *feels* like rock and roll without being it.

In 1998 the Klezmatics teamed with Israeli singer Chava Alberstein for *The Well,* a collection of new melodies Alberstein wrote based on twentieth-century Yiddish poems. While not a klezmer album per se, *The Well* underlined the group's broader, overarching commitment to yidishkayt, or Yiddish culture. The Klezmatics first met Alberstein—an Israeli answer to Joan Baez and Judy Collins—at the 1992 Berlin Jewish Culture Festival, and they have often performed together since. Reflecting Alberstein's broad stylistic palette, which includes American folk, French chanson and Brazilian samba, the sound of *The Well*—which was produced by Ben Mink, known for his work with k. d. lang and Roy Orbison—fits squarely into the amorphous musical territory of world-pop. It is a song-based album and a showcase for the lush vocals of Alberstein, who sounds like a Yiddish Edith Piaf, and Lorin Sklamberg, who duets and shares lead vocals with Alberstein on several numbers.

With no leader and with each member a potential composer, arranger, and soloist with an agenda both inside and outside the band, the Klezmatics are a likely breeding ground for creative power struggles and dissension. Yet the band has found a way to use its members' various talents and interests to the advantage of the whole group.

Says Sklamberg, whose soulful, cantorial-style vocals give the Klezmatics sound its ecstatic warmth and intimacy, "Someone will bring something in and everyone will put in their two cents, or their own spices and ideas. It changes from piece to piece. It really depends on the material. Some things really lend themselves to going to some other place, and other things it seems like, the more direct you are the better. There's no hard and fast rule about it, but we do have conflicts all the time about arrangements. Sometimes they get settled by force of personality and sometimes they don't get settled. Sometimes what happens is that nobody wants to deal with it and things just kind of get left on the sideline. We used to be much feistier than we are now in some ways. You get used to things. In some ways it's just like too much work. Other things become more important. Family and settling down has become very important to people in the band. But we're still the same people."

If there are two polarities in the band, they are symbolized by the group's onstage setup, with Svigals at stage-right and London at the extreme left. While Svigals's hauntingly bewitching violin sound is utterly modern and personal, when it comes to the band's arrangements, her creative instinct is to ground the band to the music's roots. "To play klezmer, there's definitely a language you have to learn," says Svigals. "And it takes years of study. I want the melodies to be played with depth, with the full complement of ornamentation, for example."

When it came time for Svigals to record her first solo album, she delved deep into the traditional repertoire for *Fidl*, an all-acoustic album that attempts to reclaim for the violin its starring role in the traditional kapelye, a role usurped by the clarinet around the turn of the century. In addition to her solo work, Svigals also works with an all-star female klezmer ensemble called Mikveh, including founding Klezmatics clarinetist Margot Leverett, and former Kapelye members Lauren Brody on accordion and Adrienne Cooper on vocals.

London's outside interests, on the other hand, symbolize his pull toward the more radical. His other group, Hasidic New Wave, builds a fusion of funk and free-jazz on a foundation of Hasidic prayer melodies, creating an exciting new, Jewish avant-garde music. No matter how far out he gets, however, London always maintains a connection to the music's Jewish roots. "There's just a really, really rich pool to dive into," says London, "and there's enough there that it's conceivable that the rest of my career could be spent exploring all kinds of different aspects and never really run out of things to explore."

London and Svigals aren't the only ones with careers outside the band, either. Darriau leads the appropriately named Balkan/Gypsy quartet, Paradox Trio. While his group's repertoire is ostensibly non-Jewish, Darriau's band is consistently lumped in with klezmer groups and booked at klezmer festivals. In part to rectify that misconception, but also as a logical result of Darriau's own exploration of the connections between musical styles, in 1999 he released *Source,* which consisted of what he called "Balkan-Jewish crossover repertoire," including several tunes associated with Naftule Brandwein. Darriau also plays with the Irish music group Whirligig, and leads a neoswing band, Ballin' the Jack, of which Frank London is also a member.

Other side projects by band members have included an album

of nigunim by a trio including London, Sklamberg, and keyboardist Uri Caine. Sklamberg also coproduced *The Green Duck,* a recording of Yiddish animal songs for children. Band members frequently compose music for independent films—London's score for Jonathan Berman's documentary, *The Shvitz,* is available on the Knitting Factory label, and in 1999 Tzadik Records released *The Debt,* a collection of London's music for films. In 1998, the group's music was heard in an animated short, *The Parable of the Clowns,* part of the HBO cable network's series, *Kids Are Punny.*

With one foot planted firmly in the shtetl and the other in the Knitting Factory, the Klezmatics embody the Old World/New World dialectic of the klezmer renaissance. It is their precisely cultivated combination of cutting-edge innovation rooted to a studied authenticity that keeps the Klezmatics from succumbing to the kitsch, camp, nostalgia, schmaltz, and novelty that plague some of the other bands working the neoklezmer circuit. Having carefully built a bridge from functional dance music to hard-rocking nightclub music, the Klezmatics have helped chart a path for a new generation of klezmorim.

## ITZHAK PERLMAN IN THE HOUSE

By the mid-1990s, the klezmer renaissance was in full swing. The KCB had been performing for fifteen years. The Klezmatics and Brave Old World were taking the music to places it had never been. And Andy Statman was reinvesting the music with newfound spirituality, echoing the revival of spirituality found throughout American life and among Jews in particular.

To mainstream America—and even to many American Jews

In the mid-1990s, world-renowned classical violinist Itzhak Perlman's foray into klezmer garnered the music unprecedented media attention. His "In the Fiddler's House" CDs are the best-selling klezmer recordings in history.

—klezmer, however, still remained a novelty, a nostalgic visit to the Old World. If people were more curious or comfortable visiting that world than they had been twenty or thirty years earlier, they had yet to have the opportunity to do so on a large scale. With occasional exception, klezmer concerts were still seen primarily as Jewish cultural events or as of interest only to ethnic-music aficionados, not mainstream audiences.

This changed when Itzhak Perlman decided to immerse himself in the music of his forebears. The world-famous classical violinist had grown up in a Yiddish-speaking household in Israel, and in 1987 he recorded an album with the Israel Philharmonic Orchestra of Yiddish folksongs in symphonic arrangements. But with

*In the Fiddler's House,* Perlman fully embraced the challenge of playing klezmer in a nonorchestral context.

The *Fiddler's House* project began as a documentary for the PBS-TV series *Great Performances*. First broadcast in 1995, the show followed Perlman to his ancestral homeland of Poland, where he rediscovered his musical and cultural roots in the world of the klezmorim. He was escorted on his journey through the medieval streets and synagogues of Kraków's Jewish quarter by members of several of the leading American klezmer bands, and he jammed with members of Brave Old World and the Klezmatics in various locations.

Back home in New York, over dinner at Sammy's Roumanian Restaurant on Manhattan's Lower East Side, he listened to Red Buttons and Fyvush Finkel regale him with memories of the Yiddish theater. The film culminated with an all-star concert at New York's Lincoln Center, featuring Perlman performing with Andy Statman, members of the Klezmer Conservatory Band, the Klezmatics, Brave Old World, and others. The film celebrated the music, the tradition, the revival, and Perlman's newfound interest in all of it.

The project lit a spark in Perlman not easily extinguished. Perlman asked some of the musicians he met through the film to join him in a recording studio, where they laid down the tracks for *In the Fiddler's House,* which at nearly a quarter-million easily became the biggest-selling klezmer album of all time. More live performances were scheduled, and over the course of four years several successive concert tours brought Perlman together with the KCB, Andy Statman, the Klezmatics, and Brave Old World on prestigious stages at Wolftrap, Radio City Music Hall, Tanglewood, Ravinia—places where old-time Yiddish dance music had never before been heard.

Klezmorim had never seen anything like it. Suddenly bands accustomed to performing in small theaters for audiences in the hundreds began performing before thousands in the world's finest concert halls. They played on albums that sold between ten and one hundred times as many copies as a typical klezmer release. And with Perlman's credibility, klezmer gained the sort of mainstream press attention that a hundred years of fiddling had not.

*In the Fiddler's House* took on a life of its own. The TV show became a commercially available home video. The first CD was followed by a concert album, *Live in the Fiddler's House.* Perlman brought a group of the musicians with him to David Letterman's late-night TV program, where they subsequently blew away the audience and left the ordinarily loquacious host dazed and nearly speechless, simply uttering the words, "klezmer, klezmer" over and over again.

For Perlman, the midcareer foray into klezmer was a return to something familiar. "I grew up with it, it's not something foreign to me at all," he says about klezmer music. "It's something very close and something that I feel    I find it to be very infectious, and the more I listen to it and the more I play it the more I find a great love for it and great satisfaction in playing it with these groups."

Playing klezmer was a way for Itzhak Perlman to allow himself to express more naked emotion in his playing. "It's freer," he says, comparing it to the classical repertoire upon which he built his career. "One can really improvise a particular style. I find that very intriguing, particularly when one listens to different kinds of recordings. One can listen to a similar tune played by different orchestras or played by different soloists—two different clarinetists or violinists—who give it their own style, so even though there is set melodic material, there is still an inventiveness and an improvisational quality to this music that makes one performance so much different from another.

"This is certainly not the case in classical music, where you basically—it's a little more subtle, because classical music, there's a more of a . . . stiffness in classical music."

While critics and klezmerphiles differ over the quality of the music spawned by the project, everyone agrees that the Perlman collaboration was the biggest thing to happen to the quarter-century-old klezmer revival, as thousands of concertgoers and record buyers drawn simply by the name "Perlman" were turned on to the fertile, contemporary klezmer scene. The Itzhak Perlman project was the kind of serendipitous public-relations coup money could not buy.

According to Michael Alpert, "The whole fact of Itzhak's interest in and involvement with the music brought the music to so much of a higher profile nationally, not only to Jewish audiences but also to a much broader general public than any of us had ever dreamed of twenty years ago."

Alpert recounts the moment he knew he had truly crossed over into the mainstream. "I was driving through the Cascades in Oregon a couple of years ago and stopped for gas, and the gas station attendant recognized me from the TV show," he said.

## LAND OF A THOUSAND BANDS

After the klezmer revival, hundreds of bands—some professional, some semiprofessional, and some amateur—began performing and recording. Many of them followed the early lead of the Klezmorim, and later that of Brave Old World and the Klezmatics, combining Old World klezmer with modern sounds.

## THE EUROPEAN CONNECTION

The klezmer revival and renaissance were not strictly American phenomena. Audiences across Europe welcomed first-generation revival bands such as Kapelye and the Klezmorim, and Brave Old World and the Klezmatics received early support for their experimental approaches in Germany and recorded several albums in Berlin. But Europeans did more than merely support American artists touring and performing in their countries. European musicians, a large number not Jewish, responded to the revival of Yiddish music in their midst by learning the old tunes the klezmorim used to play for their ancestors and perpetuating the music themselves.

Klezmer bands sprouted up throughout the continent. It wasn't so surprising to see this happening in Eastern European countries like Hungary, Poland, and Romania, where the klezmorim used to jam with Gypsies and other local musicians in front of audiences in market squares and taverns, and at private performances for noblemen. American players searched the small towns of Eastern Europe looking for older musicians who might still retain some long-forgotten klezmer tunes in their repertoire.

Klezmer also gained popularity in Germany, and it's not such a stretch to understand why young German musicians might be drawn to the sounds of klezmer. Perhaps it was part of an overall fascination with Jewish culture that functioned as a kind of national therapy, an attempt to work out ambivalent feelings about the legacy left them by their fathers and grandfathers. In some ways, Germany became ground zero for the klezmer revival in Europe, nurturing both the Klezmatics and Brave Old World and producing dozens of homegrown bands, more than one of which wore the moniker *Gojim*, or non-Jew, with a sort of ironic pride. Also, German-speaking audiences came with a built-in advantage over most American ones, given the similarity of the languages—they could understand a lot more of the Yiddish lyrics than all but the oldest American Jews. But the European klezmer revival wasn't confined to the graveyard of Ashkenazi culture in Germany and Eastern Europe—bands cropped up in such unlikely places as Denmark, Switzerland, and even Sweden, not exactly hotbeds of Jewish culture in this or any century.

Of course, the most obvious answer as to why klezmer gained such widespread popularity in Europe, is the same as to why American audiences responded to it, and why the klezmorim of old were hired to entertain at non-Jewish affairs. Musicians and audiences alike enjoy klezmer because when played right, it has an uncanny way of moving listeners' hearts and their feet. Klezmer is "roots 'n' soul" music that crosses linguistic and cultural boundaries.

Founded in Toronto in 1987, the Flying Bulgar Klezmer Band launched on a course that paralleled that of the Klezmatics. (Indeed, their early repertoire shares several of the same numbers.) Between the group's eponymous first recording in 1990 to its decade-ending *Tsirkus*, the Flying Bulgars grew from a straightforward revival band mixing instrumentals with vocal numbers to an ensemble breathing new life into the klezmer repertoire and style book.

Its first album boasted a folksy approach, with mandolins, violins, Balkan flutes, and woodwind instruments, and standard repertoire. Most of these elements were relegated to a secondary role or jettisoned altogether for the band's sophomore effort, *Agada,* which adopted a more modern, small jazz-combo approach and more innovative arrangements. The follow-up recording, 1996's *Fire,* is a live album featuring guest vocalist Adrienne Cooper of Kapelye; it summarizes the group's accomplishments up to that point, balancing rousing theater-style songs with more experimental fare.

On 1999's *Tsirkus,* group founder David Buchbinder reached a creative peak, with original music and songs that seamlessly incorporated global influences from pop, jazz, Afro-Cuban music, and Broadway into its Yiddish mix. The title track is a soulful, jazzy, piano-based, Yiddish rock ballad—what Steely Dan might sound like if Donald Fagen turned his focus to the music of his Jewish ancestors. On "Flora," trumpeter Buchbinder lays down a breathy, plaintive solo melody from Joseph Moskowitz atop a blanket of rich, organlike electric guitar chords. "Highwire" plays off a Hasidic-inspired clarinet melody against jazzy piano modulations, and "Infidel Tants" features wailing, frenetic ensemble and solo passages by the group's horn and reed players.

As their name indicates, the New Orleans Klezmer Allstars bring an approach native to their hometown; second-line rhythms vie with freylekhs and bulgars while Creole melodies cross-pollinate with nigunim. Formed in 1991 as an outgrowth of a weekly jazz jam at a New Orleans café, the band's open-ended, funk-based approach has made it popular with the jam-band set. The group has been the most successful of all renaissance bands in crossing over to modern-rock audiences, having warmed up audiences for popular rock bands such as Squirrel Nut Zippers and Cake, and having garnered a spot on the summer H.O.R.D.E. (Horizons of Rock Developing Everywhere) tour, the traveling festival of neohippie bands pioneered by the group Blues Traveler. Members of the NOKAS, as the band is called, also show up in other New Orleans–based funk groups, including Galactic, Royal Fingerbowl, and Michael Ray and the Cosmic Krewe.

In spite of the adventurous, open-ended approach of the Allstars, the group's original compositions are rooted in a Yiddish style that definitely says "klezmer." The songs on 1999's *Fresh Out the Past* are typical of the group's strategy. "Struttin' with Some Doner Kabob" features a wailing, Yiddish-flavored clarinet solo by Robert Wagner by way of Louis Armstrong, atop a funky Creole beat lent a Sephardic tinge by pianist Glenn Hartman and echoed by Jonathan Freilich on electric guitar. Later, Freilich tosses in some Chuck Berry–style guitar licks in answer to a honking, Ashkenazic saxophone on "The Moroccan Roller."

As the name indicates, "Aging Raver's Personal Hell" hints at contemporary electronic dance music, but does so amid swirling, minor-key sax lines and repeated acoustic piano chords. The group also isn't afraid to yuck it up musically with cartoon antics, as in "Not Too Eggy." Accordionist and coleader Glenn Hartman, who

In the 1990s, the New Orleans Klezmer Allstars combined the jazzy sound and cross-cultural sensibility of their hometown with the cadences of Old World klezmer to create a vital, contemporary fusion.

wrote his thesis on klezmer at Tulane University, has put it plainly: "We shy away from cheesy old Yiddish folk songs."

Underlining the group's deep New Orleans heritage, its original drummer was "Mean" Willie Green, best known for his work with the Neville Brothers. Green continued his association with the band after he ceased touring with the group, occasionally showing up on recordings (he plays on "Dr. Lizard" on *Fresh Out the Past*) and joining them for live gigs in New Orleans, where the band is regularly featured in the annual New Orleans Jazz and Heritage Festival.

Other groups take varying approaches to klezmer, some emphasizing particular stylistic fusions or novel approaches to instrumentation. The Texas-based Austin Klezmorim, for example, mix klezmer with a variety of jazz influences, including Charles Mingus and 1920s jazz. On *Klezmology,* the Cayuga Klezmer Ensemble of upstate New York conjure a progressive, rootsy, klez-pop fusion that would please fans of jam-rock band Phish. California's Freilachmakers Klezmer String Band explores the common ground between klezmer, traditional American string-band music, and Irish music, with violin runs vying for supremacy with fast mandolin and banjo licks. With a guitar and banjo in its lineup, the 12 Corners Klezmer Band, based in Rochester, New York, plays in a folksy style heavy on the repertoire of the 1920s. Pete Rushefsky invents new uses for the banjo as part of this klezmer ensemble, approaching it as a horn as well as a string instrument.

In spite of its name, Yid Vicious of Madison, Wisconsin, does not play a punk-klezmer fusion, although on *Klez, Kez, Goy Mit Fez* they have a lot of fun with playful, punk-rock references in song titles like "Never Mind the Cossacks" and "Anarchy in the Ukraine." Chicago's Shloinke, on the other hand, brings an indisputable garage-band quality to its brand of klezmer, as well as a new, humorous concept of coterritorial repertoire. On its eponymously titled album, the theme to *Mission Impossible* snakes its way through a version of "Hava Nagila," and a klezified version of The Doors' "The End" ("The klezmer woke before dawn . . .") is combined in a suite with "A Nakht in Gan Eyden." And if the alternative pop duo They Might Be Giants turned their attention to klezmer and Jewish-oriented songs, they'd be The Kabalas, who sprinkle Yiddish tunes among their astute cultural parodies in the tradition of Mickey Katz, including tributes to Chico Marx, The Golem, and such other overlooked Jewish cultural heroes as porn star Traci Lords, née Nora Kuzma.

By the end of the 1990s, klezmer was on the radar of "world-music" artists, who saw it as a genre worthy of exploration in the same way that Celtic, African, and Brazilian music had been for the past two decades. Thus, klezmer tunes began cropping up in the repertoires of performers such as the Los Angeles Guitar Quartet, 3 Mustaphas 3, Dutch folk group Flairck, Irish fiddler Kevin Burke, Celtic ensemble De Danaan, and English vocalist June Tabor, who recorded several Yiddish songs, including "Mayn Rue Plats" and "Di Nakht." WOMAD, Peter Gabriel's annual festival of world music in Reading, England, featured several klezmer bands in its lineup, including Brave Old World and the Polish trio, Kroke.

Rock artists also began flavoring their music with bits of klezmer, including college favorite Ben Folds Five, which employed the services of the Klezmatics on hit albums including *The Autobiography of Reinhold Messner* and *Whatever and Ever Amen*. The neohippie band Phish occasionally improvised on Hebrew numbers such as "Yerushalayim Shel Zahav" and "Avinu Malkeinu" in its live shows. Neoswing outfit Squirrel Nut Zippers also integrated klezmerish sounds into some of its material, which it explored further in its offshoot, Andrew Bird's Bowl of Fire. Klezmer was also in the repertoire of alternative-rock groups Charming Hostess, Hypnotic Clambake, and Firewater.

In the summer of 1999, the *New York Times* reported that Metreon, a new retail and entertainment complex developed by the Sony Corporation in San Francisco, "spins to the rhythm of a klezmer violin." For the suits in the marketing department, klezmer was now apparently familiar enough to be used as a subliminal tool to suggest values like "authenticity" and "timelessness" in places where they didn't already exist.

To speak of a "klezmer revival" by the end of the 1990s was to overlook the obvious: that after a quarter-century, there was no longer any question about the music's vitality. The only question remaining was, now that it was fully revitalized, where would it go?

## CHAPTER 5

# BEYOND THE PALE

The same social, cultural, and political forces that fed the klezmer revival also fed an interest in exploring other non-klezmer-based Jewish musical traditions and in creating entirely new ones out of the same material. These included the schlockiest attempts to combine modern American pop music styles with Jewish themes, resulting in music that was both bad pop and bad Jewish music, as well as some fascinating experiments that pushed forward the limits of both Jewish music and music informed by a Jewish sensibility. It's worth noting a few representative artists whose experiments in modern Jewish music vary in their debt or relationship to the klezmer tradition, but who in combining Old and New World styles, share much of the same spirit of the contemporary klezmorim.

## WOLF KRAKOWSKI'S SHTETL-ROCK

It is a long way from the Saalfelden Farmach Displaced Person's Camp in Austria (U.S. occupied zone), where Wolf Krakowski was born, to Northampton, Massachusetts, the ultramodern, ultraprogressive college town where he lives today. Yet in the course of a four-minute song, Wolf is somehow able to shrink that vast geographic and cultural distance, and even to reveal correspondences between the two unlikely worlds.

On *Transmigrations (Gilgulim)*, Krakowski teams with an ensemble of some of New England's finest roots-rock musicians on a dozen Yiddish folk and pop songs with contemporary twists. Krakowski's electric shtetl-rock combines the sound of the American roadhouse with mournful, vintage Ashkenazi melodies to create a self-styled "Yiddish world-beat soul" fusion. In the wrong hands, such musical miscegenation would sound forced at best or a novelty at worst, but Krakowski pulls it off successfully, perhaps because he himself is the very embodiment of Old World meets New.

Shortly after his birth, Krakowski's family moved to Sweden, where they lived for six years before permanently settling in Toronto. It was there, in Toronto's multiethnic, inner-city, West End neighborhood, known as the Junction, that Krakowski first confronted many of the dualities that would later inform his life and work. Not the least of these was the fact that the shul in the Junction sat literally across the fence from the railroad track, so that to this day the sounds of the khazones and the lonesome train whistle coexist inside his head—as apt a summation as any of the extraordinary fusion at the heart of *Transmigrations*.

For much of Krakowski's early life, the figurative train whistle drowned out the khazones. He dropped out of high school at seventeen and ran away with the circus, sharing a room with a sideshow pinhead named Schlitzie and his keeper, a hard-drinking French-Canadian Gypsy prone to outbursts about the "Jew" Roosevelt née Rosenfeld. "I took it all in stride," says Krakowski. "It beat the hell out of high school."

The ensuing years were a blend of Kerouac-inspired, cross-country travel, all-night jam sessions with pickup bands, stints on a commune and with a Cambridge street theater, and jobs as a carpenter, sheetrocker, and guitar maker. In 1981 the Yiddish-speaking Krakowski began documenting Holocaust survivors on audio and videotape, years before Steven Spielberg's Survivors of the Shoah project for which Krakowski worked in 1994–95. Krakowski's own videos include *Vilna,* which he calls "the first post–World War II Yiddish music video," and *My Name Is Stella: An Oral History,* the firsthand testimony of a Polish-Jewish nursing student's survival.

*Transmigrations* contains a dozen Yiddish folk, theater, and popular tunes written by the likes of Benzion Witler, Mordkhe Gebirtig, Max Perlman, and Shmerke Kaczerginski, rearranged by Krakowski variously as rootsy country-, blues-, and reggae-influenced tunes. "My life did not include music lessons or the New England Conservatory," says the self-taught guitarist. "It did however include playing with Canadian folk legends Mendelson Joe and Daisy DeBolt and all-night jams with bluesmaster Big Joe Williams. It started even before then—with my mom's Yiddish folk songs and Hebrew liturgy, mixed with the sounds of Fats Domino and the Everly Brothers on the radio."

What is perhaps most surprising about *Transmigrations* is how effortlessly the Old World—the melodies, phrasing, indeed, the Yiddish language itself—blends with the New World, the sinuous electric guitar leads, the chunky Rastafarian-styled rhythms, the gospel-style choruses, the Latin dance beats, the honking, blues-drenched saxophone solos. In Krakowski's hands, the combination seems logical and downright organic.

"My sound represents what is best, and more importantly,

On his album *Transmigrations*, singer Wolf Krakowski fashioned his own brand of electric shtetl-rock by setting classic Yiddish folk, pop, and theater songs to roots-rock arrangements.

honest, about the whole folk and pop experience as filtered through my experience and sensibilities," says Krakowski. "Not as mere 'pine-reproduction furniture' music. It is not a studied thing. It is a thing of the heart and soul. . . . I dig blues-based music above anything else. And it took a lifetime to have it all come together to the point where my experience and evolution both as a person and musician enabled me to find the bridges in the songs and the melodies without messing with them or turning it all into a novelty or a joke."

A transcultural person, as at home in the world of I. B. Singer as he is in the world of Willie Nelson and Bob Marley, Wolf Krakowski builds a musical bridge between the two on *Transmigrations*. His music is also suggestive of the possibilities that might have occurred had Yiddish, and the Yiddish world, not been destroyed by the Germans. For better or worse, American popular music has pervaded all corners of the globe, so that everywhere indigenous styles of music are combined with American popular forms to create contemporary hybrids. Thus, you have Russian folk-rock bands influenced by the Velvet Underground and R.E.M. It isn't too much of a stretch of the imagination to think that had the Eastern European Yiddish civilization survived, it may have on its own produced music remarkably like that found on Wolf Krakowski's *Transmigrations*.

Krakowski himself is aware of this dynamic. "Without being corny, I sing through them and those that were silenced sing through me," he says. "It is as if all the people who I left behind somehow 'transmigrated' over here, and their stilled voices, cloaked in the raiment of R&B, blues, country-rock, and reggae, act as a bridge from the Old World to the New, through me."

## BOB GLUCK'S ELECTRONIC MIDRASH

For many years Bob Gluck's life ran on two parallel but independent tracks. On the one hand, he was an academy-trained musician and composer whose interests ranged from Bach to Cage to Hendrix to Stockhausen. On the other hand, he was a rabbi active in the Reconstructionist movement, first as director of national outreach and then as spiritual leader of Congregation Ahavath Sholom in Great Barrington, Massachusetts. While Gluck didn't keep his two interests entirely compartmentalized—he studied and wrote about a wide range of Jewish music—for the most part the sounds of the synagogue remained in their place of origin.

Over time, however, Gluck's two main interests converged. Inspired both by a contemporary musical theory that embraces all sounds as the stuff of music, and by the progressive views of Reconstructionism, which welcomes the integration of modern culture with ancient practice, Gluck began exploring ways in which he could combine the two. In particular, Gluck was obsessed with memories of his grandparents' synagogue: the sounds of the cantor's voice, the rhythmic prayers of the congregation, and the rustling of the prayerbooks, which all served as "aural wallpaper" in his mind.

In 1995 Gluck made composed music with that "aural wallpaper," recording *Some Places I Have Been: Sacred Electronic Landscapes,* a limited-release cassette tape that drew on the Sabbath liturgy for its raw material. Three years later, he produced *Stories Heard and Retold,* a 48-minute CD that fully realized his attempt at "joining the musical sensibilities of Pierre Henry and Edgard Varese with the resonances of the sounds, melodies, and experiences of Jewish life," as he wrote in the album's liner notes.

A graduate of the Reconstructionist Rabbinical College in Philadelphia, Gluck sees a similarity between what he does in his compositions, which manipulate ambient and found sounds such as a prayer service and midrash, rabbinical commentaries that expound upon or manipulate the original text of the Bible. "If the core of Judaism is midrash, what I do is midrash," said Gluck, a native of Queens, New York, who studied at Juilliard Prep and received an undergraduate degree in electronic music from the State University of New York at Albany. "Furthermore, if the way in which ancient text is chanted is by taking short sound gestures and putting them together like in a puzzle, that for me points to the kinds of ways that I piece together a mosaic, as it were, of Jewish sounds."

The most obvious difference between traditional, rabbinical midrash and Gluck's contemporary update is that of form and technique. The rabbi's traditional tools are the sermon, the song, and the written text, but Gluck avails himself of the latest in state-of-the-art electronics. On *Stories Heard and Retold,* prerecorded sounds are sampled, looped, filtered, and altered, in order to create a kind of sound collage. Once trained as a classical pianist, Gluck now draws from a large palette of electronic instruments, tape recorders, and computers, alongside the keyboard and human voice, to create a kind of audio image. Indeed, Gluck's compositions are cinematic. "Yiddish Songs," one of three extended works on the CD, is a sound memorial for the lost civilization of pre-Holocaust, Yiddish-speaking Jewry.

While Gluck's primary intention is to create a new Jewish art music, he acknowledges that his compositions, particularly those based on traditional prayers, might have liturgical implications as well. "For people who have a Jewish liturgical life, it might help them think about or listen to the prayers that they chant and the music they hear in a different way from an aesthetic point of view, and that can enrich their prayer life," he said. For others, including those who might not be familiar with the specific cultural or religious references or allusions, the piece can work more generally as a soundscape or as a window into a particular world or vision. "Once our ears become more attuned to a wider range of sounds that go beyond the melodic sounds that we're used to, then the palette that is available is vast, really endless," said Gluck.

# KING DJANGO'S HASIDIC SKA

For thirty years fans of the Rastafarian-drenched Jamaican dance music called reggae have perhaps unknowingly and unconsciously been inundated with imagery borrowed from Judaism, with such latter-day prophets as the late Bob Marley lamenting the contemporary exile in "Babylon" and longing for return to the promised land of "Zion." Thus when New York–based ska artist King Django —born Jeff Baker—released *Roots and Culture* in 1998, an album of Yiddish, Hebrew, and English reggae and ska with Jewish themes, it seemed wholly natural and fitting. The Jamaican grooves on the album are so authentic, in fact, that an unsuspecting listener could be forgiven for not even noticing that the original song "Seventh Day" is about observing the Jewish Sabbath, and that other horn-drenched tunes were based on such traditional liturgical Hebrew and Yiddish folk fare as "Heveinu Shalom Aleichem," "Lomir Alle Zingen," and "Ya'aseh Shalom."

As a member of such venerable ska groups as Skinnerbox and the Stubborn All Stars, Baker's Jamaican music credentials are impeccable. He invited a number of his Jamaican music cronies from these groups, as well as such other well-known bands as the Toasters, the Slackers, and the New York Ska Jazz Ensemble (here transformed into the New York Ska *Jews* Ensemble) to lay down the basic rhythm tracks for *Roots and Culture*.

But Baker wanted to do more than just cover a few Jewish tunes reggae style. He recruited some of klezmer's best, including clarinetist/mandolinist Andy Statman and violinist Alicia Svigals of the Klezmatics, to add their authentic Old World touches to the effort. And he corralled Yiddish scholar Michael Wex—who often collaborates with the Klezmatics and many other top groups—for lyric consultation and an all-around Yiddish hekhsher, or kosher seal of approval.

Baker was not the first musician to attempt a klezmer/ska fusion. Back as early as 1986 an Amsterdam band named De Bend, led by Henk Pender, attempted to combine the herky-jerky sounds of Jamaican dance music with the rhythms of the freylekhs. But in

Django's case, the result is a seamless interweaving of the Jamaican and Eastern European styles. On the jumpy ska version of "Lomir Alle Zingen," for example, Andy Statman's clarinet wails in the background as if Naftule Brandwein were a member of the Wailers. Most convincing are Baker's vocals, which reveal a great kinship between Yiddish and the Jamaican cadences of Bob Marley.

Mixing reggae and Yiddish music came as naturally to Baker — who grew up in Brooklyn with Yiddish-speaking grandparents — as mixing polkas and waltzes and Gypsy melodies came to the Old

Brooklyn-born Jeff Baker, a.k.a. "King Django," made his mark on the New York ska scene before combining the sounds of Jamaican dancehall music with classic Yiddish song.

World klezmorim. In his case, it was simply another version of co-territorial repertoire. "I grew up listening to and playing reggae music, and I grew up being Jewish, so it was pretty natural," he says of the fusion. Ironically, the project first came about when the head of a record label—who happened to be Jewish—asked Baker if his ska group would record an album of Christmas songs. Baker declined the offer. A few days later, the label executive came back to Baker and said, "I've got it—'Ska Mitzva,'" and the idea of a Jewish/Jamaican fusion album was born.

## WALLY BRILL'S YIDDISH TECHNO

In the 1990s, spiritual-based singing from other times and cultures was all the rage. Record buyers found the music of West African Islamic singer Salif Keita and Pakistani Sufi vocalist Nusrat Fateh Ali Khan—music that grew directly from religious liturgical traditions—reached them in a deep and profound way, transcending cultural differences in stark contrast to the coldly constructed, computerized music that made up the bulk of radio's Top 40 pop hits. Even new recordings based on Gregorian chant came out of nowhere to become chart-busting hits.

There was precedent for this recontextualization of spiritual singing in Jewish music. In the earlier part of the century, virtuoso cantors such as Yossele Rosenblatt, Samuel Malavsky, and Ben Zion Kapov-Kagen took their songs of worship out of the shul and into the concert hall and the recording studio. In doing so, they turned themselves and their music into pop artifacts, and they were treated accordingly by listeners who collected their albums and caught them in concert every time they came to town, much as we do today with our favorite pop and opera stars.

Producer Wally Brill was introduced to a collection of the old cantorial recordings by his girlfriend's father in 1995. He heard the same kind of ecstatic spirituality that had earlier attracted him to Salif Keita and Nusrat Fateh Ali Khan, and thus was born *The Covenant*, an album that sampled the vintage cantorial vocals and wove them into modern electronic dance music, in the same way that the group Enigma used chant, and Deep Forest used Eastern European folk music.

Brill's album is a dreamy, almost psychedelic whirlwind of musical juxtapositions. Jazzy trumpets bump up against synthesizer bleeps; Indian tablas and Australian didgeridoos punctuate cantorial melodies; contemporary recitations by Holocaust survivors and observers of the millennial scene are foreground to Brian Eno–like ambient backgrounds. Occasionally the result reminds a listener of some of Led Zeppelin's more adventurous excursions into Middle Eastern music, such as "Kashmir."

Some may balk at Brill's tampering with these ancient melodies by placing them in such nonsacral contexts as the contemporary, cosmopolitan dance club or juxtaposing them with sounds that bear no relation to the music's original intent. But to do so misses a key point: It would have been impossible for Brill to have created these new musical collages across time and space if the original creators, the cantors, hadn't already themselves taken the music out of the holy realm and turned it into a popular form. In a way, these cantors anticipated the many black gospel artists who in the postwar era would take Church music and, by combining it with rhythm and blues in a pop context, create what we call "soul" music. What Brill understood was that Yossele Rosenblatt was just as much a "soul" singer, and what he did on *The Covenant* was merely to lend old-time Jewish soul a contemporary patina.

# JOHN ZORN AND RADICAL JEWISH CULTURE

While John Zorn would probably object to his music being lumped together with klezmer, the fact is that much of the music he has touched as a performer, composer, recording artist, producer, and record-label executive in the 1990s fits in alongside the more progressive efforts of the klezmer renaissance. Some of his own compositions, and those by others whose music he released on his Tzadik record label, evolve from the same Yiddish musical tradition on which klezmer is based. Other works bear a looser connection, musically speaking, to the klezmer tradition, having more obvious roots in Sephardic or Middle Eastern music, jazz, and the music of Jewish composers.

Zorn's name for this musical movement is Radical Jewish Culture. The term itself took on a life of its own by the late nineties, used somewhat promiscuously to describe a generic musical movement beyond John Zorn himself, even though it was the official name of several Zorn-curated festivals in New York and elsewhere, as well as the name he gave to a series of recordings on Tzadik. Zorn founded Tzadik—the word is Hebrew for "righteous one"— in 1995 as an independent venue for his own work and the work of a stable of other downtown-oriented artists, many of whom play on each other's albums and share a musical sensibility similar to Zorn's: one that sees no hierarchy in music, no distinction between high and low, art and pop. For Zorn and his fellow avant-gardists, there are two kinds of music, good and bad, and the challenge is to come up with new and exciting styles through unlikely juxtapositions.

Born in 1953, Zorn grew up in Flushing, New York, and attended the United Nations International School in Manhattan, where he studied music and began a love affair with odd musical juxtapositions. Bach, Bartok, and Berg were on the teenage Zorn's play list, right next to the Beatles, the Beach Boys, and the Doors. At Webster University, a small, liberal arts college in St. Louis, Zorn was exposed to the experimental jazz coming out of Chicago in the early seventies, and it was there that he began combining improvisational strategies with written music.

By the mid seventies, Zorn was living in downtown Manhattan, where a lively scene of experimentation and cross-fertilization

In the 1990s, avant-garde composer/saxophonist John Zorn spearheaded Radical Jewish Culture, a movement of downtown musicians exploring Jewish identity through original composition and improvisation.

thrived in clubs and lofts. It was in this fertile milieu, where punk bands shared bills with classical-noise fusion groups, that Zorn's dissonant, anarchic aural collages of splattered saxophone riffs, distorted electric guitars, and industrial noise began garnering him the sort of notices that made him a leader of the avant-garde. Zorn was known for playing *parts* of his saxophone, producing squeaks and duck calls with just his mouthpiece, or playing with his mouthpiece immersed in a glass of water. In the mid-to-late eighties, Zorn's "game" compositions, such as "Cobra," featured group improvisations triggered by visual cues. In the late eighties and early nineties, he wrote several pieces commissioned and recorded by the Kronos Quartet, perhaps the world's best-known, contemporary-classical string quartet. In groups like Naked City, Pain Killer, Spy vs. Spy, and News for Lulu, he collaborated with other leading and well-known figures of the avant-garde, including George Lewis, Bill Frisell, Wayne Horvitz, and Fred Frith.

A genre unto himself, Zorn's music fit everywhere and nowhere, much to his chagrin. Different works invoke jazz, neoclassical, minimalism, surf, punk, metal, hard-core, noise, and various world musics, especially Japanese—sometimes all in one piece. His works were as likely to reference those of free-jazz pioneer Ornette Coleman, to whom he has been frequently compared, as they were to recall Raymond Scott's visionary cartoon music or Ennio Morricone's spaghetti-western film scores.

To fully appreciate the significance of Zorn's Jewish work in its proper context, one needs to understand that when John Zorn declared his full-fledged allegiance to Jewish music in the mid nineties, he was at the apex of the avant-garde, a central figure of musical postmodernism. Whatever he touched had instant credibility and hip cachet, at least with those who embraced the idea of

Zorn as king of the avant-garde. Thus, his decision to remodel himself as a Jewish composer suggested something about the creative potential of Jewish music. Also, for perhaps the first time in American pop-cultural history, "Jewish" was "cool," a development Zorn recognized and promoted by appearing in public wearing T-shirts with Hebrew words, and with tzitzit—the ritual fringes usually worn only by the most traditionally observant Jews— peeking out from underneath. For Zorn, this was all part of a mission to inspire pride in a new, radically formed Jewish identity.

"For younger Jews, if you don't have a positive thing to identify with, you don't even want to identify as a Jew," says Zorn. "If everybody thinks it's just awkward people with glasses who stumble around and can't dance . . . you know what I mean? That's not what it is at all. So we almost have a *duty* and responsibility to show you can be hip and Jewish, like Lou Reed, like Allen Ginsberg, like Marc Ribot. It's about busting stereotypes, it's about challenging the status quo, and it's about fighting for rights and equality." By the end of the decade, Zorn had done much to achieve this, even to the extent of turning the wearing of tzitzit into a quasi political and cultural statement of positive Jewish identity.

Zorn's overtly Jewish music began with "Kristallnacht," given its debut in Munich in 1992 at the first Radical Jewish Culture festival, which also included performances by Lou Reed, Gary Lucas, and the New Klezmer Trio. A powerful, alternately poignant and demented tone poem meant to evoke the Nazi "night of broken glass" (the pogrom in which thousands of synagogues and Jewish-owned businesses in Germany were destroyed and nearly a hundred dred Jews murdered, signaling the beginning of the Holocaust), "Kristallnacht" was as much a manifesto as a work of music. Once the audience took its seats, Zorn ordered the doors locked and told no one to leave. The musicians in Zorn's ensemble came onstage wearing yellow Jewish stars sewn onto their sleeves. The piece began with passages of Old World–style klezmer clarinet played by David Krakauer, followed by the pummeling, eardrum-shattering noise of breaking glass, intended to evoke the horror of the Holocaust. (The recorded version warns the listener against "prolonged or repeated listening" to this section at the risk of "temporary or permanent ear damage.") It was a stunning moment, the birth pangs of a movement, and Zorn returned to New York emboldened and determined to pursue and explore this avenue in his music.

That exploration would reach its fulfillment in Zorn's Masada, aptly named after the hilltop fortress in the Judean desert where in 73 C.E. a band of Jewish patriots took their lives rather than surrender to and be enslaved by the Roman conquerors. Undoubtedly Zorn was attracted to the image of the relentless resisters, refusing to succumb to or assimilate into the mainstream—a theme that runs through his entire career. For Zorn, Masada was several things at once: a jazz quartet, a group of chamber ensembles of various shapes and sizes, and a set of over two hundred original compositions in traditional Jewish modes that Zorn has written for these groups. But Masada was more than just a metaphor or a vehicle— it was a conceptual framework and a redoubt from which Zorn could expand the Jewish musical tradition.

In Masada the jazz quartet, which includes trumpeter Dave Douglas, drummer Joey Baron, and bassist Greg Cohen, Zorn plays alto saxophone and leads the group through his compositions built on traditional Jewish scales and modes but played with methods gleaned from straight-ahead jazz and free improvisation, with snatches of blues, ballads, and traditional melodies thrown into the mix. In the course of five years from the mid-to-late nineties, Masada released over a dozen albums, live and studio recordings, which were hailed not merely as great Jewish music but as some of the best jazz of its era.

By 1999, a year in which the jazz mainstream was preoccupied with everything Ellington on the occasion of the Duke's centennial, *Boston Globe* jazz critic Bob Blumenthal declared that "jazz is in the Masada era," calling Zorn's group the "signature ensemble of the music's fin de siècle," and its music "as melodic and inviting as . . . anything offered by his contemporaries." Masada's music is full of energy and surprises—cacophonous group improvisations growing out of or leading into remarkable solo investigations of melodic themes, an abstract musical rendition of the call-and-response-type prayer ceremonies of a Hasidic *shtibl,* or prayer room. If klezmer has been erroneously tagged "Jewish jazz," then, notwithstanding the occasional claims that it derives its ensemble approach from saxophonist Ornette Coleman's free-jazz quartets, Masada might well be the genuine article.

But Zorn's Jewish music project didn't end there. Zorn writes for and conducts the Masada Chamber Ensembles, an array of duos, trios, quartets, sextets, and other pairings of strings, keyboards, and clarinets, ensembles sometimes referred to collectively as Bar Kokhba, after the quasi-messianic leader of the final Jewish revolt against the Romans in 132–35 c.e. Their work, contained on two excellent double CDs, *Bar Kokhba* and *The Circle Maker,* includes some of Zorn's most accessible jazz- and classical-styled Jewish compositions in a range of styles, from "Gevurah," a Latin-jazz version of the Yiddish theater tune "Vus du Vilst, Dus Vill Ich Oich," to "Nezikin," a highly percussive, dissonant, contemporary-classical workout for string trio. "Mahshav," an alternately poignant and lighthearted melodic piano-clarinet duet, could sit comfortably on any album of traditional klezmer; indeed, the most shocking thing about it is not that it is experimental, but that this gorgeous, Old World–style melody was written by John Zorn.

Zorn wasn't functioning in a musical or aesthetic vacuum. One result of his newly raised Jewish consciousness was that he began noticing patterns where he had not seen them before. "I'm not sure why it is, but all of a sudden it was like some weird kind of revelation, suddenly realizing that most of the musicians that I've been really strongly associated with have been Jewish," he says. "It was like, wait a minute, how come all these cats are Jewish? . . . That began to interest me. And I'm not quite sure if I have an answer as to what that's about."

Not only were they Jewish, but Zorn sensed that there was an "awakening," both creative and spiritual, going on. "This is something that's going on all over, it's not just happening here in New York," he says. "There are musicians all over who are awakening their Jewish soul. That's what makes this a phenomenon. It's a lot bigger than any one person or one event."

Gary Lucas, for example, a protégé of Leonard Bernstein's who in the early eighties was a guitarist in Captain Beefheart's experimental-rock band, had made his own musical response to Kristallnacht in Germany at the Berlin Jazz Festival with Zorn on the bill in 1988. It was the fiftieth anniversary of the Night of Broken Glass, and Lucas stunned the audience with an unannounced piece he called "Verklärte Kristallnacht," a knowing reference to Arnold Schoenberg's "Verklärte Nacht" that juxtaposed the Israeli national anthem, "Hatikvah," with phrases from "Deutschland Uber Alles," amid wild electronic shrieks and noise. A few years later, Lucas went on to compose an original score to the German

Expressionist silent film, *Der Golem,* based on a kind of Jewish Frankenstein myth, which he performed at the 1992 festival in Munich.

The premonitions of Radical Jewish Culture were also being felt on the West Coast. In California, refugees from Hotzeplotz and the Klezmorim formed the New Klezmer Trio. Clarinetist Ben Goldberg had been growing restless performing music he felt merely recapitulated earlier styles rather than creating new ones. "I wrote a kind of manifesto then that said something like, 'Think of the difference between John Coltrane and Sidney Bechet, yet we consider them to be of the same lineage,'" he recalls. "If klezmer music had been similarly evolving since the twenties, then we certainly wouldn't be here today trying to sound just like Naftule Brandwein. That was important to me."

As a result, Goldberg began thinking about the imaginary line between "traditional" and "avant-garde" music. "I wanted to take the kind of pent-up, stuttering, neurotic energy of klezmer and spread it over a long form and see what happened." In 1988 he began jamming with former bandmates Kenny Wolleson and Dan Seamans, and building on a firm foundation in traditional klezmer, they began exploring the "claustrophobic, quick and darting, hurried, nervous" aspects of the music in extended pieces.

In 1991 the group released its first album, *Masks and Faces,* which mixed klezmer with strategies gleaned from such jazz and avant-garde visionaries as Charles Mingus, Thelonious Monk, Steve Lacy, Lee Konitz, and Andrew Hill, prefiguring the shape of avant-klez to come. A decade later, it still sounds startlingly fresh and original and stands as a benchmark for subsequent attempts at a progressive, klezmer-jazz fusion. Zorn issued the group's second album, *Melt Zonk Rewire*—which further explored the outer bounds of what one might call "free-klez," an approach to klezmer that employs theories and techniques drawn from free jazz—on Tzadik in 1995, and reissued *Masks and Faces* the following year.

With the publicity following the Radical Jewish Culture festivals that Zorn curated in New York, San Francisco, and Munich, musicians who were already exploring their Jewish identities through experimental music began coming out of the woodwork, trying to get in touch with Zorn and sending him demo tapes. "I didn't know Naftule's Dream was around, for example, until I started the label and people started sending me things," he says. He began to receive tapes from all over the United States and Europe. Some of these, including Naftule's Dream and Ahava Raba, a German group that mixes Eastern European music with classical, pan-Asian folk musics and Mongolian throat singing, eventually wound up being released on Tzadik.

"There's all these people," says Zorn. "That just doesn't happen overnight. They've been thinking about this shit for a long time— certainly as long if not longer than I've been thinking about it. The cliché word is renaissance. But it's an exciting time, there's a lot going on, and a lot of people are considering this. I think it's because there's this generation of post-Holocaust Jews who are now feeling well, hey, wait a minute, this is cool, this is hip, this is me, let's keep it going."

Zorn followed up on that impulse and began inviting his friends to explore their heritage through music as part of Tzadik's Radical Jewish Culture series. With the series, Zorn set out to ask the question, "What is Jewish music?" "Each one has a personal answer to the question, but the answer cannot be articulated in words," says Zorn. "The answer is in the music. Sometimes it's mixed with classical, sometimes it's mixed with jazz, sometimes it's tinged with a straighter, folk kind of approach, sometimes there's rock involved."

In just a few short years, this resulted in a body of work consisting of nearly three dozen CDs (not including Masada's dozen recordings) by two dozen different artists covering a vast array of styles, ranging from the neo-Hasidic traditionalism of *Nigunim,* a collaboration by Frank London and Lorin Sklamberg of the Klezmatics, and keyboardist Uri Caine, to *In These Great Times,* John Schott's quietly impressionistic chamber-opera, to the guitar-noise of Marc Ribot's group Shrek.

Some of the music very obviously refers to specific traditions in Jewish music: *Nigunim,* which directly accesses Hasidic prayer melodies; David Krakauer's albums, which are firmly rooted in the classic klezmer of Dave Tarras and Naftule Brandwein; and Anthony Coleman's Afro-Cuban reworkings of Yiddish and Sephardic folk songs. Other works require a certain suspension of disbelief to be accepted as Jewish music. Sometimes it's merely a case of packaging music in a way that overtly acknowledges the Jewish backgrounds of the composers and performers: provocative titles such as *Yo! I Killed Your God* or *Selfhaters,* Hebrew song titles, and album artwork laden with Kabbalistic imagery. More often, however, the Jewish connection is somewhere between obscure and explicit, ranging from the Yiddish-theater quotations in *Bar Kokhba*'s "Gevurah" to the klezmer melodies buried deep at the heart of the blistering, hard-core, guitar-punk instrumentals of Kletka Red.

One moment on one of the albums stands out as representative of the whole. Easily overlooked as a novelty, "Abie the Fishman" on Gary Lucas's *Busy Being Born* encapsulates the ideological foundations of Radical Jewish Culture as much as any other single work. The song is built upon a simple, childlike taunt, which references a scene in the Marx Brothers classic film, *Animal Crackers:*

"Wait a minute, I know you," says Chico Marx in his indistinct European-accented English to a proper and pretentious art collector, "you're Abie the Fishman."

In a single swipe, Lucas reveals the Marx Brothers in a whole new light; as forerunners of Radical Jewish Culture, as cultural terrorists whose movies are filled with subversive moments exposing pomposity and hypocrisy, as mischievous pioneers of identity politics. It's no accident that the victim of this seminal "outing" is an art collector whose money buys highbrow cultural status, precisely the sort of cultural dynamic opposed by the avant-garde movement, or "avant-ghetto," as Lucas prefers it. In "Abie the Fishman," the issue of social status is tied to questions of Jewish identity and assimilation, which makes it all the more subversive.

That Gary Lucas plucked this moment, with "Abie the Fishman," out of twentieth-century American pop culture and put it in the employ of Radical Jewish Culture on what is ostensibly an album of children's music — thereby giving a generation of American children a new, radical playground chant — is in itself a most playful act of subversion. He carries the subversion forward throughout the rest of the album, juxtaposing straightforward renditions of Hebrew hymns and pointedly ironic, "fiddler on the roof" schmaltz with other original works of Jewish fantasy.

UNEXPECTED MOMENTS OF subversion are strewn throughout Tzadik's Radical Jewish Culture series. On *Sephardic Tinge*, keyboardist Anthony Coleman reposits the classic Yiddish theater tune "Belz" as a bit of Afro-Cuban piano jazz — a pointed commentary on the cultural divide between the prevailing Yiddish/Ashkenazi/Eastern European Jewish heritage and the equally rich but unfortunately overlooked Sephardic/Ladino heritage, a tradition with roots in Jewry's "Golden Age" pre-Inquisition Spain.

After clarinetist David Krakauer left the Klezmatics in the mid-1990s, he went on to establish himself as one of the most innovative and adventurous soloists in contemporary klezmer.

Having lived much of his life in New York City rubbing elbows with its large Hispanic population, Coleman's musical aesthetic is highly informed by the Latin rhythms of salsa, mambo, and montunos. Coleman, who attended the New England Conservatory in the late seventies alongside the Klezmer Conservatory Band founder, Hankus Netsky, decided to explore this aspect of his heritage from the point of view of someone whose family name was originally Cohen.

*Sephardic Tinge*, on which Coleman is joined by Masada members Greg Cohen on bass and Joey Baron on drums, also includes jazz versions of traditional Sephardic melodies, as well as covers of

Thelonious Monk and Jelly Roll Morton rendered with a Sephardic tinge—a playful reference to Morton's interest in what he called the "Spanish tinge" in jazz. *Morenica* ("Little Dark One"), the follow-up, continues in the same vein, with more original, piano-based tunes, including the provocatively titled "Ghetto (Ich Bin Ein Marrano)."

Where Coleman's piano jazz albums are lush and lyrical, recordings by his group Selfhaters are as nasty and violent as their title suggests. With liner notes citing Theodore W. Adorno, Saul Bellow, Richard Wagner, and Sander L. Gilman, author of "Jewish Self-Hatred: Anti-Semitism and the Hidden Language of the Jews," Coleman is clearly working out some deeply theoretical ideas in the compositions on *Selfhaters* and the follow-up, *The Abysmal Richness of the Infinite Proximity of the Same*. The numbers on these albums tend to eschew conventional song forms and adopt the style of classical abstractionists such as Morton Feldman. Even the "cover versions" of jazz songs like "You Don't Know What Love Is" and "The Mooche" are altered beyond recognition. Despite the wailing clarinets, insistent percussive effects, and harsh group dynamics, these numbers are no less effective, and perhaps even more haunting than Coleman's conventional piano jazz.

Such radical reinterpretations of traditional klezmer are found throughout the Radical Jewish Culture series. The Boston-based group Naftule's Dream was formed by the members of the traditional klezmer group, Shirim, as an outlet for their more experimental inclinations. The individual musicians in the sextet boast a vast range of experience. Trombonist David Harris was a charter member of the Klezmer Conservatory Band and Frank London's Les Miserables Brass Band. Clarinetist Glenn Dickson is a graduate of the New England Conservatory who has performed in rock bands and played Greek and nineteenth-century American music. Other musicians have played ska, rock, New Orleans, South Indian classical, military marches, and avant-garde jazz. These influences get remanufactured as Naftule's Dream, a borscht of free-klez, speed-klez (both descriptions are song titles) and anarchic punk-klez—what metal band Metallica might play if it were a mostly unplugged klezmer band.

On *Hijacking*, Kletka Red, a guitars and drum trio from Germany, puts classic klezmer melodies into a blender and spits them out as blistering, hard-core punk-rock. But the melodies survive, even with the industrial effects, reggae beats, and Velvet Underground–inspired lead guitar lines of Leonid Soybelman, whose Yiddish vocals lend a surprisingly warm, human feeling to the otherwise violent sound. Another German-Jewish group, Psamim, skirts the folk-classical divide on *Abi Gezint!*, reworking Yiddish and Sephardic folk songs in chamber arrangements for string ensemble and accordion. Acoustic trio Davka, from San Francisco, reimagines klezmer melodies as jazzy, percussive, world-beat excursions on *Judith*. On *The Watchman*, composer/cellist Erik Friedlander's Chimera, a chamber group for cello, bass, and clarinet, plays neoclassical compositions suggestive of Old World melodies. Zeena Parkins's *Mouth=Maul=Betrayer*, a collage of voice, sampled sound, and instrumental composition, traces the subterranean history of the Jewish Mafia back to its European roots in medieval Germany, where Jewish thieves spoke a little-known argot they shared with musicians—a sly bit of radical Jewish culture. And on *Sojourn*, clarinetist Marty Ehrlich explores the rich potential of nigunim and Yiddish melody in a jazzy manner not unlike that of Andy Statman.

Zorn's Great Jewish Music series, in which downtown artists perform versions of songs by composer-performers Burt Bacharach, Mark Bolan (the T. Rex founder, née Feld), and French recording artist Serge Gainsbourg, pushed the limit of what some listeners would accept as "Jewish music." Zorn introduced the series with a mini-essay on the back of the Burt Bacharach tribute that explained his intentions in part. "Burt Bacharach is one of the

Boston-based Naftule's Dream are the avant-garde alter ego of the traditional-style group, Shirim. Improvisational musicians versed in free-jazz and rock music, they are affiliated with John Zorn's Radical Jewish Culture movement.

great geniuses of American popular music—and he's a Jew." He goes on to write, in what is a crucial key to understanding Zorn's outlook, "The Jews are a tribe who continue to believe that if they devote themselves to a place they love and contribute to the society selflessly that they will be embraced and accepted into it. In many cases this has proved to be a fatal error, yet there they go again, stubbornly believing in their own ability and vision."

On some level, Bacharach, Bolan, and Gainsbourg stood apart from the mainstream in spite of their commercial success. While Bacharach songs such as "Close to You," "Walk On By," and "Promises Promises" were huge popular hits, they were also subversive bits of moody complexity. New interpretations by performers like Sean Lennon, the Melvins, Living Colour's Vernon Reid and Faith No More's Mike Patton examined the brittle shards and convoluted structures of these deceptively simple pop songs. When Fred Frith closes the first of the two Bacharach disks repeatedly intoning, "You are from another part of the world," suddenly Bacharach's songs take on an entirely new subtext.

In conversation, Zorn talks about what interests him in the work of these disparate songwriters. What is the Jewish element in Serge Gainsbourg's music, he asks himself rhetorically? "If you look hard enough you can find it, is the simplest answer you can come up with," he says. "But it's not that simple. I think there absolutely are elements that tie in with his identity, and why shouldn't there be? I mean, he experienced shit that only Jews have experienced, and it's going to come out!

"There's a feeling there [in all Jewish music]. Feelings are not meant to be written down, they're meant to be felt. Leonard Bernstein's music, I feel it there. Sometimes you can actually come out and say it with things like the *Kaddish* symphony, but you look at

*West Side Story,* I think it's there too. I think it's in Irving Berlin's 'White Christmas,' so how deep can it go?"

If the normative klezmer world was not quite ready to embrace Zorn as one of its own—not that he was applying for membership—there was still plenty of give-and-take between the two worlds. Frank London and David Krakauer of the Klezmatics show up as musicians on *Kristallnacht,* Krakauer plays in the Masada Chamber Ensembles, and both would go on to make multiple solo albums for Tzadik. The musicians in the New Klezmer Trio were all card-carrying members of revival-era groups, Naftule's Dream was an alter-ego to the conventional klezmer band Shirim, and Michael Alpert and Stuart Brotman of Brave Old World and Lorin Sklamberg of the Klezmatics also played on various albums in the series.

Eventually, Zorn's influence and that of the other Radical Jewish Culture artists so pervaded the downtown scene that on the cusp of the millennium, the prevailing mode of experimental, avant-garde music seemed largely synonymous with Radical Jewish Culture. *New York* critic David Yaffe called the presence of avant-Jewish bands "a phenomenon comparable in scope to the avant-garde loft scene of the seventies"—ironically, the very scene out of which Zorn first emerged.

The Knitting Factory, the downtown nightclub where Zorn first presented many of his projects and Radical Jewish Culture festivals, expanded its Jewish music programming and hosted an annual "Jewsapalooza" festival featuring traditional and experimental klezmer bands. The club, which first opened in 1987, also hosted an annual "Cyber-Seder," featuring alternative-rock royalty such as Lou Reed and the members of hypno-pop band Yo La Tengo offering biblical commentary alongside Zorn and others. In the fall of 1993, the Knitting Factory sent Hasidic New Wave, Gary Lucas, and the New Klezmer Trio to Prague, Budapest, and eastern Germany on the "Jewish Avant-Garde Music Tour."

The Knit, as it is affectionately known to insiders, also took a cue from Zorn and created its own Jewish music imprint—Jewish Alternative Movement, or JAM—as a subset of its in-house Knitting Factory record label. "It's radical, it's new, but you don't need to be a Jew," trumpeted its catalog, which went on in provocative fashion to say, "Play that funky music, Jew Boy!" JAM issued several compilations of downtown Jewish bands, including *A Guide for the Perplexed*, and was home to Frank London's experimental band Hasidic New Wave, whose three CDs feature free-jazz, fusion, and funk-fueled improvisations often based on preexisting Hasidic dance tunes.

In addition to his work as a performer, composer, and record label executive, Zorn has continued his role as a catalyst of the downtown Jewish music scene. He was instrumental in expanding live Jewish music programming beyond the Knitting Factory in 1998 to Tonic, another downtown club. Situated on the site of a former kosher winery on New York's Lower East Side, Tonic introduced "Klezmer Sundays" as a regular feature—probably the first time since the demise of the Jewish ghetto that klezmer could be heard on a weekly basis in that neighborhood.

"I think we're getting a new generation of younger Jews who are proud of their heritage, who don't want to pass for white, who want people to know that they're Jewish," says Zorn. "Their Jewish heritage is becoming a stronger part of their identity, and it's becoming part of their music. Now, each person has his own particular take on that history . . . his own particular attachments or revulsions to the Jewish side of his identity. . . .

"I think it's important for the world to know that Jews have had a very strong role in the creation of popular music and serious music of several nations . . . of the world's art. And why not celebrate that, why not explore that, why not put that out to all the people who think that we're just a bunch of managers shoveling money around?"

Why not indeed?

## CHAPTER 6

# DISCOGRAPHY

T his discography is intended to be a descriptive, informative guide to recorded klezmer available on CDs. Every
effort has been made to be as comprehensive and as accurate as possible.

---

**KEY**

1. Album titles in **boldface** type and marked by a rectanglar bullet are highly
   recommended. A list of these appears on pages 166.
2. Where relevant, page numbers referring back to the text, to more in-
   depth discussion of the recordings, appear in parentheses at the end of
   the entry.
3. (NR) = the recording was not reviewed for this book, but is included
   merely for informational purposes.
4. When albums are released under names different from the name given at
   the head of an entry, the name credited on the album appears in parentheses following the album title.
5. Years in parentheses refer to the original year of an album's release.
6. Record labels and catalog numbers are included for the latest version of
   an album's American release.
7. Every effort has been made to provide accurate information, but given
   the highly fluid nature of small and independent record labels, some of
   the recording details might be outdated or no longer relevant by the time
   of publication. A few of these works may be hard to find or out of print;
   consult the specialty Jewish-music retailers listed on page 248.

## THE ESSENTIAL KLEZMER LIBRARY

*A Jumpin' Night in the Garden of Eden*, Klezmer
 Conservatory Band

*Blood Oranges*, Brave Old World

*Fidl: Klezmer Violin*, Alicia Svigals

*Gimel (Three)*, Masada/John Zorn

*Jews with Horns*, The Klezmatics

*King of the Klezmer Clarinet*, Naftule Brandwein

*Klezmer Pioneers: European and American Recordings
 1905 – 52*, Various Artists

*Mother Tongue*, Budowitz

*Metropolis*, The Klezmorim

*Yiddish-American Klezmer Music 1925 – 56*, Dave Tarras

### (Ten More for Good Luck)

*Art of the Klezmer Clarinet*, Margot Leverett

*Bar Kokhba*, Masada Chamber Ensembles/John Zorn

*Bessarabian Symphony*, Rubin and Horowitz

*Chicken*, Kapelye

*Family Portrait*, The Klezical Tradition

*Klezmer Madness*, David Krakauer Trio

*Klezmer Music*, Andy Statman Klezmer Orchestra

*Klezmer Music: Early Yiddish Instrumental Music 1908 – 27*,
 Various Artists

*Possessed*, The Klezmatics

*Yiddish for Travelers*, Metropolitan Klezmer

## AHAVA RABA
*Kete Kuf* (1999) Tzadik TZ7133

Group founder Simon Jakob Drees, of Germany, traveled throughout Asia, including China, the former Soviet Asian republics, and the Indian subcontinent, and brought back a pan-cultural musical palette that draws freely from the traditions of all these lands as well as from Eastern European folk and Western classical music. Thus, for example, the title track combines operatic cantorial music, Mongolian folk singing, and contemporary minimalism.

## ALEXANDRIA KLEZTET
*Y2Klezmer* (1999) Kleztet CD1

This Washington, D.C.–area quartet (Alexandria refers to Virginia, not Egypt) was formed in 1998 by ex–Cayuga Klezmer Revival clarinetist Seth Kibel, and the group continues in the vein of that progressive band, with an emphasis on rhythmic jazz variations of traditional material and Kibel's own compositions. "Klezmerobics" features a very Middle Eastern–style melody over a throbbing, Jamaican dance-hall-derived bass line, and "Fon Der Choope" and "Rozhinkes Mit Mandlen" include some Cayuga-style rock dynamics, but this album doesn't quite live up to the legacy of that remarkably inventive band.

## AMBARCHI/AVENAIM
*The Alter Rebbe's Nigun* (1999) Tzadik TZ7131

Oren Ambarchi and Robbie Avenaim are allegedly former students of Lubavitcher Hasidism (a Hasidic sect tracing its origin back to Reb Schneur Zalman of Liadi, the *alter rebbe*) and currently members of an Australian punk band called Phlegm. On *The Alter Rebbe's Nigun,* they attempt to combine these two wildly disparate influences on four long pieces based on the four "worlds" of Kabbalah. Much of this is rendered in the vocabulary of extreme hard-core-punk, industrial-rock, free jazz, squealing electronic sounds, spoken word, and guitar noise—sometimes all at once—but sure enough, brimming under the surface cacophony are Yiddish modes, giving this a kind of otherworldly, cosmic-spiritual soundtrack feel.

## ATZILUT
*Souls on Fire: Music for the Kabbala* (1998)

This acoustic, nine-piece ensemble plays what it calls "ecstatic Hebrew mystical music," a mixture of Jewish liturgical music, Arabic music, and klezmer. On *Souls on Fire*, the emphasis is on world-beat-style improvisation with khazn Jack Kessler singing Kabbalistic texts. The instrumental arrangements are heavy on Indian-style percussion, and the violin playing on the occasional klezmer melody lacks Old World–style ornamentation. An intriguing attempt at cross-cultural musical fertilization.

## AUFWIND
*Lomp noch nit farloschn* (1989) (NR)
*Gassn singer* (1992) Nebebhorn Musik 011
*Junge jorn* (1995) (NR)
*Awek di junge jorn* (1996) Misrach MSR 0144-2

Founded in 1984 in East Berlin as an act of resistance against official East German policy banning all but officially sanctioned performers, this group of Germans taught themselves Yiddish and learned klezmer and Yiddish folk songs on their own, isolated behind the Iron Curtain. Since then they have traveled to the United States, traded licks with top musicians, and won respect for their mixture of Old World melodies and Yiddish folk tunes, some rendered in a cappella choral arrangements à la jazz-cabaret groups like the Manhattan Transfer.

## AUSTIN KLEZMORIM
*Texas Klez* (1991) Music BAM1 (NR)
*East of Odessa* (1995) Global Village 170

As the name of the group suggests, some of the playing by the Austin Klezmorim is more Texas than Odessa, such as Howard Kalish's gleeful fiddle solo on "Birobidjan." But the Austin Klezmorim is actually a horn-heavy group with accordion and vocals, drawing more on New Orleans jazz than western swing. Many of the group's arrangements on *East of Odessa* are surprisingly straightforward, evocative of the classic Yiddish bands of the 1920s. Its repertoire includes folk songs ("Tumbalalaika") and theater tunes ("Rozhinkes mit Mandelin"), dance numbers, and a few innovative original selections, including the centerpiece, the eight-minute "Big Megillah," a witty bit of hipster jive-jazz retelling the story of Purim. In sum, an eclectic, well-played grab bag of various approaches.

## STEVEN BERNSTEIN
**▌ *Diaspora Soul* (1999) Tzadik TZ7137**

On *Diaspora Soul,* trumpeter Steven Bernstein, the founder/leader of downtown jazz band Sex Mob and the musical director of John Lurie's Lounge Lizards, recasts a selection of traditional Jewish melodies in funky, "Gulf Coast" arrangements—equal parts New Orleans, Afro-Cuban, and R&B. Bernstein's arrangements, drenched in saxophones, organ, percussion, walking bass, and his own eloquent trumpet, transform Yiddish songs like "Roumania, Roumania," prayers like "Oseh Shalom," and transcriptions of cantorial solos into funky cigar music without losing their essence.

## BOJBRIKER KLEZMORIM
*Bojbriker Klezmorim* (1996) Syncoop 5756 CD 191

Accordion and clarinet heavily color this Dutch sextet's blend of theater tunes, dances, and Old World wedding marches, with a sensibility heavily informed by French chanson and German lieder. Arrangements are quite basic, and the album includes a medley of Israeli/Hebrew folk songs that (for better or worse) would not be out of place at a 1950s American bar mitzvah.

## NAFTULE BRANDWEIN
**▌ *King of the Klezmer Clarinet* (1997) Rounder 1127**

Naftule Brandwein's status as a giant of klezmer clarinet is fully supported by this collection, which is, remarkably, the only reissue devoted in its entirety to one of the two most influential of the immigrant-era musicians (the other being Dave Tarras). The simple fact is Brandwein was not a prolific recording artist, and as such, what does exist of his recorded work is well represented by these twenty-five tracks recorded between 1922 and 1926, with four selections from his final session in 1941. Many of these songs are standards of the contemporary klezmer repertoire—indeed, this is probably the recording you are most likely to find in any contemporary musician's private library. The word *essential* doesn't even begin to describe how significant the music is on this disk, coproduced by Henry Sapoznik and Dick Spottswood. (Pp. 59–64, 69–70)

## BRAVE OLD WORLD

*Klezmer Music* (1990) Flying Fish FLY 560
▮ *Beyond the Pale* (1994) Rounder 3135
▮ *Blood Oranges* (1999) Red House RHR 134

On *Klezmer Music,* the group's first CD, the Old World quotient outweighs the Brave. The group is feeling its way, trying to figure out just what Brave Old World is going to be. A vehicle for Michael Alpert's Yiddish vocals? A modern group playing nineteenth-century-style Eastern European arrangements? An historical reenactment of various klezmer and Yiddish styles?

*Beyond the Pale* is a great leap forward, the recording on which Brave Old World first attempted its more ambitious themes and suites. It is here that the group's identity coalesces: the broad worldview, with its European-American thematic, musical, and political concerns, and the introduction of nonklezmer influences into its mix (hence, "beyond the pale," a pun on the Pale of Settlement, the region to which Jews were restricted in Western Russia). Original lieder melodies meet haunting, elegant horas. "Doina Extravaganza" borrows ideas from contemporary classical music, and songs bleed into one another. As much as it draws on Old World forms and melodies, Brave Old World appears here as a contemporary ensemble. Also, with *Beyond the Pale,* Kurt Bjorling replaces Joel Rubin on clarinet, bringing a more personal, "hot" feel to the group. His jazz-influenced approach can be heard on his rich solo on "Rufn di Kinder Aheym."

With *Blood Oranges* the group truly lives up to its promise, elevating its brand of klezmer to the level of a new Jewish art music without leaving behind its "hot" origins in dance music or its Old World poignancy. *Blood Oranges* is a dynamically modern suite—there is no longer any question that this group is making innovative klezmer, as opposed to reviving old tunes. Michael Alpert plays the role of badkhn to the hilt, introducing the band to "all Yiddishland, from San Francisco to Brest-Litovsk."

In the same way that the Beatles' *Sgt. Pepper's Lonely Hearts Club Band* wove together all that had come before in an entirely new and innovative fashion, *Blood Oranges* is one of the greatest achievements of the entire klezmer revival, setting the standard against which all subsequent efforts of its kind would be judged. From a foundation firmly rooted in klezmer, *Blood Oranges* succeeds in its attempt to create, as Alan Bern writes in the liner notes, "an affirmation of music which simply celebrates its own freedom." (Pp. 108–114)

## WALLY BRILL

### *The Covenant* (1997) Six Degrees/Island 314-524 422-2

Electronica meets the Kabbalah on this remarkably innovative recording by musical auteur/producer Wally Brill, who samples cantorial recordings from the early twentieth century and builds atmospheric grooves and world-beat textures around them with synthesizers and live musicians. Akin to what the popular world-music group Deep Forest has done with Eastern European folk music, Brill's experiment creates some starkly suggestive juxtapositions: one Auschwitz survivor's reminiscence of life in the death camp is punctuated by cantor Samuel Malavsky wailing "Ribon Ho-Olomim" atop an industrial/hip-hop percussion loop. While not klezmer, the impetus for this sort of cross-generational fertilization springs from the same well as some of the more experimental klezmer fusions. (Pp. 144–145)

## EMIL BRUH

### *Klezmer Violinist and Instrumental Ensemble* (1985) Global Village 102

This reissue of a 1950s album features violinist Emil Bruh in small, orchestral arrangements of Yiddish theater and folk melodies. Bruh's playing veers in and out of Gypsy territory, occasionally leaden with schmaltz, but once in a while striking a real klezmer chord. This rare example of midcentury violin is available on cassette only and includes surface noise.

## BUDOWITZ

**▌ *Mother Tongue* (1997) Koch/Schwann 3-1261-2**

This European-based group is klezmer's answer to classical music's "early music" ensembles. Led by Joshua Horowitz, a scholar of Old World klezmer who plays tsimbl and nineteenth-century button accordion (manufactured by a man named Budowitz), the group plays on vintage instruments in arrangements the players believe reflect the way klezmer was performed in the 1800s in Eastern Europe. This is klezmer as elegant chamber music that doesn't lose its essence as "folk" or dance music, in keeping with a late nineties move to neotraditionalism among some klezmorim. Includes an exhaustive and informative thirty-page booklet by Horowitz.

## WARREN BYRD AND DAVID CHEVAN

*Avadim Hayinu: Once We Were Slaves* (1998) Reckless DC RMCD-1031

This piano-bass duo performance—recorded before a live audience in April 1998—explores the musical and spiritual connections between African Americans and Jewish Americans. Pianist Warren Byrd and bassist David Chevan employ the jazz idiom to construct an eloquent, intercultural dialogue on a selection of traditional Jewish prayer melodies and black gospel tunes.

## DON BYRON

**▌ *Plays the Music of Mickey Katz* (1993) Elektra/Nonesuch 79313-2**

Clarinetist Don Byron, who was a member of the Klezmer Conservatory Band for seven years, lovingly revisits musical parodist Mickey Katz on this album. Mostly forgotten or consigned to the bin as a jokester or musical prankster, Katz is resuscitated by Byron, who makes a strong case for the bandleader/comedian as a forerunner of Radical Jewish Culture, one who drew upon the deep well of yidishkayt to comment, sometimes acerbically, on American culture, and Jewish American culture in particular. Byron assembled an all-star cast to help him re-create many of Katz's most sophisticated, concerto-style arrangements: violinist Mark Feldman and trumpeter Dave Douglas of the Masada Chamber Ensembles, pianist Uri Caine, and vocalist Lorin Sklamberg of the Klezmatics.

## SHLOMO AND NESHAMA CARLEBACH
*Ha Neshama Shel Shlomo* (1998) SISU NDN 183656

The work of the late Shlomo Carlebach is far too exhaustive to be treated in any comprehensive way here. His innovations in updating Hasidic-style prayer melodies for the folk-rock era merit an entire book of their own. This posthumously released recording—completed just a few weeks before he died in 1994—serves as a kind of passing of the torch to his daughter, Neshama, who boasts a deep, rich voice of her own. Since her father's death, Neshama Carlebach has dedicated her life to bringing his inspirational music and stories to audiences around the world. On this recording, she is a warm, affecting, soulful emissary, utterly worthy of the gregarious passion her father brought to contemporary Jewish music.

## CATSKILL KLEZMORIM
*Beyond the Borscht Belt* (1998) Divine Noise DN 001

Formed in 1995, based in Oneonta, New York, the Catskill Klezmorim features two vocalists and seven musicians on an eclectic selection of vocal and instrumental favorites. They give "Abi Gezunt" a swing-jazz feel and go Gypsy on the fiddle tune, "Csardas." Folksy one minute, they can tackle a soulful doina the next, and are versatile enough to include an Israeli medley and the Sephardic favorite "Ocho Kandelikas."

## CAYUGA KLEZMER REVIVAL
▌ *Klezmology* (1998) Corncake CCD-663-27

This little-known upstate–New York group revamped Old World melodies and rhythms and made them speak to contemporary audiences on this, their only recording. They do a "Honga Tanz" that would not be out of place at a neohippie, jam-rock concert. Banjo, violin, and electric guitar hold a dynamic, three-way conversation on an "Odessa Bulgar." One medley, "Shamil/Golden Wings," is a fusion of hard-rock and Hasidism akin to Jethro Tull's similarly progressive fusion of rock and English folk. The group is now defunct, which is too bad—outside of the Klezmatics, few groups have been able to pull off this sort of klezmer-pop fusion with such wit and musical sophistication.

## CHICAGO KLEZMER ENSEMBLE

*Sweet Home Bukovina* (1998) Oriente/Rien CD 13

Founded in 1984 by clarinetist Kurt Bjorling, the Chicago Klezmer Ensemble is one of the world's finest practitioners of acoustic, Old World–style klezmer. Bjorling is a careful student and arranger and brings an elegance of classical proportions to the group's arrangements, which breathe with inordinate grace. The group also includes such well-known contemporary players as violinists Josh Huppert and Deborah Strauss, pianist Eve Monzingo, and bassist Al Ehrich, all of whom find ways to inject personality into their playing while remaining true to the core melodies.

## CINCINNATI KLEZMER PROJECT

*Klezmer's Greatest Hits* (1998) Mastersound/Intersound 3591

Sooner or later some band was bound to claim this album title for its own, and it could have done worse than the Cincinnati Klezmer Project. The album isn't a bad primer on some of the basic dance genres and the most popular melodies in the repertoire, and clarinetist Michele Gingras acquits herself well as the leader of a small ensemble with no other lead instrument. Mixed in are Yiddish theater and folk tunes, as well as a few Hebrew/Israeli numbers, and even a selection from *Fiddler on the Roof.* One could quibble as to whether these and other vocal numbers belong on an album called *Klezmer's Greatest Hits,* but then again, this is probably quite representative of how American audiences would have heard these tunes at a typical, post–World War II simkhe.

## ANTHONY COLEMAN

▌ *Sephardic Tinge* (1995) Tzadik TZ7102

*Selfhaters* (1996) Tzadik TZ7110

*I Could've Been a Drum* (Roy Nathanson and Anthony Coleman)
  (1997) Tzadik TZ7113

*The Abysmal Richness of the Proximity of the Same* (Selfhaters)
  (1998) Tzadik TZ7123

*Morenica* (Sephardic Tinge) (1998) Tzadik TZ7128

Inspired by the hidden connections between Jelly Roll Morton's jazz,

Latin music, and the Sephardic tradition, keyboardist Anthony Coleman came up with a beautiful Jewish-Latin fusion on his original piano trio album, *Sephardic Tinge,* which he recorded with bassist Greg Cohen and drummer Joey Baron of Masada. In addition to Coleman's original compositions, the album includes versions of songs by Morton and Thelonious Monk, as well as a gorgeous, Afro-Cuban version of the Yiddish folk classic, "Belz." Coleman continues in the same vein on *Morenica,* relying more on original composition and the jazz piano tradition.

Coleman's Selfhaters albums couldn't be more different from his Sephardic Tinge projects. The music on *Selfhaters* and *The Abysmal Richness of the Proximity of the Same,* arranged for small ensembles (quartets and quintets) that variously include trumpet, clarinet, trombone, saxophone, accordion, cello, banjo, organ, and voice, exploits dissonance and group improvisation while exploring Jewish identity. On *Selfhaters* these themes play out in a series of jazz-based, free improvisations, including virtually unrecognizable "versions" of jazz standards "You Don't Know What Love Is" and "The Mooche." On *The Abysmal Richness of the Proximity of the Same,* Coleman employs long forms and strategies adopted from modern composers such as John Cage and Morton Feldman. On both albums the results are strikingly suggestive, and not anything close to easy listening.

The Nathanson/Coleman duet album *I Could've Been a Drum* bears a closer resemblance to Coleman's Selfhaters than his Sephardic Tinge music. Roy Nathanson plays a variety of saxophones and recorder, and Coleman makes use of electronic samples, piano, and organ on mostly experimental tracks. "L'Amore," for example, sounds like Godzilla snoring while his next door neighbor practices saxophone scales (and not very well at that); "Rumle," on the other hand, is a relatively lyrical duet between the two musicians.

## MIKE CURTIS KLEZMER QUARTET (see also Oomph)
### *Street Song* (1997) Louie 006
The jazz backgrounds of the musicians in the Mike Curtis Klezmer Quartet hold them in good stead, as they confidently swing traditional shers,

horas, and freylekhs without breaking them. Clarinetist Curtis and keyboardist Dave Leslie (who were members of the band Oomph) also write a few originals. On some numbers, like Leslie's "Kasimierz" and "Alcazaba," the group plays a kind of Latinesque, jazzy, cocktail-klez. A curious fusion.

## DAVKA

*Davka* (1994) Interworld CD-809132
*Lavy's Dream* (1996) Interworld 922
*Judith* (1999) Tzadik TZ 7135

Together since 1992, this San Francisco–based, classically flavored acoustic trio has been composing original Yiddish instrumental music infused with a world-beat pulse. Daniel Hoffman's Jewish violin dances over drones and counterpoint laid down by Moses Sedler's cello, and a variety of percussion instruments and hand drums, including *dumbek* and *zarb,* give the music an exotic, cosmopolitan feel; a whirlwind journey from India to Africa to the Middle East to the British Isles and back to Eastern Europe. On *Judith,* Brave Old World's Stuart Brotman lends a hand on bass and cymbalom. Whether or not it was intended, this album works as an extended suite of instrumental songs. Close your eyes and imagine you are a Polish nobleman in the eighteenth century being entertained by a trio of virtuoso, cosmopolitan klezmorim.

## DI GOJIM

*Grine Medine* (1991) Syncoop 5751 CD 131
*Noch a Sjoh* (1993) Syncoop 5753 CD 161 (NR)
*Fun sjtetl un sjtets* (1996) Syncoop 5756 CD 201 (NR)

This Dutch acoustic sextet, heavy on horns with tuba, clarinet, trombone, and trumpet in its front line, acquits itself quite well on a selection of popular klezmer standards and a few vocal numbers. As captured on the live album, *Grine Medine,* the group's ironic sense of humor and its spirited ensemble approach, punctuated by accordion and banjo, seems modeled on the early American revival outfit Kapelye.

## DI NAYE KAPELYE
■ *Di Naye Kapelye* (1998) Oriente RIEN CD 17

The name *Di Naye Kapelye* means "the new band" in Yiddish, but since 1989, the Budapest-based group has played a decidedly Old World–flavored, traditionally based klezmer. Influenced by the highly percussive, grassroots sounds of Gypsy, Hungarian, and Romanian village folk styles, the group's music draws heavily upon the field research of violinist/vocalist Bob Cohen, conducted among surviving Jewish and Gypsy musicians in Hungary, Romania, and Moldova. The result bears the dynamic immediacy of a street band.

## MARTY EHRLICH
*Sojourn* (1999) Tzadik TZ 7136

*Sojourn* features breathtakingly gorgeous new compositions by clarinetist/saxophonist Marty Ehrlich played by his trio, the Dark Woods Ensemble, including cellist Erik Friedlander and bassist Mark Helias, with guitar accompaniment by Marc Ribot. Previously noted for his new-classical work and for collaborations with such avant-garde jazz greats as Anthony Braxton, Julius Hemphill, and Muhal Richard Abrams, Ehrlich's acoustic arrangements are alternately jazzy, intimately classical, and darkly melodic and folklike. Occasionally frenzied and discordant, always richly textured and painterly, Ehrlich's compositions sometimes reference Hebrew melody ("Eliyahu HaNavi" in "Eliahu: Second Variation"). In addition to his original compositions, he includes an impressionistic version of Bob Dylan's "Blind Willie McTell" and a rendition of "The Modzitzer Nigun."

## ENSEMBLE KLEZMER
*Live in Prag* (1997) Extraplatte EX 317-2

This recording captures this Vienna-based, violin-bass-accordion trio at their 1994 concert in Prague. Leader Leon Pollak is well versed in the core klezmer repertoire, as well as Hasidic music and Yiddish theater tunes, a few of which he sings here. Pollak's playing and arrangements occasionally show the influence of his longstanding career as a classical musician, but for the most part the trio format provides a good showcase for his approach and repertoire.

## EPSTEIN BROTHERS ORCHESTRA
■ *Kings of Freylekh Land: A Century of Yiddish-American Music*
  (1995) Spectrum/Wergo SM 1611-2

This album captures the Epstein Brothers, who played with Dave Tarras and Naftule Brandwein and are at the twilight of their careers (in the case of clarinetist Max Epstein in his seventieth year as a professional musician). It is an invaluable document both for the repertoire—which includes Old World dances and listening pieces, Yiddish theater tunes, Hasidic melodies, Oriental fox-trots, and cabaret songs—and the style, opening a window on to what Jewish music must have sounded like in the "lost period" between World War II and the revival of the 1970s. Another lovingly produced and exhaustively annotated effort by Joel Rubin and Rita Ottens.

## GIORA FEIDMAN
*Jewish Soul Music* (1973) Hed Arzi 14297
*The Incredible Clarinet* (1981) Pläne 88725
*The Singing Clarinet of Giora Feidman* (1987) Pläne 88582
*The Magic of the Klezmer* (1990) Pläne 88708
*Gershwin and the Klezmer* (1991) Pläne 88717
*Viva El Klezmer* (1991) Pläne 88712
*The Dance of Joy* (1993) ROM 105CD
*Klassic Klezmer* (1993) ROM 106CD
*Feidman in Jerusalem* (1994) Pläne 88768
*Klezmer Chamber Music* (1995) Pläne 88785
*Klezmer Celebration* (1997) Pläne 88809
*Silence and Beyond: Feidman Plays Ora Bat Chaim*
  (1997) Koch/Schwann 3-6499-2

Giora Feidman is nothing if not prolific, and for that alone he deserves credit for spreading the gospel of klezmer, such as it were, throughout the world. Feidman has undoubtedly been the door through which many have come to klezmer, especially in Europe.

His recordings, however, are not representative of anything else in klezmer. Indeed, while to many around the world Feidman is synonymous with klezmer (not the least for the simple reason that so many of his albums use the word in their titles), his recordings truly belong in a category of their own. Freely mixing and matching klezmer-derived melodies with other Yiddish, Israeli, and non-Jewish styles, almost all his albums place Feidman's genuinely skillful, soulful, and occasionally jazzy clarinet playing in a polished, classical-symphonic context, an aesthetic utterly alien to klezmer's roots as a folk music. This might appeal to fans of "symphonic pops" music, but it is unlikely to stir the hearts of the true klezmer aficionado.

Like most of Feidman's albums, *Jewish Soul Music* takes a broad view of klezmer repertoire, including Hebrew prayers, Israeli folk songs, Broadway show tunes, original melodies, and Yiddish dance numbers. This modest, early effort featuring Feidman backed simply by acoustic guitar and bass, however, is free of the emotional bombast and pretension that mars most of what was to come. His clarinet playing here is warm and familiar, whereas on subsequent albums it is unduly cold and garish. If you must own one Feidman album, this is the one.

Otherwise, buyer beware. (Pp. 100-101)

## FINJAN KLEZMER ENSEMBLE
*Crossing Selkirk Avenue* (1993) Red House RHR 57
*Dancing on Water* (2000) Rounder 3160 (NR)

As the liner notes explain, Selkirk Avenue was the main drag running through the section of Winnipeg where Eastern European immigrants— Poles, Ukrainians, and Jews—all settled. This nostalgic tribute to that neighborhood weaves the sounds of swing, bluegrass, and jazz through the acoustic, mostly immigrant-era-style klezmer played by this Winnipeg-based sextet. Finjan boasts a wide instrumental palette. With members doubling- and even tripling-up on different instruments, they cover all the standard bases of clarinet, violin, bass, and accordion, and add piano, saxophone, guitar, harmonica, guitar, banjo, mandolin, bouzouki, drums, and vocals. The group is at its best when it is pushing itself creatively—when played straight, the music lacks distinction.

## KAILA FLEXER

*Listen* (Kaila Flexer and Third Ear) (1995) Compass 7 4226 2

*Next Village* (1999) Compass 7 4259 2

Violinist Kaila Flexer comes from a klezmer family (her great-grandfather and great-uncle were klezmers in Poland), and she continues the tradition, albeit from a wider vantage point than just klezmer. A founding member of the klezmer revival group Hotzeplotz, Flexer has gone on to make her mark as an ensemble leader playing what she calls "country & Eastern," an innovative fusion of American and Eastern European folk musics with a jazzy approach by a virtuoso ensemble, including accordion, marimba, and percussion. While these are not klezmer albums, each includes several klezmer-based tunes, which will undoubtedly please fans of world-folk or David "Dawg" Grisman.

## FLYING BULGAR KLEZMER BAND

*The Flying Bulgar Klezmer Band* (1990) Traditional Crossroads TCRO 4293

*Agada: Tales from Our Ancestors* (1993) Traditional Crossroads TCRO 4294

*Fire* (1996) Traditional Crossroads TCRO 4295

▌ *Tsirkus* (1999) Traditional Crossroads TCRO 4292

This Toronto-based group, founded in 1987, made its recording debut in 1990 with a pretty straightforward revivalist approach, although trumpeter David Buchbinder—the founder, leader, and chief visionary of the group—reimagines the klezmer standard "Baym Rebn's Sude" in an Afro-Cuban jazz setting. *Agada* is a great leap forward, and here David Buchbinder indulges his more radical desire to combine klezmer with a jazz aesthetic. "Cooking Bulgar(s)" opens the album in a conventional manner before it morphs into a Tito Puente–style salsa number. *Fire* summarizes the group's accomplishments up to that point in a live program featuring vocalist Adrienne Cooper appearing with the band.

*Tsirkus* makes a bold statement with the title cut, a Steely Dan–style, midtempo jazz-rocker with Yiddish lyrics sung by Dave Wall and a psychedelic, circus-music bridge wrapped inside. "Flora" follows, a striking trumpet–electric guitar duet on melodies by Joseph Moskowitz. The album continues in this progressive vein, with jazzy interpolations of traditional melodies and new Yiddish songs carved from poems and folk ballads, putting the Flying Bulgars in league with the Klezmatics and Brave Old World.

## FREILACHMAKERS KLEZMER STRING BAND
*The Flower of Berezin* (1998) EDDAL98

This Sacramento, California–based quintet plays an intriguing fusion of old-time klezmer melodies and old-time American string-band music, with occasional detours into Irish and Balkan territory. There are no horns in this band—as the name suggests—just mandolins, banjos, guitars, balalaikas, bass, and fiddle. The result is lively and virtuosic playing. The musicians have done their homework, studying the original music and coming up with a sound that will surely please fans of traditional string-band music.

## ERIK FRIEDLANDER
▌ *The Watchman* (1996) Tzadik TZ7107

Chimera, cellist Erik Friedlander's quartet with clarinet, bass clarinet, and string bass, performs eight of his original compositions, ranging in length from a minute and a half to twelve minutes. Inspired by the short fiction of Jewish-American author Mark Helprin, the new-classical-cum-jazz-styled works are, like Helprin's stories, full of drama and heroism, including the Middle Eastern–tinged "Najime."

## BOB GLUCK
▌ *Stories Heard and Retold* (1998) Electronic Music Foundation EMF 008

This electronic sound collage built with found sounds, ambient recordings, and original, computerized compositions takes a listener on a journey backward in time, from a contemporary worship service (Jewish renewal guru Zalman Schacter-Shalomi is heard davening), to prewar, Yiddish-speaking Europe, all the way back to the Bible, where a listener experiences firsthand the tribulations of "Jonah under the Sea." In the process, Bob Gluck makes us understand that "Jewish music" is more than just melodies played on conventional instruments—it permeates all aspects of ritual life, from milling about in the antechamber before services to turning the pages of the *siddur*, or prayerbook. (Pp. 139–141)

## GOJIM
*Tscholent* (1994) Extraplatte EX 207-2
*In a schtodt woss schtarbt* (1997) Extraplatte EX 307-2 (NR)

Flute, acoustic guitar, soprano saxophone, and accordion dominate this Austrian ensemble of non-Jews (hence the group's name), which on *Tscholent* plays a mix of Yiddish dance tunes and folk songs with a Bavarian folk feel. The Central European sensibility suggests turn-of-the-century Vienna rather than Old World shtetl. The unfortunate imitation of a horse on Gojim's version of "Odessa Bulgar" might have precedent in klezmer history: according to noted klezmer historian Martin Schwartz, the B-side of an early Naftule Brandwein record contained comedic imitations of barnyard animals. It's not clear from the liner notes if Gojim intended the parallel.

## BEN GOLDBERG (see also New Klezmer Trio)
*Junk Genius* (Goldberg/Schott/Dunn/Wollesen) (1995) Knitting Factory
    Works KFW 160
*Here by Now* (1997) Music & Arts CD-1004
*Eight Phrases for Jefferson Rubin* (1998) Victo CD057
▌ *What Comes Before* (Goldberg/Schott/Sarin) (1998) Tzadik TZ7120

Beginning with his work in the Klezmorim in the mid-to-late 1980s and continuing through his leadership of the New Klezmer Trio in the 1990s, Ben Goldberg has been one of the most talented and innovative clarinetists in klezmer.

Of the four recordings listed here, only the Goldberg/Schott/Sarin trio effort, *What Comes Before,* is presented as a "Jewish" recording, by virtue of its inclusion in Tzadik's Radical Jewish Culture series. The centerpiece of this effort is the seventeen-minute "Night Prayer Song," which like much of Goldberg's work outside of the New Klezmer Trio is hauntingly quiet and atmospheric.

Ostensibly Jewish or not, Goldberg's playing and composition is always deeply informed by his experience with klezmer. Anyone who appreciates Goldberg's work with the New Klezmer Trio might want to delve deeper into Goldberg's experimental oeuvre, which is only partly touched on here.

*Junk Genius* unleashes Goldberg, along with frequent collaborators John Schott on guitar, Trevor Dunn on bass, and Kenny Wollesen on drums, on a selection of bebop tunes by Bud Powell, Charlie Parker, Dizzy Gillespie, and Miles Davis. In the hands of these progressive-minded musicians, classics like "Koko," "Hot House," and "Donna Lee" take on entirely new shadings.

Goldberg showcases his talents as both player and composer on *Here By Now*, credited to the Ben Goldberg Trio and including accompaniment by bassist Dunn and drummer Elliot Humberto Kavee. This is the solo effort most like his New Klezmer Trio work. *Eight Phrases for Jefferson Rubin*, performed by a sextet including guitarist Schott and drummer Michael Sarin, is a mostly delicate tribute to Goldberg's childhood friend who died tragically at age thirty-five.

## GOLDEN GATE GYPSY ORCHESTRA
*The Travelling Jewish Wedding* (1981) Rykodisc 10105

Formed in 1976 by over a dozen amateur and semiprofessional musicians in the Marin County region of California, this freewheeling, acoustic-folk ensemble included Hasidic nigunim, Israeli love songs, Ukrainian and Russian dances, Sephardic folk, Brahms, and tango on its first and only recording, all with a strong, Gypsy-like approach that for better or worse blurs the distinction between klezmer and the co-territorial repertoire.

## GREAT JEWISH MUSIC (Various Artists)
*Great Jewish Music: Burt Bacharach* (1997) Tzadik TZ 7114-2
*Great Jewish Music: Serge Gainsbourg* (1997) Tzadik TZ 7116
*Great Jewish Music: Marc Bolan* (1998) Tzadik TZ 7126

A wildly eclectic cast of downtown artists, many part of John Zorn's stable, pay tribute to composer-performers Burt Bacharach, Marc Bolan, and Serge Gainsbourg on Tzadik's "Great Jewish Music" series, which seeks to make the case that their Jewish heritage informed the composers' music.

This sort of approach works best with the Bacharach volume. Given the widespread familiarity of most of these songs, the new approaches highlight their hidden recesses and subtexts. Thus, "Trains and Boats and Planes" takes on a whole new meaning as Fred Frith repeatedly intones, "You are from another part of the world." If nothing else, the album is a hoot just for the strange versions of songs like "The Look of Love," "What's New Pussycat," and "What the World Needs Now Is Love," by Sean Lennon, Elliot Sharp, and acid-jazz trio Medeski, Martin, and Wood.

Serge Gainsbourg boasts the dubious distinction of being the first recording artist to have a number-one hit in Great Britain with a single banned by all broadcasters. His sexually suggestive "Je t'aime . . . moi non plus" shocked the censors with its lascivious-sounding French words and heavy breathing (the record barely made the charts in the United States). Born Lucien Ginzburg to Russian-Jewish parents, Gainsbourg was to become a superstar of French popular music, one whose dark, moody, passionate concerns, as reflected in song titles such as "Ce Mortel ennui," "Un Poison violent, C'est ca l'amour," "Les Amours perdues," and "69 Annee erotique," need no translation. Twenty-one of his songs are given the Tzadik treatment by the usual suspects, including psychedelic-pop group Cibo Matto, Medeski, Martin, and Wood, Fred Frith, Wayne Horvitz, and, in a rare vocal appearance, by John Zorn himself, in arrangements that don't have to veer from the originals in order to highlight their dark, haunted quality.

Marc Bolan was the stage name for Mark Feld, the leader of seminal British glam-rock band T. Rex. His imaginative, theatrical antics and fantasy-infused songs paved the way for a slew of acts that followed, including David Bowie, Elton John, the Ramones, and Johnny Rotten. Again, in the hands of such ultrahip, downtown performers as Arto Lindsay, the Melvins, Medeski, Martin, and Wood, Gary Lucas, Sean Lennon, and Cake Like, the dark undercurrent of longing that infuses the material is transparent, most obviously in Kramer's version of the familiar glam anthem, "Get It On." (Pp. 160–161)

## HARRY'S FREILACH
*Klezmer Tov!* (1998) Nightingale NGH-CD-457

German clarinetist Harry Timmermann has a powerfully individual sound, and the small-band arrangements featured on his group's album are tasteful showcases for his considerable talent. Unfortunately, the same cannot be said for the group's accordionist, who still seems stuck in the beer hall.

## HASIDIC NEW WAVE
■ *Jews and the Abstract Truth* (1997) Knitting Factory KFW 192
*Giuliani Über Alles* (EP) (1998) Knitting Factory
*Psycho-Semitic* (1998) Knitting Factory KFR 203
■ *Kabalogy* (1999) Knitting Factory KFR 239

Probably no group can more rightly claim to make progressive, improvisational jazz genuinely rooted in Jewish music than Hasidic New Wave. Especially on its first album, *Jews and the Abstract Truth*, which consists almost entirely of Hasidic melodies put through its blender of postbop, Frank Zappa–inspired fusion, Hasidic New Wave sets the standard for innovative, authentically Jewish jazz, or "Hebe Bop," as the title of one of the group's songs calls it.

On *Jews and the Abstract Truth*, where newcomers to Hasidic New Wave should begin, coleaders Greg Wall and Frank London dig deep into the contemporary Hasidic repertoire for the kernels and nuggets of solo and all-group improvisations. The followup, *Psycho-Semitic*, builds on the debut's foundation, adding more original compositions to its repertoire and indulging its members' more avant-garde leanings. For the uninitiated, this will probably be the group's most difficult album to comprehend.

*Kabalogy* spreads the compositional duties all around, with electric guitarist David Fiuczynski, drummer Aaron Alexander, and bassist Fima Ephron sharing writing chores with Wall and London. More accessible perhaps than *Psycho-Semitic*, *Kabalogy* includes Ephron's lovely, lyrical,

Middle-Eastern-meets-Miles-Davis-flavored ballad, "Benigni," and Greg Wall's swing-fusion title track. Frank London's "H.W.N." opens a window on the group's strategy by following a two-minute-long vocal nign with an instrumental version of the same. Wall also pays tribute to one of the group's main influences with "The Frank Zappa Memorial Bris," which clocks in at exactly one minute. The group's arrangement of "Satmer Hakafos Nign #3" is downright Ellingtonian even as it refers back to *Jews and the Abstract Truth*.

The *Giuliani Über Alles* EP is worth seeking out for its five different versions of the group's devastatingly pointed, hard-core-rap remake of the punk group Dead Kennedy's song, "California Über Alles," featuring new lyrics tailored to New York Mayor Rudy Giuliani's so-called quality of life crackdown. A version of the song also closes *Kabalogy*.

## SHELLEY HIRSCH

### *O Little Town of East New York* (1995) Tzadik TZ7104

Electronic soundtracks pulse underneath Shelley Hirsch's dramatic, autobiographical recitations of life in Brooklyn in the 1950s and 1960s, on an album that functions much like an aural short-story collection. Hirsch's characters and anecdotes are full of color and vibrancy, and her sound treatments bring them fully to life, capturing the tensions pulling apart the fabric of one of the last of the inner-city Jewish neighborhoods.

## I. J. HOCHMAN

### *Master of Klezmer Music: Fun Der Khupe* (1993) Global Village 114

The earliest of the vintage recordings collected here date back to 1918, and unfortunately they sound like it, but there is gold underneath the scratches. Hochman's six- and seven-piece ensembles were among the best playing parade-style arrangements. This collection includes some incredibly inventive and witty arrangements, such as the cartoonlike "Zion March," a suite that incorporates what was to become the Israeli national anthem, "Hatikvah." It also includes some early examples of recorded Yiddish song, with Hochman's group backing vocalists Joe Feldman and Sam Goldin, and a comic number featuring Yiddish comedian Gus Goldstein.

**HOT PSTROMI (see Yale Strom)**

**JEWISH TRIO**
*Introversions* (1995) Music Sources

This unique trio is a vehicle for the improvisations of multi-instrumentalist Samuel Heifetz, a Latvian native whose musical arsenal includes oboe, English horn, piano, and recorder. Joined by electric guitarist Boaz Ben-Moshe of Israel and bassist Bruce Kaminsky of Philadelphia, Heifetz builds extended, sometimes impressionistic, improvisational suites on traditional religious and folk melodies as well as original compositions. Some arrangements are extremely sparse, but when the musicians start swinging, Heifetz's oboe works surprisingly well in the role of the clarinet on this warm, intimate, jazzy recording.

**KABALAS**
*Martinis and Bagels* (1995) Dionysus ID 123343
*The Eye of the Zohar* (1998) Dionysus ID 123349
▌*Time Tunnel* (1999) Dionysus ID 123379

In the spirit of Mickey Katz, the Kabalas dissect contemporary pop culture with shameless wit on songs like "Wall Martt Polkaa" and "Photograph of Aunt Rachel Doing the Cha-Cha at Cousin Ira's Bar Mitzvah (circa 1963)." They don't limit themselves to Jewish themes or music— polkas and waltzes appear alongside freylekhs—but their albums are sprinkled with accordion-heavy renditions of traditional shers and bulgars amid the zany original tunes, some of the best of which are based on figures from Jewish folklore like the Golem and the Dybbuk, and on American-Jewish entertainers Chico Marx and porn star Traci Lords, née Nora Kuzma. Call this midwestern quartet the They Might Be Giants of neo-klez.

**HARRY KANDEL**
*Master of Klezmer Music: Russian Sher* (1991) Global Village 128
*Master of Klezmer Music, Vol. 2: Der Gassen Nigun* (1997) Global Village 138

Harry Kandel was one of the most prolific recording artists of the early immigrant period, recording over 90 sides from 1917 to 1927. As a result, his is a rich and important legacy, and the music contained on these two disks is a treasure trove of early recorded klezmer. Many of the selections on these two disks were recorded by groups of up to a dozen musicians, and although they manifest the American influence of Kandel's stint performing with John Philip Sousa in the Pennsylvania State Militia Band, they also boast wonderful ensemble playing and subtle, Old World touches. More than that, they are primers of the core repertoire.

While the sound is by no means pristine, with a few exceptions the quality of *Russian Sher* is better than other recordings in Global Village's Master of Klezmer Music series. Nearly the first half of *Der Gassen Nigun* is virtually unlistenable, but the second half—including the poignant title track, which features virtuosic xylophone-playing by Jakie Hoffman in the tradition of the tsimbl and shtroyfidl, and the rousingly Dixielandish numbers, "Cohen Visits the Sesquicentennial" and "Jakie Jazz 'Em Up"— is almost immaculate, and perhaps worth the price of the whole. (Both "Der Gassen Nigun" and "Jakie Jazz 'Em Up" are also available on the compilation *Jakie Jazz 'Em Up*.)

## KAPELYE

*Future and Past* (1981) Flying Fish FLY 249 (NR)
▌ *Levine and His Flying Machine* (1984) Shanachie 21006
▌ *Chicken* (1986) Shanachie 21007
▌ *On the Air: Jewish-American Radio* (1995) Shanachie 67005

One of the original revival bands, Kapelye mixed classic klezmer with Yiddish theater tunes, novelty numbers, and an overall approach that emphasized nostalgic yidishkayt. All its albums are commendable and rendered with deep, abiding care, attention to detail, and instrumental proficiency. *Chicken* stands out in particular, not the least for Henry Sapoznik's "Banjo Doina," and for "Der Badkhin," a full-fledged suite that mixes genuine, folkloric badkhones with Michael Alpert's and Henry Sapoznik's comedic interpretations of the tradition.

*Levine and His Flying Machine* could do just as well as a representation of prime Kapelye, with its mix of vocal novelties like the title track, Ken

Maltz's several remakes of Naftule Brandwein solos, and Michael Alpert's dramatic vocals on several theater tunes. *On the Air: Jewish-American Radio* is also outstanding for its mix of vintage radio transcriptions juxtaposed seamlessly with Kapelye's updates of classic Yiddish radio, replete with commercial voice-overs and a comic Yiddish version of "Sixteen Tons." (Pp. 90–95)

## MICKEY KATZ

▌ *Simcha Time: Mickey Katz Plays Music for Weddings, Bar Mitzvahs, and Brisses* (1994) World Pacific/Capitol CDP 7243 8 30453 2 7

While Mickey Katz is best remembered for his music parodies—think of him as the Catskills version of "Weird" Al Yankovic—this album makes the case for Katz as more than just a novelty artist. Included here are the entire contents of Katz's mid-fifties album, *Mickey Katz Plays Music for Weddings, Bar Mitzvahs, and Brisses,* plus a few cuts from the soundtrack to "Hello, Solly," and some previously unreleased gems. The emphasis here is not on Katz-as-comedian but on his genius as a bandleader, composer, and musician. His band's arrangements, by Nat Farber, are also works of subversive vision prefiguring Radical Jewish Culture. Until someone releases a box set of the complete Mickey Katz catalog, this reissue will have to serve as the testament to his considerable musical talent and wit.

## KING DJANGO

▌ *King Django's Roots and Culture* (1998) Triple Crown 3006-2

An extraordinarily seamless fusion of reggae and Yiddish song by King Django—a prominent, New York–based ska performer born Jeff Baker—that reappropriates the biblical imagery that infuses so much of Rastafarian music. If Bob Marley sang in Yiddish, it would have sounded like this. Includes guest appearances by Andy Statman and Alicia Svigals. (Pp. 141–144)

## KLAZZJ (see Yale Strom)

## KLETKA RED

*Hijacking* (1996) Tzadik TZ7111

Klezmer doesn't get any more punk or metallic than it does in the hands of Kletka Red, the vehicle for Berlin guitarist/vocalist Leonid Soybelman, who with the help of guitarist/violist Andy Ex and drummer Tony Buck slices old Naftule Brandwein tunes and horas to pieces with blistering shards of electric guitar noise and feedback. Noisy, provocative, highly suggestive, definitely not for the weak of heart, but still a tribute to the strength of the original melodies that somehow survive the transformation. A poignant metaphor, perhaps, for the survival of the Jewish people?

## KLEZAMIR

*Klezamir Cooks for Tante Barbara* (1995) KL 101C

*Back in the Shtetl Again* (1998) KL 102

Flutist Amy Rose soars on the opening track of *Klezamir Cooks for Tante Barbara,* enough to make a believer out of anyone who doubts that flute can fill in for clarinet as the lead instrument of the kapelye. But Klezamir is a lot more than a showcase for Rose's flute. It is a versatile outfit tackling instrumental classics, Yiddish theater tunes, vocal novelties, and klezmer swing. Rose plays jazzy piano on a swinging version of "Bay Mir Bistu Sheyn," featuring multi-instrumentalist Jim Armenti wrapping clarinet lines around the vocals. Armenti also contributes guitar, vocals, and superb mandolin on a medley of "Khsidim Tants" and "Tsurik fun der Milkhome."

If *Cooks for Tante Barbara* was Klezamir's attempt to make a Kapelye-type album, on *Back in the Shtetl Again,* the Massachusetts quintet stretches out in some novel ways, patterned after the innovations of the renaissance bands. The Hasidic song "Vos Vet Zayn" boasts a funky, hip-hop break, while "Noshville Bulgar" is a clever bit of country-and-western klezmer. "Yankls Freylekh" features some jazzy piano accompaniment, and the electric guitar on "Miserlou" gives the Greek-derived folk song a surreal aura.

## KLEZGOYIM

*Out of the Eyebrow* (1996) Globe Records LC 5153

Formed in 1993 in Bremen, this versatile sextet of non-Jewish Germans

—hence the cheeky moniker—renders loyal, all-instrumental versions of Yiddish songs, Hasidic melodies, and classic klezmer from the 1920s to the 1950s with a lineup that includes two clarinets, accordion, guitar, drums, and banjo. The all-acoustic group's witty, original contributions to the contemporary repertoire include a combination doina/tarantella, a bit of frenzied Middle Eastern kitsch ("Freylekhe Kneydlekh," by the KCB's Merryl Goldberg), and a Yiddish tango. Bassist/tuba player Ralf Stahn is the group's secret weapon, giving the ensemble's arrangements a muscular boost and lending a beautiful lead melody line to "Di Sapozhkelekh."

## KLEZICAL TRADITION
▌ *Family Portrait* (1999) TKT

An effortless authenticity pervades this debut recording by this New England–based acoustic quartet. It's a spirited, witty journey from Old World to New via traditional melodies, immigrant-era instrumentals, and Yiddish theater songs. With spoken-word accounts in English and Yiddish (translation provided) of immigrant-era life, dance tunes, and ballads, the recording works simultaneously as a kind of aural documentary and vibrant entertainment. All the performances are invested with a high degree of virtuoslty and a deeply rooted yidishkayt. Vocalist Fraidy Katz, one of the finest Yiddish singers alive, sounds like she could have just walked off a Second Avenue stage.

## KLEZMATICS (see also Alicia Svigals, Frank London, Paradox Trio, David Krakauer)
▌ *Shvaygn=Toyt* (1989) Piranha PIR 20-2
▌ *Rhythm + Jews* (1992) Flying Fish FLY 591
▌ *Jews with Horns* (1995) Xenophile 4032
▌ *Possessed* (1997) Xenophile 4050
▌ *The Well* (with Chava Alberstein) (1998) Xenophile 4052

The Klezmatics combine a deeply rooted commitment to klezmer tradition with a contemporary approach that eschews limitations as long as the result is good music. Everything the group has ever recorded is rich, golden, and worth seeking out, but *Jews with Horns* and *Possessed* are their most fully realized efforts to date.

*Shvaygn=Toyt,* the group's debut album, was recorded in Berlin and includes performances by Les Miserables Brass Band, a side group of Frank London's that at the time included future Klezmatics member Matt Darriau and several players from the Klezmer Conservatory Band. It is the group's most "traditional"-sounding album, and includes several numbers that remain standards of its live repertoire, including "Ale Brider." It also boasts a rare vocal turn by violinist Alicia Svigals, who harmonizes with Lorin Sklamberg on the boozy Bavarian folk song, "Schneider-Zwiefacher."

*Rhythm + Jews* also includes a few cuts that have become Klezmatics standards. Their remake of Naftule Brandwein's "Fun Tashlikh," which kicks off the album, is in some ways the signature tune of the renaissance, the very template of progressive klezmer. The song is simultaneously faithful to the original, yet tweaks it enough with a psychedelic break, Middle Eastern percussion, and Lorin Sklamberg's Sufi-like wailing vocals to make it wholly contemporary.

Other instrumental numbers on the album, such as "NY Psycho Freylekhs" and "Bulgar à la The Klezmatics" use a similar approach. The album also showcases soloists David Krakauer on "Clarinet Yontev" and Alicia Svigals on "Violin Doyna," and contains the original version of another Klezmatics concert staple, "Shnirele Perele," a mystical, Hasidic song about *meshiekh*—the Messiah—which has become a renaissance anthem of sorts.

*Jews with Horns* unabashedly announces the Klezmatics' subversive streak and identification with downtown New York on the opening cut, "Man in a Hat," which employs the choral harmonies of pop vocal group Moxy Fruvous behind Lorin Sklamberg's witty, gay lyrics: "Met a man in a hat with a tan/Man-hat-tan, I met a Manhattan man." When the next song, "Fisherlid," opens with echoey guitar lines courtesy of downtown guitarist Marc Ribot, the point is driven home that while the modes remain the same, the attitude has changed, and in case you haven't yet picked up on it, this is not your grandfather's klezmer. Even so, the repertoire still consists in large part of new arrangements of traditional melodies.

While their work is still firmly rooted in recognizably Yiddish modes, the compositional balance shifts on *Possessed,* on which the majority of songs were written by Frank London, Alicia Svigals, and other group members. (Matt Darriau replaces clarinetist David Krakauer on this and subsequent albums.) Among these are "Mizmor Shir Lehanef (Reefer Song)," a prayerlike, mystical ode to marijuana with lyrics by contemporary Yiddish poet Michael Wex (the chorus goes "Reykher a splif, kanabis," meaning "Smoke a spliff, cannabis"). The album also includes several songs with English lyrics by Pulitzer prize–winning playwright Tony Kushner, some of which are part of a suite of melodies written for his adaptation of S. An-ski's classic Yiddish play, "The Dybbuk."

*The Well,* recorded with Israeli folk-pop singer Chava Alberstein and produced by Ben Mink of k. d. lang fame, is a bit of a side journey for the group, an all-vocal album that reimagines Yiddish song as contemporary world-pop with an Old World flavor. A celebration of modern Yiddish poetry that Alberstein set to music, it is a lovely piece of work in its own right—including several duets between Alberstein and Lorin Sklamberg—but ultimately a detour on the Klezmatics path of blazing new trails for klezmer. (Pp. 114–124)

## KLEZMER CONSERVATORY BAND

*Yiddishe Renaissance* (1981) Vanguard VCD 79450
*Klez!* (1984) Vanguard VCD-79449
▌ *A Touch of Klez!* (1985) Vanguard VMD-79455
*Oy Chanukah!* (1987) Rounder 3102
▌ *A Jumpin' Night in the Garden Of Eden* (1988) Rounder 3105
▌ *Old World Beat* (1991) Rounder 3115
▌ *Live! The Thirteenth Anniversary Album* (1993) Rounder 3125
▌ *Dancing in the Aisles* (1997) Rounder 3155

Modeled on the big bands of the 1920s and 1930s, and taking much of its repertoire from old 78s, the Klezmer Conservatory Band is more than a repertory band. Its albums reflect an eclectic approach, and include Yiddish folk and theater songs, immigrant ballads, nigunim, dance tunes, novelty numbers, Yiddish swing, and more. Several of the top contemporary klezmorim have passed through the ranks of the KCB at one time or another, and several of the band's recordings boast the earliest recorded works of Don Byron, Frank London, Alan Bern, and David Harris, as well as longtime members such as vocalist Judy Bressler and violinist Miriam Rabson, both of whom are tops on their instruments. And all the KCB's recordings feature the brilliant arranging and conducting genius of leader Hankus Netsky, a prime force behind the klezmer revival and renaissance.

Most KCB albums include a diverse selection of material, split between instrumentals and vocal numbers, classics and obscurities, although the balance tips heavily in favor of vocals on *Klez!* The group's third album, *A Touch of Klez!*, stands out for the dual lead lines by Frank London and Don Byron on Mickey Katz's "Mazeltov Dances," and the group's jazzy, riotous version of Mickey Katz's "Tsatske Kazatske," for which Judy Bressler penned new, KCB-oriented lyrics and which features her athletically comic, vocal sound effects. Highlights also include remakes of such novelties as "Yiddisher Charleston" and "Miami Beach Rumba," which were early-twentieth-century precursors to renaissance-era efforts to combine Yiddish music with other, non-Jewish styles.

*Oy Chanukah!* grew out of a program the group recorded in 1985 for the American Public Radio network, and it includes narrative segments by a variety of nonband members. Original compositions first surface on *A Jumpin' Night in the Garden of Eden,* the last album to include Frank London and Don Byron, and the group's arrangements show heightened sophistication, tight ensemble playing, and more of an Old World flavor. Highlights include violinist Miriam Rabson's wild solo on "Pearl from Warsaw," Merryl Goldberg's original composition, "Freylekhe Kneydlekh," which is a showcase for the KCB's turn-on-a-dime group dynamics, and more comic vocal antics from Judy Bressler, this time with Donald Duck–like vocals on a version of Mickey Katz's "Dos Geshrey fun der Vilder Katshke (The Cry of the Wild Duck)."

*Old World Beat* is very much in the same vein as *A Jumpin' Night*, with approximately the same proportion of classic, vocal, and original material, and virtuoso performances. Likewise for *Dancing in the Aisles*, which includes a rousing rendition of the Hasidic march, "Kol Rina," a haunting version of the classic folk song, "Miserlou," and "Freylekh Fantastique," a witty, klezmerized pastiche of classical music themes borrowed from Beethoven, Mozart, Tchaikovsky, Grieg, Rossini, and Mendelssohn. As one might expect, *Live! The Thirteenth Anniversary Album* captures the excitement of the KCB's live show—a veritable Yiddish revue.

Choosing one KCB recording to call "essential" is pretty much a roll of the dice. (Pp. 96–103)

## KLEZMER PLUS!
*Old-Time Yiddish Dance Music* (1991) Flying Fish FLY 488

This horn-heavy band replicates the bouncy style played by commercial bands in the postwar years before the revival. In addition to being a mentor to many first- and second-generation revivalists, clarinetist Sid Beckerman is the scion of a klezmer dynasty that has included uncles, cousins, and his father, Shloymke Beckerman, a contemporary of Naftule Brandwein and Dave Tarras. This is his first and one of his only recordings. Saxophonist Howie Lees studied with Beckerman's father, and was a much-in-demand musician on the Hasidic scene in the 1960s and 1970s. Trumpeter Ken Gross, who also has family roots in the immigrant klezmer era, rounds out the front line on a rousing selection of classic, Americanized klezmer dance music backed by arch-revivalists Peter Sokolow and Henry Sapoznik.

## KLEZMOKUM
*Jew-azzic Park* (1995) BVHAAST 9506
▌ *ReJew-Venation* (1998) BVHAAST 9809

This Amsterdam-based, acoustic ensemble is in pursuit of the ever-elusive fusion of klezmer and jazz. Burton Greene, the expatriate American who leads the group, arranges, composes, and plays piano, is clearly well versed in both genres. His ideas are well executed on a doina/dance medley that skillfully veers in and out of traditional styles and jazzy improvisation, and on the Dave-Brubeck-meets-Sephardic "El Rey Por Muncha Madruga," both on *ReJew-Venation*. The ensemble occasionally goes outside the klezmer tradition—dipping into the Sephardic and Israeli repertoire as well as Rumanian- and Armenian-derived melodies—for its source material. Greene is also one of the first musicians to take up the challenge implicit in John Zorn's hefty Masada songbook, covering Zorn's "Nevala" on *ReJew-Venation*. His players, who include two clarinetists, a tuba player, a drummer, and a vocalist, are not always up to the task of capturing the phrasing and ornamentation that distinguishes klezmer; sometimes what comes out sounds more generic, like one of Paul Winter's world-fusion jazz projects.

## THE KLEZMORIM

▌ *First Recordings 1976–78* (1989) Arhoolie CD 309
▌ *Metropolis* (1981) Flying Fish FLY 258
▌ *Notes from Underground* (1984) Flying Fish FLY 322
▌ *Jazz-Babies of the Ukraine* (1987) Flying Fish FLY 465

As perhaps the first and most popular of the revival groups to tour and record, the Klezmorim's recordings are at the very least of historical interest, for this is the music that rekindled the first wave of interest in klezmer. And not surprisingly, the recordings are lively and fun. But they are also responsible for some of the fundamental misconceptions about klezmer: that it is zany, wacky cartoon music, that it is Jewish vaudeville, that it is indistinguishable from Greek, Turkish, or Arabic music. Indeed, the Klezmorim's recordings contain all these elements and more, seamlessly interweaving these ostensibly nonklezmer styles into its mix. Then again, these are precisely the aspects that draw many to the music.

The group's first two albums, *East Side Wedding* and *Streets of Gold*, are now available on one CD, *First Recordings 1976–78*. In fact, the two recordings were very different species, and it is worth going to the trouble of programming your CD player to listen to them as they originally appeared (the songs are out of sequence, but the credits indicate which songs came from which album), to get a sense of the group's musical development as it happened. The songs from *East Side Wedding* show the group's strong roots in Balkan folk music, both instrumentally and in terms of song style. With *Streets of Gold,* the group took the full plunge into a primarily Yiddish repertoire and expanded its lineup from a small, string-based ensemble into a large band with horns.

On *Metropolis,* which was produced by Stuart Brotman and holds the distinction as the only klezmer album to have been nominated for a Grammy Award, the Klezmorim dispense totally with stringed instruments in favor of an all-horns, clarinet, and percussion approach, which they would favor for the rest of their career as a band. The resulting brass-band quality of the arrangements is strikingly sophisticated and ahead of its time, anticipating projects like Lester Bowie's Brass Fantasy and Frank London's Les Miserables Brass Band. For klezmer, it emphasizes the New Orleans marching-band quality some find in the music, although Donald Thornton's "Tuba Doina" is as poignant as any violin or clarinet solo.

*Notes from Underground* carries on the horn-heavy approach of *Metropolis,* but the emphasis is more strongly on the New Orleans jazz/ klezmer crossover repertoire, with Oriental fox-trots like "Egyptian Ella," the cartoonlike medley of "Betty Boop/Gangsters in Toyland," and even a version of Duke Ellington's "The Mooche." Again, however, the horn arrangements are downright dizzying.

*Jazz Babies* was recorded before a live audience in Amsterdam over several days in the summer of 1986. The album includes some vocal shtick, as well as some superb playing by clarinetist Ben Goldberg (who went on to form the New Klezmer Trio), particularly on a trio version of "Oy Tate," featuring clarinet, tuba, and percussion. The centerpiece of the program is a comic-theatrical suite of tunes that follows the group from Minsk to the opera, where they leap onto the Orient Express on their way to Bulgaria, before hightailing it to Harlem, where the production ends with a version of Cab Calloway's "Minnie the Moocher." It's great conceptual fun and somewhat suggestive of the cosmopolitan wanderings of the klezmorim through history. (Pp. 76–82)

## KOL SIMCHA

*Traditional Jewish Music* (1990) Kol Simcha (NR)
*Voice of Joy* (1994) World Class HSWC 11301-2
*Symphonic Klezmer* (1996) Claves CD 50-9627
*Crazy Freilach* (1997) Claves CD 50-9628
*Klezmer Soul* (1997) World Class HSWC 11303-2

Founded in Switzerland in 1986, Kol Simcha (Hebrew for "voice of joy") plays a polished, easy-listening style of klezmer that veers from hard-swinging to cool, "contemporary" jazz to sleepy, klezmer-tinged New Age music. Its members—several of whom are graduates of Berklee College of Music in Boston—bring a wide range of experience in classical, jazz, and commercial music to the quintet, creating a tight sound that layers warm, klezmer-derived melodies played by clarinet and flute over a pulsing, jazz rhythm section, in some cases suggesting what klezmer might sound like if the Dave Brubeck Quartet were to give it a swing. It is clearly music meant for the concert stage and not the dance hall.

*Voice of Joy* features mostly original compositions that explore and expand upon klezmerlike melodies and rhythms. The same approach works to much better effect on *Crazy Freilach*—the group simply shows more command of the idiom and more wit and invention in terms of composition. With its fleet improvisations, "Flatbush Minyan Bulgar" in particular stands out as a piece that could easily be covered by a contemporary jazz artist like Pat Metheny or Paul Winter.

On *Symphonic Klezmer,* the group interpolates elements of klezmer melody and rhythm into several ambitious, extended symphonic compositions performed by the Swiss orchestra Sinfonietta de Lausanne. Unfortunately, the group's reach is stronger than its grasp on this effort, and the bombastic arrangements overwhelm the core of the music. *Klezmer Soul* is a retrospective, compiling the more quiet, meditative pieces from the previous four albums.

## LEOPOLD KOZLOWSKI

*The Last Klezmer* (1994) Global Village 168

This recording boasts the same strengths and weaknesses as the documentary film upon which it is based. In spite of the title, Kozlowski, a Holocaust survivor and scion of the Brandwein klezmer dynasty, mostly plays original piano music based in the tradition of Yiddish theater and folk music as opposed to klezmer. Many of these tunes go by in a minute and a half or less; they are not recorded performances so much as snippets or extracts from an audio journal. At its best it offers a fascinating glimpse into Kozlowski's musical sensibility, through which so much of twentieth-century Eastern European Jewish history is channeled; at worst it is a lot of tedious, indulgent musical noodling to which few will want to listen more than once.

## DAVID KRAKAUER (see also the Klezmatics)

▌ *Klezmer Madness!* (David Krakauer and The Krakauer Trio)
   (1995) Tzadik TZ7101
*The Dreams and Prayers of Isaac the Blind* (with the Kronos Quartet),
   (1997) Nonesuch 79444-2
▌ *Klezmer, N.Y.* (David Krakauer's Klezmer Madness!)
   (1998) Tzadik TZ7127

David Krakauer was an early member of the Klezmatics, appeared on several of the group's CDs, and played on the first Itzhak Perlman klezmer concert tour and album. A clarinetist of some renown in both classical and avant-garde circles, Krakauer left the Klezmatics to pursue his solo projects in 1996. The result, like much of the work of his former bandmates, has been some of the most successful fusions of Old and New World klezmer. Of all those recording on John Zorn's cutting-edge Tzadik label, with perhaps the exception of Frank London, Krakauer is the most deeply versed in traditional klezmer. Whether he is putting on the funk James Brown style on "Funky Dave," or attempting a more ambitious, compositionally oriented piece on "Doina/Death March Suite" (both on *Klezmer Madness!*), the spirit of Naftule Brandwein is never far behind.

On *Klezmer Madness!*, Krakauer builds upon the repertoire of immigrant-era klezmer clarinetists Brandwein and Dave Tarras, updating their material with the vibrant, multicultural and multitextural sound of contemporary New York. Thus, "Bogota Bulgar" adds the South American rhythms of Los Macondos, a Colombian *vallenato* percussion ensemble, to Brandwein's "Heyser Bulgar." "The Ballad of Chernobyl," with original Yiddish lyrics by Michael Alpert, features eerie, industrial sampling effects in the mix. "Living with the H Tune" is a playful romp based on that bane of every Jewish musician's existence, "Hava Nagila." The album's centerpiece, however, is the "Doina/Death March," which begins with a duet full of fury and alarm between Krakauer and drummer David Licht and ends with a wailing nign by Michael Alpert.

Krakauer's imagination and creativity, as well as his considerable jazz chops, are fully unleashed on his second album, *Klezmer, N.Y.*, a full-fledged concept album, in which Krakauer envisions a musical summit meeting of his two clarinet idols—Naftule Brandwein and jazz great Sidney Bechet. There is no historical record of the two ever meeting, but in fact they were contemporaries in New York for fifteen years, from the late 1920s to the 1940s. Compositions like "The Meeting" and "Bechet in the Roumanian Wine Cellar" are atmospheric works that feature wailing electric guitars and other electronic effects not ordinarily associated with klezmer. But more than that, they are celebrations of the expressive role of the clarinetist, among which Krakauer ranks at the top.

*The Dreams and Prayers of Isaac the Blind* is a collaboration with the famed Kronos Quartet on a suite by contemporary composer Osvaldo Golijov, based on the thought of the medieval Kabbalist rebbe of Provence. While not klezmer music per se, the piece borrows heavily from klezmer and Yiddish motifs. "Kronos is an accordion in the prelude, a klezmer band in the second movement," writes Golijov in the liner notes, and Krakauer's duets with the quartet have a strong, Old World feel to them. A great example of klezmer's richness as raw material for both composer and improviser.

## WOLF KRAKOWSKI
▐ *Transmigrations* (1997) Kame'a Media 7001

What Wolf Krakowski has made here is not a klezmer album—there is little if any klezmer music on this recording—but rather a unique attempt at fusing Yiddish song and American roots music. The result, a kind of electric shtetl-rock, shares a kinship with some of the more rock-oriented efforts of other klezmer renaissance groups. A European-born, native Yiddish speaker who was raised in Toronto, Krakowski brings to the material an equal appreciation for the source material (Yiddish folk, theater, and popular song) and for the rural and urban American musical settings he uses to display it: blues, country, R&B, and reggae laid down by the roots-rock outfit the Lonesome Brothers. (Pp. 135–139)

## KRAMER

*Let Me Explain Something to You about Art* (1998) Tzadik TZ7119

Downtown rock artist and impresario Kramer—a veteran of bands including Bongwater, Shockabilly, Butthole Surfers, and Galaxie 500—wraps manipulated spoken-word reminiscences of growing up Jewish in America around minimalist-style electronic music supplemented with strings and accordion by Deni Bonet in a formula somewhat akin to Steve Reich's "Different Trains." His narrators offer stark juxtapositions and observations about life's ordinary and heroic struggles atop an ever-changing loop of pulsing sounds that glide effortlessly from Old World to world-beat to contemporary, industrial textures, sometimes merging all together.

## KROKE

*Trio* (1996) Oriente RIEN CD 04
*Eden* (1997) Oriente RIEN CD 09

Formed by three graduates of the Cracow Academy of Music in 1992, Kroke plays with the finesse of a classical chamber group but invests their arrangements of traditional and original material with great emotion. Kroke's arrangements emphasize the music's solemn, serene, trancelike qualities, partly a result of the violin-accordion-double-bass instrumentation. On *Eden*, some gorgeously moving playing is marred by some very unfortunate attempts at vocalese—the sort of wordless jazz vocals favored by groups like the Manhattan Transfer. If you can filter out these and the occasional theatrical shouts, the music retains its great dignity in the hands of Kroke.

## SY KUSHNER JEWISH MUSIC ENSEMBLE
■ *KlezSqueeze!* (1997) Bon Air

On *KlezSqueeze!,* accordionist Sy Kushner puts together a timeless mix of ancient and modern. With Ukrainian native Alexander Fedoriouk on tsimbl and former Andy Statman sideman Martin Confurius on bass, Kushner plays classic klezmer and Hasidic tunes in the Old World trio format, but with the accordion and occasionally the tsimbl assuming the lead role of the violin or clarinet. Few could pull this off successfully, but if any could it is Kushner, who has been a major force in Jewish music since the 1960s when he led the Mark 3 Orchestra. Peter Sokolow contributes excellent liner notes.

## STEVE LACY
*Sands* (1998) Tzadik TZ7124

On *Sands,* avant-jazz musician Steve Lacy paints eleven musical portraits of himself and others on solo soprano saxophone excursions that are intimate and revealing. Recorded at his home in Paris where he has lived for nearly thirty years, the album provides the listener an introduction to Lacy's uniquely improvisational manner of composition. Several of the pieces are based on written texts by Allen Ginsberg and William Burroughs, and Lacy's longtime partner Irene Aebi contributes vocals on a piece by Samuel Beckett. Only one track, "Jewgitive," explicitly addresses the MacArthur Fellow's relationship to his Jewish background, although it does so with great beauty and eloquence. By placing Lacy's new work in the context of Radical Jewish Culture, the artist and executive producer John Zorn presumably want us to consider it a product of a Jewish sensibility, much like the Mark Rothko painting on the CD cover.

## LA'OM
, , . . . *spielt!* (1997) Raumer RR11197
■ *Riffkele* (1998) Raumer RR13299

This Berlin-based quintet draws heavily on the repertoire of Dave Tarras, Naftule Brandwein, and tsimblist Joseph Moskowitz, although they recast the arrangements to fit the group's particular aesthetic. While the group has a strong, Eastern European "street-folk" feel, given its acoustic instrumentation (mandolin, bass, accordion, violin, and clarinet) and muscular ensemble dynamics, the live recording *Riffkele* suggests strongly that La'om is very much an "art" or "concert" band in the vein of Brave Old World.

La'om is still working out its approach on its debut album, , , . . . *spielt!,* and you can practically hear the musicians falling in love with the music. But it's on *Riffkele* that the group really catches fire. The rearrangement of Dave Tarras's "Dem Trisker Rebn's Chussid" is representative of the whole. Tarras's familiar clarinet melodies are shared by accordion, violin, mandolin, and bass—all the instruments *except* clarinet—and each musician has a go at making a personal statement out of Tarras's original in tag-team fashion. On this number and others, including "Fun Tashlikh," the musicians are adept at finding previously unexplored nuances in staple tunes from the classic klezmer repertoire. La'om also exhibits great sensitivity on the issue of non-Jewish Germans playing klezmer and addresses it head on in the liner notes of both albums.

## LE GRAND KLEZMER
*Oy!* (1998) Zemer Atik ZA 02

Central European klezmer groups often but not always seem fated to get the rhythms and inflections of klezmer wrong, so the music too often comes out sounding like ersatz polka or Gypsy music. This French sextet, formed in 1994, falls into that category. The music is sweetened with too much or incorrect harmonization, and inflections owe more to Irish music and bluegrass than Yiddish.

## MARGOT LEVERETT
▌ *The Art of Klezmer Clarinet* (2000) Traditional Crossroads TCRO 4296

On *The Art of Klezmer Clarinet,* Margot Leverett—a founding member of the Klezmatics and with that group's Alicia Svigals a member of the all-female klezmer supergroup, Mikveh—explores the classic klezmer repertoire of Dave Tarras, Naftule Brandwein, and Shloymke Beckerman. She achieves the nearly impossible feat of rendering the music with authenticity and respect while simultaneously making a highly personal statement about the art of klezmer clarinet—the instrument and its history. Her arrangements for small ensembles—duos, trios, quartets—recall Dave Tarras's postwar efforts, but here she elevates what was originally intended to be functional dance music to shimmering art music. With this album, Leverett will have to be ranked with the virtuosos of her generation, and the klezmer clarinet lineage will have to be amended by adding Leverett's name to the pantheon of Tarras, Brandwein, Beckerman, and Andy Statman.

### FRANK LONDON (see also Hasidic New Wave, the Klezmatics)

▌ *The Shvitz* (1993) Knitting Factory Works KFW 144
▌ *Nigunim* (Frank London/Lorin Sklamberg/Uri Caine)
  (1998) Tzadik TZ7129
▌ *The Debt* (1999) Tzadik TZ7507
▌ *Shekhina* (2000) Nujumusic
*Di Shikere Kapelye* (Frank London's Klezmer Brass Allstars) (2000) Piranha
  CD-PIR 1467 (NR)

In his work as a composer, performer, bandleader, and recording artist, and as a cofounder of groups including the Klezmer Conservatory Band, the Klezmatics, and Hasidic New Wave, trumpeter Frank London looms over the klezmer revival and renaissance as an archetypal figure, with one foot in the Old World and another in the New.

London brings to his more experimental works a deep knowledge of traditional klezmer, Hasidic prayer music, and Yiddish swing. As a movie soundtrack, *The Shvitz* lacks the coherence of a stand-alone album, but still it is a great catalog of London's musical approaches: from Klezmatics-style progressive-klez (his bandmates from that group perform on several tracks) to downtown avant-klez (guitarists Marc Ribot and Elliott Sharp put the pedal to the shtetl-metal on several tracks). A highlight is DJ Nastee's dance-club remix of the old Yiddish labor song, "Ale Brider," here called "(How to) Sweat," featuring Klezmatics vocalist Lorin Sklamberg rapping homoerotic love poetry from the Song of Songs.

London and Sklamberg also collaborate on the surprisingly neotraditional *Nigunim*. Joined by downtown keyboardist Uri Caine, the trio emphasizes the haunting beauty of these Hasidic prayer and dance melodies, with Sklamberg's cantorial-style Yiddish vocals and accordion set off against London's Old World–style trumpet. Except perhaps for the last track on the album—which sets a nign down on a funky bed of Hammond B-3 organ—this is an album that you can play for your grandmother with no fear of offending her Old World sensibilities, and at no expense to the integrity of the performance.

*The Debt* collects London's various compositions for film and theater other than those for *The Shvitz*. The album makes no claims to being Jewish or klezmer music—it is part of Tzadik's Film Music series—and like *The Shvitz* it is a veritable catalog of the composer's transcultural, multiphonic obsessions, ranging from lounge-jazz to electric noise to choral works to Latin dance grooves. But London is too steeped in Jewish music for it ever to be too far off his compositional radar, and fans won't be disappointed by this definitive representation of London's most experimental work, with an all-star team of downtown jazz, including John Medeski, Ben Perowsky, Anthony Coleman, Mark Feldman, David Krakauer, Yoron Israel, Bob Musso, and Sebastian Steinberg of the funk-rock group Soul Coughing.

## LOX AND VODKA
### *Heavy Shtetl* (1997) S11A4J8C

Don't be misled by the title of Lox and Vodka's album; the group plays classic-style, small-combo klezmer mixed with Yiddish theater tunes. The ensemble playing is above average, with fleet communication between clarinetist Tom Puwalski and accordionist Zoltan Racz on Sid Beckerman's "Fast Freilach." Mandolinist Chip Cliff has obviously spent time listening to Andy Statman and learned his lessons well. The group's own "Ellis Island Freilach" is a witty, seamless musical pastiche that tells the story of how klezmer and jazz met in America, one of several numbers that cleverly fuse jazz and klezmer. Unfortunately one cannot say the same for the group's vocal arrangements, which are the very essence of schmaltzy, bar mitzvah–band music.

## GARY LUCAS
### ▌ *Busy Being Born* (1998) Tzadik TZ7121

Ostensibly a children's album by the former guitar sideman from Captain Beefheart, *Busy Being Born* is a brilliantly eclectic array of original songs ("The Mensch in the Moon," "Sandman"), guitar instrumentals, straightforward versions of Hebrew folk songs and "Fiddler on the Roof" favorites, and witty reworkings from subcultural icons like the Marx Brothers, cartoons, obscure and not-so-obscure movie ("Exodus") and TV themes ("Masada"). While it is definitely not only for kids, your kids *will* be the coolest ones on the block if they own this album, which includes a reworking of one of the great "outing" moments in the history of cinema: "Abie the Fishman" from the Marx Brothers film, "Animal Crackers." (Pp. 152–53, 155–56)

## MACHAYA KLEZMER BAND
*Machaya Klezmer Band* (1991)
*What a Machaya!* (1995)

This Maryland-based ensemble plays classic-style klezmer and Yiddish theater tunes. On *Machaya Klezmer Band* their choice of repertoire draws heavily from the tried-and-true: "Mayn Rue Platz," "Papirossen," "Bay Mir Bistu Sheyn" for the vocals, "Russian Sher," "Oy Tate," "Firn di Mekhutonim Aheym," "Der Heyser Bulgar" for the instrumentals. On *What a Machaya!* they stretch out a bit by adding a few well-played, obscure gems to staples such as "Yidl Mit'n Fidl" and "Shnirele Perele." The use of the electronic keyboard and the dumbek, which mars the group's first album by giving it a presumably unintended, contemporary world-beat feel, is less intrusive on the second.

## MASADA (see John Zorn)

## MAXWELL STREET KLEZMER BAND
*Maxwell Street Days* (1987) Global Village 116
*Maxwell Street Wedding* (1991) Global Village 136
*You Should Be So Lucky!* (1996) Shanachie 67006

Based in Chicago and named after that city's famed Jewish thoroughfare, the Maxwell Street Klezmer Band, which has been together since 1983, is as much an all-around Yiddish-revival group as a klezmer outfit. With a repertoire including Yiddish vaudeville, theater and folk songs, the group's albums will appeal to fans of the better-known Klezmer Conservatory Band. Instrumental arrangements owe as much to the Borscht Belt–style of Mickey Katz as to immigrant-style klezmer. *You Should Be So Lucky!* includes such Yiddish classics as "A Yiddishe Mama" and "Tumbalalaika." Led by cantor Lori Lippitz, the group also includes a few Soviet émigré musicians.

## SHERRY MAYRENT
**(see also Wholesale Klezmer Band)**
*Zogn a Nign* (1991) Oyfgekumener OYF 001 (NR)
▌ *Hineni* (1995) Oyfgekumener OYF 003

Taken in sum, the dozen original compositions by composer/clarinetist Sherry Mayrent that comprise *Hineni* are at once a creative achievement of elegance and an eloquent personal statement of the connection between music and spirituality. Mayrent has arranged her Old World–flavored compositions for trio, and her Wholesale Klezmer Bandmates Owen Davidson and Lynn Lovell effortlessly converse with her on accordion and bass, respectively. These contemporary doinas, khosidlekh, freylekhs, terkishers, and horas are testimony to the richness and lasting power of these age-old genres, given new life and vitality in Mayrent's arrangements.

## MAZELTONES
*Seattle/Romania* (1986) Global Village 103 (NR)
*Odessa/Washington* (1987) Global Village 118 (NR)
*Meshugge for You* (1989) Global Village 137
*Zei Gezunt* (1991) Global Village 151
*Latkes and Lattes* (1993) Global Village 159

Formed in Seattle in 1983, the now-defunct Mazeltones, led throughout the years by violinist/vocalist Wendy Marcus, was one of the earliest and most prominent regional groups of the revival period. Along with standard klezmer dance tunes, their albums are chock full of kitsch—an erratic, grab-bag approach mixing theater tunes, Sephardic and Israeli numbers, Yiddish swing (particularly in the style of the Barry Sisters), folk songs (in Yiddish and English), children's and holiday songs, and other novelties, making them something of a guilty pleasure.

Occasionally the group transcended the merely novel and attained creative heights, particularly when its ever-changing lineup included Margot

Leverett on clarinet *(Meshugge for You)*. Among the other notables to pass through the group were drummer Aaron Alexander, on his way to Hasidic New Wave, and clarinetist/saxophonist Shawn Weaver of Shawn's Kugel, who together power a swinging version of "Der Heyser Bulgar" on *Zei Gezunt*.

## METROPOLITAN KLEZMER

■ *Yiddish for Travelers* (1998) Rhythm Media RMR 001

This recording by the New York–based sextet plus guests is distinguished by just plain great, versatile ensemble playing on two dozen selections offering a broad sweep of mostly pre–World War II klezmer and Yiddish music. With a wide range of instrumentation from which to draw, including woodwinds, horns, accordion, violins, bass, tuba, drums, and vocals, they mix repertory staples ("Russian Sher," "Der Gasn Nigun," "Oy Tate") with lesser-known and overlooked tunes from Yiddish film soundtracks and immigrant-era klezmer bands. For the most part they deliver exuberant, classic-style arrangements, but occasionally they tweak things: "Sheyn vi di Levone" has a jazzy, rhythmic shuffle bordering on western swing, the typically paradelike "Oy Tate" is turned into a snakey bit of Middle Eastern music, and a loyal version of "Rozhinkes Mit Mandlen" is followed by a groovy, lounge-jazz arrangement. Extra points for drummer Eve Sicular, who drives the band with great spirit and wit.

## MINNESOTA KLEZMER BAND

*Bulka's Song* (1998) Frozen Chosen FCP198

More than half of the selections on this wildly inconsistent recording are by pianist/composer Joseph Vass, written in a schmaltzy, faux-Yiddish style with classical, jazz, Latin, and Gypsy influences. Some of the playing isn't half bad, especially that of Russian-born violinist Yuri Merzhevsky. Vass's "Minnesota Tango," "Simchat Torah," and "Ashes and Dust" are dark, dreamy, and jazzy enough to fit in on any of several Radical Jewish Culture albums. But the group's humorous efforts are not half as funny as they think they are, they make a rhythmic mess of Dave Tarras's "Bb Minor Bulgar," and the original songs are bogged down by overwrought vocals and sentimental lyrics.

## REA MOCHIACH AND ALON COHEN
*Slichot (Forgiveness)* (1997) Rawkus Primitive PTV 1125-2

This hard-to-find CD was produced by electronic recording artists Rea Mochiach, aka Dumbeat, and Alon Cohen, aka Lonely Men of Faith. On *Slichot,* the two apply their cutting-edge sampling techniques to Sephardic cantorial melodies from the Days of Awe liturgy. The result is like a call to prayer on Jupiter, or the soundtrack to a science-fiction movie. From beneath the din of white noise and electronic blips emerge the ancient sounds of khazns out of time. See Wally Brill's *The Covenant* for a similar but ultimately more successful effort.

## MODERN KLEZMER QUARTET
*Hora & Blue* (1993) Global Village 156

This side project by four members of Chicago's Maxwell Street Klezmer Band is one of the most successful attempts at exploring Yiddish music from a jazz approach, albeit an approach that for the most part steers clear of klezmer in favor of folk and theater tunes for its source material. The title track is a witty inversion of a Romanian hora modeled on the Paul Desmond/Dave Brubeck classic "Take Five," featuring a Coltrane-esque soprano saxophone improvisation by Shelley Yoelin, who also plays a muscular tenor on "Shein Vi Di Levology" and other numbers. Pianist Bob Applebaum shines on a Bill Evans–like intro to "Belz," and the quartet plays "Tzena Tsamba" with a calypso lilt. Breezy fun.

## JOSEPH MOSKOWITZ
▌ *The Art of the Cymbalom: The Music of Joseph Moskowitz, 1916–53*
  (1996) Rounder 1126

One listen to Joseph Moskowitz's "Buhusher Chusid," recorded in 1916, and you will be an instant convert to his joyful virtuosity. Moskowitz made the Hungarian cymbalom (a variant of the traditional tsimbl) sing and swing in a way few others could, bringing to it an encyclopedic and orchestral approach. The preeminent immigrant cymbalomist, Moskowitz performed a wide-ranging repertoire that included Hungarian, Gypsy, Ukrainian, Turkish, Greek, and Yiddish melodies, along with tunes from the classical repertoire and even American ragtime. These are all represented on this collection of twenty-four recordings, almost all of which include rhythmic piano backup.

## MUZSIKAS
*The Lost Jewish Music of Transylvania* (1993) Hannibal HNCD 1373

Before the Holocaust, Hungary was home to a thriving, independent Jewish civilization. Aided by two Gypsy musicians who regularly played with Jewish musicians before the war, this Hungarian folk quartet has recovered a partial repertoire of Hungarian Jewish village music of the Transylvanian region, which they document here with the aid of the Gypsies and their ensemble. Well-known Hungarian vocalist Marta Sebestyen also contributes to the effort. The music, played mostly on violins, cymbalom, and bass, is clearly cousin to Russian and Romanian klezmer, although as played here on this beautifully annotated, sharp recording, it has strong stylistic variations—a particularly "rough" quality —from Hungarian and Gypsy music.

## MYSTIC FUGU ORCHESTRA
*Zohar* (1995) Tzadik TZ7106

John Zorn, in the guise of "Rav Tzitzit," teams with Yamantaka Eye on this subversive effort—either a brilliantly inventive, postmodern pastiche or a sick joke (perhaps a bit of both). By purporting to be "newly discovered recordings from the mystical tradition of the Kabbalah," the record echoes claims by the fourteenth-century author of the *Zohar,* Moses de Leon, to have discovered the book originally authored by Rabbi Simeon ben Yohai centuries earlier.

The 24-minute recording consists of the faint sound of human voices humming Ashkenazic-style melodies, davening, or making weird, animal-like noises over the dim drone of a harmonium, barely audible underneath the noise of hiss, pops, and scratches of vintage recordings. While the structural method of the piece may be patterned after that of the original *Zohar,* and while it may succeed as a piece of conceptual art, it is quite unlikely that listeners will be deriving any mystical insights from this modern-day *Zohar* at any time in the near or distant future.

**NAFTULE'S DREAM** (see also Shirim)
▌ *Search for the Golden Dreydl* (1997) Tzadik TZ7118
▌ *Smash, Clap!* (1998) Tzadik TZ7125

A Boston-based group led by clarinetist Glenn Dickson, Naftule's Dream is the experimental alter ego of the more traditional but no less creative group, Shirim (see separate entry). The group's musicians bring a wide variety of musical backgrounds to the band, and the result is a wide-open, new-jazz approach to klezmer, alternately funky, dark, humorous, and electric. And with a tuba and trombone in the lineup as well as clarinet, drums, piano, and accordion, there's as much New Orleans influence here as with the New Orleans Klezmer Allstars.

"Oy Tate" on *Search for the Golden Dreydl* is typical of the ensemble's approach. The number begins with a pretty straightforward statement of the traditional melody atop a funky drumbeat and builds to a cacophonous, all-group blowfest led by Dickson, before closing with a reprise of the melody. The aptly titled "Farshtunkene Hobo (The Stinky Hobo)," composed by pianist Michael McLaughlin, is a boozy, blowzy, teetering, roly-poly march; besides needing a bath, this is one hobo who has had too much slivovitz to drink, and oy, does he sound it! A very funky, New Orleans–like piano riff hides inside Dickson's original composition, "The Unseen," which, like other songs, taps hard-rock music for some of its chordal dynamics.

On *Smash, Clap!*, the group integrates its Old World rhythms with chord clusters reminiscent of Cecil Taylor, more hard-rock textures, and psychedelic groove music on a dozen original tunes. "Yid in Seattle" might be an already dated attempt at reconciling grunge-rock and klezmer, with its accordion playing a very Nirvana-like chord progression. "Yash the Chimney Sweep," written by Glenn Dickson, is another cute, timeless personality portrait. Song titles like "Free Klez" and "Speed Klez" are telling, but except for the electric guitar, the music is all acoustic even if it doesn't always sound it. This isn't klezmer for the faint of heart, but neither does it stretch the definition so far that it can't bear the name Naftule. From what we know of the late, great Brandwein, he may very well have approved of Naftule's Dream. He might have even joined them.

## NEW KLEZMER TRIO (see also Ben Goldberg)
▌ *Masks and Faces* (1991) Tzadik TZ7112
▌ *Melt Zonk Rewire* (1995) Tzadik TZ7103

Formed by members of revival bands Hotzeplotz and the Klezmorim, the New Klezmer Trio rendered traditional melodies with an approach borrowed from such avant-garde jazz visionaires as Charles Mingus, Thelonious Monk, Steve Lacy, Lee Konitz, and Andrew Hill. On *Masks and Faces,* the communication among clarinetist Ben Goldberg, bassist Dan Seamans, and drummer Kenny Wollenson seems almost telepathic on sparse, intimate numbers like "Rebbe's Meal" (an update of the classic staple, "Baym Rebn's Sude") and "Washing Machine Song." To the uninitiated, Goldberg's jagged aesthetic might seem harsh or even violent, but once one grows accustomed to his point of view, the arrangements seem as logical to contemporary listeners as a flute-tsimbl duet must have sounded two hundred years ago.

*Melt Zonk Rewire* opens with an electrifying version of a gasn nign, a street song, which is also the melody to the Yiddish folk song, "Di Sapozkelekh (Boots)." Goldberg's clarinet seems to be channeling an electric guitar. The rest of the album mostly consists of original compositions and frenetic improvisations. The group's breakup after *Melt Zonk Rewire* turned out to be only a hiatus—they regrouped in late 1999. (Pp. 153–54)

## NEW ORLEANS KLEZMER ALLSTARS
*Manichalfwitz* (1996) Gert Town GT 1117
▌ *The Big Kibosh* (1997) Shanachie SHA 6026
▌ *Fresh out the Past* (1999) Shanachie SHA 9015

The New Orleans Klezmer Allstars have probably been more successful than any other renaissance-era band in "crossing over" to a rock 'n' roll audience. Listening to their albums, it's no surprise why. The group pays less heed to traditional repertoire than other renaissance bands. Instead, they flaunt a wild, frenzied, witty approach that draws heavily on the New Orleans tradition of mixing and matching different styles to come up with original party music (perhaps paralleling the approach of some Old World klezmorim, particularly those living in cultural crossroads cities like Odessa, the New Orleans of the Pale).

While the Allstars emphasize the partylike aspect of the music, it isn't at the expense of klezmer modes or textures, and their original compositions can be quite suggestive. On *Manichalfwitz,* which features Neville Brothers drummer "Mean" Willie Green on half the tracks (Galactic's Stanton Moore, no slouch himself, plays on the other half), the group riffs around with some klezmer standards, but as will be the case on future albums, the Allstars are at their best when indulging their idiosyncratic musical imaginations ("The Bar Mitzvah of Raymond Scott"). On this early effort, though, the arrangements are crowded and the group has yet to learn how to manage its large lineup, including two reed players, violin, accordion, electric guitar, drums, and bass.

These problems are mostly solved on *The Big Kibosh,* on which the group is more willing to explore recognizably klezmerish modes on well-executed arrangements. On "Klip Klop," for example, a clarinet repeatedly plays a klezmerlike figure over a hip-hop-fueled drum beat, while an electric guitar wah-wahs in the background. A saxophone answers the clarinet in the "B" section, and a whole different ensemble keeps trying to interrupt the funk with a tacky version of "Hava Nagila." A telephone starts ringing at one point, and when someone picks it up you hear some classic-style khazones. It sounds like a recipe for a messy gumbo, but the spices are all artfully measured, and it's a fun, satisfying dish.

The centerpiece of *The Big Kibosh* is "The Wedding Suite," a witty trio of original compositions. The opener, "Di Zilberne Chasene (The Silver Wedding)," one of the NOKAS's few tunes based on a traditional melody, builds an energy-packed groove of the kind favored by contemporary jam-rock bands, which explains why Deadheads or Phishheads would be fans of the NOKAS. The album ends with the 16½-minute acid-jazz jam, "Bweep, Bweep," featuring Glenn Hartman's Hammond B-3 organ undergirding Ben Ellman's funky tenor saxophone.

On *Fresh out the Past,* the group ditches the violin and traditional melodies and fully indulges its penchant for mixing up stylistic grooves. "Mean" Willie Green reappears to help out on the Moroccan-flavored "Dr. Lizard," while "Struttin' with Some Doner Kebab" is powered by a riff lifted from Louis Armstrong's "Struttin' with Some Barbecue." A rock and roll guitar riff surfaces in "The Moroccan Roller," and on "Aging Raver's

Personal Hell," a Middle Eastern saxophone melody blows over a parody of an electronic dance beat played on acoustic piano. This is the edgiest, most innovative of the group's three albums. Newcomers to the NOKAS might want to begin with *The Big Kibosh* and see where that leads them.

## NEW SHTETL BAND
■ *Jewish and Balkan Dance Music* (1987) Global Village 121

As the title indicates, *Jewish and Balkan Dance Music* explores the connection between klezmer and Greek, Turkish, Gypsy, and Romanian melodies. But the Albuquerque-based acoustic quintet founded and directed by clarinetist Stewart Mennin does not merely recreate new versions of old arrangements. Rather, they play a mostly modern style that shows the influence that jazz and American popular music have had on contemporary Balkan music. Ensemble pieces like "Sami Malik's Tune" and "Açaj Pene Rakije," while clearly remaining loyal to the melody, prefigure some of the more adventurous later klezmer-jazz fusions, like those of Paradox Trio.

Mennin, who doubles on saxophone, is both an accomplished player and arranger. On "Kramptweiss" and "Terkisher Yale-Ve-Yove Tants" he plays in the spirit of Naftule Brandwein, who also was smitten with the Balkan repertoire. Mennin shares lead lines with trumpeter Neil Alexander on "Garsona," which anticipates similar instrumental efforts by Hasidic New Wave and Masada. Alexander also turns in a few vocals on this overlooked gem of an album.

## NEW YORK KLEZMER ENSEMBLE
*The New York Klezmer Ensemble* (1984) MA-500

This modest cassette album is most notable for the presence of two generations of the noted Musiker klezmer clan—clarinetist Ray and his son, Lee. These Broadway-style arrangements of mostly familiar tunes from the classic wedding repertoire are very brassy, Americanized, almost orchestral; in addition to clarinet, the octet includes trumpet, trombone, and French horn. This is probably a very good representation of what people were listening to at weddings and other Jewish-music events in the fifties, sixties, and seventies.

## NUNU!
*JezzKlezMer* (1994) Transformer TFR 94001
*Klezmo-Copter* (1997) Tiptoe/Enja TIP-888 828 2

This Munich-based sextet with members from Germany, Austria, and Hungary mixes jazz, folk, rock, flamenco, blues, and African percussion with some traditional klezmer melodies and Yiddish songs. The lead instrument is alto saxophone, there is no clarinet, the violin is more Gypsy than klezmer, and the electric guitarist seems to have listened to too many Van Halen albums: not a typical recipe for klezmer. Still, on *Klezmo-Copter* the group finds its way to covering Naftule Brandwein and Sholem Secunda in a manner that suggests these guys have been listening closely to the Klezmatics.

## ODESSA EXPRESS
*Babel: Yiddish and Klezmer* (1993) Syncoop 5753 CD 159

This Dutch acoustic sextet sprinkles a few klezmer instrumentals from the core repertoire among the Yiddish show tunes that are its primary focus. Female vocalist Tineke Langedijk phrases with a sprightly edge, and the musicians on clarinet, violin, accordion, bass, and guitar bring a spirited, freewheeling approach to the ensemble numbers not far removed from the theater pit.

## OLD WORLD FOLK BAND
*Crossing New Borders* (1998) Old World Productions OWFB 2314

With a dozen musicians, the Harrisburg, Pennsylvania–based Old World Folk Band recalls the classic large ensembles of the 1910s and 1920s, but *Crossing New Borders* doesn't merely reconstruct the sound of vintage 78s. With several émigrés from the former Soviet Union in the group and two vocalists, they showcase the Russian/Jewish folk song tradition on numbers like "Kalinka" and "Moscow Nights" in stirring, theatrical fashion. They also find time for a version of Brave Old World's "Chernobyl."

## OOMPH (see also Mike Curtis Klezmer Quartet)
*Between Two Worlds* (1993) Global Village 135

On *Between Two Worlds,* the Portland-based Oomph attempts a multifaceted fusion of klezmer and modern styles, including contemporary jazz, rock, pop, and world-beat music, or what the group called "Interconti-nental Klezmer." The quintet tries out its approach, which includes Jack Falk's vocals and scat singing (jazz nigunim?), on a mix of instrumental classics, prayer melodies, theater songs, and original compositions.

This approach creates some unusual hybrids. "Mizmor L'David," a Ha-sidic melody based on the Twenty-third Psalm, is given a jazz-gospel ren-dering on tenor saxophone and piano. An electric guitar on "Mazltov Shver un Shviger" puts the song halfway between reggae and tango. "Mayn Yidishe Meydele" suggests Latin-rock guitarist Carlos Santana as the leader of a bar mitzvah band. The Naftule Brandwein classic "Hora Mit Zibeles" gets a bluesy, New Orleans twist.

Some of the more adventurous numbers, such as "Yankl's Tants," fea-ture unusual keyboard modulations and harmonizations that sometimes clash with the klezmer modes, but when one's ears adjust to the unex-pected changes, odd orchestrations, and the occasional, ill-advised use of a synthesizer, this is an effort that actually grows on you.

### ORIGINAL KLEZMER JAZZ BAND
*The Original Klezmer Jazz Band* (1984) Menorah 6000
*Kosher Kitschin'* (1988) Menorah 6001
*Jammin' on 7* (1993) OKJB-3

This group was founded in the early 1980s by Peter Sokolow to revive the unique Jewish-jazz crossover repertoire performed by musicians includ-ing Irving Berlin, Ziggy Elman, Benny Goodman, Mickey Katz, and Dave Tarras. Sokolow had played with Tarras as a young man, and thus was a bridge between the classic-era klezmorim and the revivalists. The record-ings, which include Kapelye cofounder Henry Sapoznik and several vet-eran, Jewish club-date musicians, are jazzy novelties. They include Oriental fox-trots like "Egyptian Ella" and numbers such as "Yiddishe Charleston" and "Bagel Call Rag"; more jazz than klezmer, they are never-theless of great historical interest, particularly as windows on the give-and-take between jazz and klezmer from the 1920s to the 1940s. Look for a new, two-volume CD reissue compiling all three hard-to-find record-ings by the Original Klezmer Jazz Band.

## PARADOX TRIO / MATT DARRIAU

*Paradox Trio* (1996) Knitting Factory Works KFW 171 (NR)
*Flying at a Slant* (1997) Knitting Factory Works KFW 206
▋ *Source* (1999) Knitting Factory KFR 237

In the diaspora there has always been give-and-take between Jewish musicians and their co-territorial brethren. Indeed, as a non-Jewish member of the Klezmatics and one equally versed in Celtic, klezmer, and Balkan music, Matt Darriau is the very incarnation of such exchange. His quartet, Paradox Trio, is his venue for exploring the Balkan tradition in much the same progressive fashion that the Klezmatics approach klezmer, building upon the traditional melodies and rhythms and combining them with strategies adopted from jazz and other world musics. In addition to Darriau on saxophones, clarinets, and kaval (a Balkan flute), the instrumentation includes cello, percussion, and electric and acoustic guitars.

On *Source,* Darriau and his group explore the Balkan/Jewish crossover repertoire, with particular reference to Naftule Brandwein, who in his own time recorded several terkishers, and Jewish-Romanian cymbalist Joseph Moskowitz, whose repertoire also strongly reflected a pan-Balkan perspective. *Source,* which features Klezmatics vocalist Lorin Sklamberg on a few numbers, also revisits a few compositions Darriau recorded with the Klezmatics, this time from a Turkish perspective—in a sense carving out a new Balkan/Jewish fusion.

## ZEENA PARKINS

*Mouth=Maul=Betrayer* (1996) Tzadik TZ7109

Using voice samples as well as electric harp, piano, violin, cello, drums, vibes, electric guitar, mandolin, and electric harp, Zeena Parkins and her "Gangster Band" perform two long-form compositions—"Maul" and "Blue Mirror"—that purport to explore the history of the Jewish underworld in Europe and New York. Atonal, dissonant chamber music, harsh electric blues, and industrial noise alternately form a bed underneath narration in "Rotwelsch," a Yiddish-based thieves' argot used in Germany since the Middle Ages. "Italyid" examines the sometimes ambivalent relationship between Italians and Jews in organized crime, and "Chase" is fittingly noir-ish, an ominous soundtrack to an imaginary gangster film. New York mayor Fiorello LaGuardia and Virginia Hill, mistress of renowned Jewish criminal Bugsy Siegel, also lend spoken-word appearances to this scorching, violent, electronic/acoustic sound collage that pays tribute to "tough Jews," cousins to the klezmorim of old.

## ITZHAK PERLMAN

*Tradition* (1987) Angel CDC-7 47904 2
*In the Fiddler's House* (1995) Angel 7243 5 55555 2 6
*Live in the Fiddler's House* (1995) Angel 7243 5 56200 2 7

Itzhak Perlman's two *Fiddler's House* recordings, featuring the internationally famous classical violinist playing with four of the top contemporary klezmer bands, are the best-selling klezmer CDs of all time. Perlman is not, however, the greatest contemporary klezmer violinist, although he is probably the most virtuosic student of the music and acquits himself well on these collaborations with the Klezmatics, Brave Old World, the Andy Statman Klezmer Orchestra, and the Klezmer Conservatory Band.

*In the Fiddler's House* is a studio recording, and *Live in the Fiddler's House*, the follow-up, was recorded before an audience at New York's Radio City Music Hall. To his credit, Itzhak Perlman does not push his way in front of the bands he performs with here; this isn't the egotistical star turn it might have been. Rather, he approaches each as a member of the ensemble, playing *with* them and not in front of them. He is an eager participant, however, and on *In the Fiddler's House,* his enthusiasm for the music reaches creative heights on his collaborations with Andy Statman on "Flatbush Waltz" and the Klezmatics' Alicia Svigals on "Dybbuk Shers."

One could argue regardless of Perlman, and with the four bands included here, that these albums make worthwhile introductions to the contemporary scene, the musical equivalent of a tasting menu. But anyone interested in the full-course meal should proceed directly to the original recordings by Perlman's backup bands.

Predating the *Fiddler's House* project, *Tradition* teams Perlman with the Israel Philharmonic Orchestra on symphonic arrangements of Yiddish folk and theater songs.

## POZA
*Odessa: Jewish Music from Russia* (1996) Playasound PS 65181

Odessa was the New Orleans of the Old World Pale of Settlement—the place where the largest number of cultural influences mixed and mingled and fused. This modest album presents mostly trio arrangements of Odessa street songs—the music typically played at Odessan coffeehouses, taverns, and celebratory gatherings. Odessa is a port city at the crossroads of Asia, the Mediterranean, and Eastern Europe, and the music that comes from the area has strong Turkish, Greek, and Romanian influence.

Poza leader and accordionist/vocalist Alik Kopyt shares the spotlight on these fifteen folk songs and instrumentals with clarinetist Raymond Van Houten. Van Houten does not play with typical klezmer ornamentation—his style owes more to Greek music—but these arrangements are probably typical of the music the Jewish residents of Odessa would hear at weddings.

## PSAMIM
*Abi Gezint!* (1999) Tzadik TZ7132

This German-Jewish string quartet with accordion plays gorgeously lush, classical-style arrangements of Eastern European and Yiddish folk and theater tunes as well as Hasidic nigunim and a few Sephardic songs. Imagine the Kronos Quartet as a klezmer ensemble.

## REBBE SOUL
*Fringe of Blue* (1995) Global Pacific GPD 371
*RebbeSoul-O: A One-Man Musical Journey* (1997) RebbeSoul 11132

*Fringe of Blue* veers from keyboard-drenched New Age to soulful, world-beat-spiced renditions of traditional Hebrew prayer melodies and Yiddish folk songs, with occasional forays into jazz-fusion—a kind of musical journey through Jewish history. *RebbeSoul-O* is a more personal look at

Bruce Burger's own spiritual journey from his secular upbringing through his rediscovery of his cultural and musical roots.

## MARC RIBOT

*Yo! I Killed Your God* (1999) Tzadik TZ7134

Mostly live recordings, the bulk of them made in the early nineties at the New York City punk venue CBGB's, and mostly consisting of guitar noise and instrumentals, truly stretching the concept of Radical Jewish Culture to the breaking point. Ribot's bands, collectively known as Shrek, contain some of downtown New York's finest, including Soul Coughing's bassist Sebastian Steinberg and Chris Wood of acid-jazz group Medeski, Martin, and Wood.

## YEHOSHUA ROCHMAN

*The Klezmer Violin of Yehoshua Rochman* (1998) Tara Music TM 702-2

The arrangements on this collection of mostly Hasidic nigunim and prayer melodies by Israeli violinist Yehoshua Rochman are drenched in tacky, simplistic electronic keyboards meant to give it an exotic, New Agey, world-beat flavor. Instead, they merely sugarcoat Rochman's already sweet, sentimental sound.

## JOEL RUBIN

*Hungry Hearts: Classic Yiddish Clarinet Solos of the 1920s*
   (1988) Wergo SM 1615-2

▌ ***Bessarabian Symphony: Early Jewish Instrumental Music***
   (with Joshua Horowitz) (1994) Spectrum/Wergo SM 1606-2

*Zeydes un Eyniklekh* (with the Epstein Brothers Orchestra) (1995)
   Spectrum/Wergo SM 1610-2

▌ ***Beregovski's Khasene*** (Joel Rubin Jewish Music Ensemble) (1997)
   Weltmusik SM 1614-2

In most of his work as a recording artist, clarinetist Joel Rubin takes a neotraditional approach, reconstructing recordings from earlier periods with meticulous attention to detail and technique. The resulting albums are of superior quality in terms of recording quality, performance, and scholarship.

*Hungry Hearts,* originally released on cassette in 1988 as *Brave Old World* by the Joel Rubin Klezmer Ensemble, shows Rubin working out the repertoire and arrangements he would develop with greater success on subsequent efforts: the clarinet/tsimbl duets that would surface on *Bessarabian Symphony,* the Old World wedding repertoire he would explore in depth on *Beregovski's Khasene,* and the classic-era ensemble works he would perform with the Epstein Brothers on *Zeydes un Eyniklekh.* The recording is also noteworthy for the presence of Michael Alpert and Stuart Brotman, who would go on to form the group Brave Old World with Alan Bern and Rubin, as well as Hankus Netsky, making this sort of a klezmer-revival all-star effort.

A recording of sheer textural beauty and virtuosity, *Bessarabian Symphony* teams Rubin with another leading neotraditionalist, Joshua Horowitz, a master of both button accordion and tsimbl perhaps best known for his work with Budowitz. On this album, the two explore the simple beauty of the Old World–style klezmer duo on a program drawn mostly from the traditional wedding repertoire and grouped in traditional suites, echoing the approach of "early music" groups in the classical sphere.

*Zeydes un Eyniklekh* joins Rubin with the Epstein Brothers, Max, Julie, and Willie, American-born klezmorim who all played with Dave Tarras and who were prominent on the Hasidic scene after World War II. Joined by Peter Sokolow, Danny Rubinstein, and Pat Merola, the musicians jammed for two days on tunes from Tarras's highly influential repertoire, heavy on Greek- and Gypsy-tinged bulgars, and performed very much in Tarras's Americanized style.

Drawn largely from the fieldwork of Soviet ethnomusicologist Moshe Beregovski, the repertoire on *Beregovski's Khasene* opens a window on the wedding music of the Jewish Ukraine. These rarely heard melodies are presented in lovely, delicate, acoustic arrangements, and are performed by a sextet including several Hungarian musicians.

## SABBATH HELA VECKAN
*Klez* (1995) Prophone PCD 024

This mostly traditional, Scandinavian acoustic sextet hits some interesting, dark notes on a particularly moody accordion-bass duet version of the klezmer staple, "Der Gasn Nign." Likewise, a spare version of "Firen Di Mekhutonim Aheym," led by clarinetist Peter Bothen, with accordion and trombone accompaniment, is poignant and effective, as are other slow, meditative selections. The group is less successful on the upbeat dance and vocal numbers, but the one original composition, "Klezmophobia," is a blast of distorted trombone that segues into a woozy "Nigun" and suggests that Sabbath Hela Veckan has an experimental vision worth further exploration.

## SALOMON KLEZMORIM

*First Klez* (1991) Syncoop 5752 CD 136

This Dutch ensemble was founded in 1989 as a vehicle for clarinetist Marcel Salomon and his accordion partner, Theo van Tol. The two are joined here on some tracks by Nienke Lootsma on violin, Michiel Weidner on cimbalom, and drummer David Licht of the Klezmatics, but for the most part this is a duo affair. Salomon adventurously tackles lesser-known repertoire in traditional fashion, with particular attention given to the Balkan/klezmer crossover repertoire. Call it stately, well-played, occasionally even innovative chamber-klez.

## JOHN SCHOTT

*In These Great Times* (1997) Tzadik TZ7115

Guitarist John Schott has composed a song cycle around early twentieth-century texts by Franz Kafka, Austrian poet and playwright Karl Kraus, and Yiddish-American poet Jacob Glatshteyn, works that variously address the condition of Jews in Europe and, although written well before the Holocaust, seem eerily prophetic in light of what was to come. With jazz- and classical-flavored instrumental pieces for guitar, bass, and drums bookending vocal turns in Yiddish, Hebrew, and German by Metropolitan Opera tenor John Horton Murray, the work has the feel of an impressionistic, contemporary chamber-opera.

## ABE SCHWARTZ

*Master of Klezmer Music, Vol. 1: The First Recordings 1917* (1987) Global Village 126

The first of a planned series of reissues of the prolific output of Abe

Schwartz focuses on three recording sessions from 1917. Underneath the poor, scratchy recordings are gems of early ensemble playing and classic melodies, but given the poor sound quality these are unlikely to be of interest to any but the most serious scholar.

## SHAWN'S KUGEL

*Simcha!* (1997) Popover PP-D5000

Multi-instrumentalist Shawn Weaver (woodwinds, guitar, mandolin, kalimba, vocals) was a member of the Pacific Northwest's Mazeltones for nine years. On his solo debut he goes his own way, taking an eclectic offering of original freylekhs, klezmer, Sephardic, and Israeli music mixed with jazz ("Baba Blues," "Zemer Atik") and world-beat ("Shalom Aleichem/Sei Yona"), and the Rolling Stones' "Paint It Black" as the Balkan dance tune it always wanted to be.

## SHIRA

*Soaked and Salted* (1995) Shira 1002

This Madison, Wisconsin–based quartet kicks off its album of klezmer-jazz fusion with "Take Five Books of Moses," a clever spin on the Dave Brubeck/Paul Desmond classic, featuring a very Middle Eastern–sounding saxophone melody. The rest of the album continues in a similar vein, albeit for the most part one that jazzes up Jewish material instead of vice versa, but titles like "My Yiddishe Mambo" and "Hava Nagebop" are better in theory than in practice.

## SHIRIM

*Of Angels and Horseradish* (1990) Northeastern NR 5005 (NR)

*Naftule's Dream* (1993) Northeastern NR 5014

▌ *Klezmer Nutcracker* (1998) Newport Classic NPD85640

*OY! It's Good: The Art of Yiddish Song* (2000) Newport Classic NPD 85653 (NR)

Shirim is allegedly the "traditional" alter ego of avant-garde group Naftule's Dream, but Shirim's arrangements are not exactly note-for-note reproductions of the classics. *Naftule's Dream* opens with a dreamy, jazzy version of the traditional Yiddish folk song, "Sha, Shtil (Shh, Be Quiet)," with Betty Silberman's rich, dusky vocals dueling with Glen Dickson's clarinet. Dickson's title track is a sophisticated, impressionistic tribute to the great Naftule Brandwein, and the group's version of the folk song "Zhankoye," here titled "Az men fort kayn Sevastopol," is a stretched-out bit of progressive jazz. The album does include a fair share of conventional material, but you can feel the group itching to break out into the sort of stylistic no-man's-land where they allow themselves to go as the group Naftule's Dream.

Shirim goes halfway there on the clever, brilliantly executed *Klezmer Nutcracker*. Half the album recasts the familiar music of Pyotr Tchaikovsky's *Nutcracker Suite* as klezmer, down to the song titles—"Dance of the Latkes Queens," "March of the Macabees," "Waltz of the Ruggelah," "Kozatsky 'til You Dropsky." The other half lends similar treatment to a host of classics by the likes of Satie, Brahms, Chopin, and Mahler; like Tchaikovsky's *Nutcracker,* these classics were originally based in Eastern European folk idioms and thus seemed ripe for klezmerization. This would have been a disastrous novelty in less capable hands, but instead it is a marvelous bit of cultural transmigration that stands on its own as great music.

## SHLOINKE
▋ *Shloinke* (1998)

This Chicago-based sextet may not be the best-sounding group ever to tackle traditional klezmer, but they are surely one of the wittiest. Mixed in with some remarkably faithful versions of staples like "Ot Azoy," "Der Gasn Nign," and "Firn di Mekhutonim Aheym" are all sorts of clever pop-culture jokes and references. The theme to "Mission Impossible," for example, proves to be the missing link between "Baym Rebn in Palestina" and "Hava Nagila," and Jim Morrison of The Doors turns out to have been a Catskills tummler. And the oldest known written version of a klezmer tune? The theme to "Underdog," of course. It's as if Mickey Katz stumbled upon a garage-rock band on his way to a bluegrass festival.

## RONNY SOMECK AND ELLIOTT SHARP
*Revenge of the Stuttering Child* (1997) Tzadik TZ7117

Israeli poet Ronny Someck and composer/multi-instrumentalist Elliott Sharp join forces on an album that is much more than the typical spoken-word-accompanied-by-music effort. Someck's deep, rich, Israeli Hebrew is a musical instrument in itself, and Sharp arranges his ensemble in and around it. English translations of the poems, all of which address Jewish life in Israel, America, Europe, or the Arab world, are provided.

## GLENN SPEARMAN

*Blues for Falasha* (1999) Tzadik TZ7130

Before his death in 1998, free-jazz saxophonist Glenn Spearman began a spiritual and musical exploration of his Jewish roots as the son of a white Jewish mother and a black Christian father. He wound up focusing on the tribe of Ethiopians called Falasha, who claim ancient descent from biblical Jews. He composed this suite of four songs for his double trio with the Falasha in mind, mixing atmospheric percussion, spoken-word recitation, African textures, prepared piano, and his own soulful tenor saxophone improvisations.

## ANDY STATMAN

▌ *Jewish Klezmer Music* (Andy Statman and Zev Feldman)
  (1978) Shanachie 21002
▌ *Klezmer Music* (Andy Statman Klezmer Orchestra)
  (1983) Shanachie 21004
▌ *Klezmer Suite* (Andy Statman Klezmer Orchestra)
  (1984) Shanachie 21005
▌ *Songs of the Breslever Chassidim: Today* (with Yaacov Klein)
  (1994) Shoresh
▌ *Songs of Our Fathers: Traditional Jewish Melodies* (with David Grisman)
  (1995) Acoustic Disc ACD-14
▌ *Between Heaven and Earth: Music of the Jewish Mystics*
  (1997) Shanachie 64079
▌ *The Hidden Light* (The Andy Statman Quartet)
  (1998) Sony Classical SK 60814

With *Jewish Klezmer Music,* the sounds of Old World klezmer were recorded for the first time since well before World War II. In duo and trio arrangements, bassist Martin Confurius, Andy Statman, on clarinet and mandolin, and Zev Feldman, on tsimbl, perform a selection of tunes they learned from vintage 78s by Dave Tarras, Naftule Brandwein, I. J. Hochman, Harry Kandel, and Abe Schwartz. Unfortunately, this album—one of the gems of the klezmer revival—is out of print and has yet to be reissued on CD.

Andy Statman's first ensemble album, *Klezmer Music* (sometimes referred to as *The Andy Statman Klezmer Orchestra* due to ambiguous cover design), is a showcase for his developing clarinet style, without shortchanging his mandolin playing (featured on "Rumanian Dance" and "Ukrainer Chosid'l," among others). The repertoire is wide-ranging, and the song titles alone show Statman's cosmopolitan music interests ("Rumanian Dance," "Pearl from Warsaw," "Ukrainer Chosid'l," "Terkisher," "Onga Bucharesti"). The arrangements are simple and folk-like, featuring Marty Confurius's violin-like bowed bass and Bob Jones's tsimbl-like guitar on "Ariela Perle." David Steinberg rounds out the quartet on French horn and trumpet.

On *Klezmer Suite,* Statman's clarinet playing is enrapturing, and some of the selections are new ones by his mentor, Dave Tarras, written at the peak of his compositional maturity. The album reunites the quartet from *Klezmer Music,* and in spite of the guitar, songs like "Opfirn di Makhetonim in Ternovka" have a pronounced Old World feel to them. The occasional use of drums and percussion on this album didn't add anything of great value to the ensemble's sound, but neither did it mar Statman's ever-expanding genius and idiosyncratic approach to repertoire. Here he favors lyrical, Hasidic melodies that offer particular room for personal expression.

*Songs of Our Fathers,* recorded with Statman mentor David Grisman, is a lovely duet album featuring two of the world's great mandolinists (Statman also plays clarinet) on a selection of traditional and contemporary Hebrew prayer melodies, nigunim, and klezmer dance tunes. A lavishly illustrated and annotated booklet enhances the value of this recording.

On *Between Heaven and Earth: Music of the Jewish Mystics,* Statman fully realizes his decades-old goal to combine the improvisational approach of jazz musicians such as John Coltrane and Albert Ayler with the source material of Jewish liturgical music, in this case Hasidic nigunim.

His group is pointedly no longer billed as the Andy Statman Klezmer Orchestra—it is now given the very jazzlike name, the Andy Statman Quartet, and by this point Statman makes no claims to be playing anything like traditional klezmer. Pianist Kenny Werner, bassist Harvie Swartz, and drummer Bob Weiner are sympathetic accompanists on this highly personal, spiritual excursion for Statman—which produces some of the only music deserving of the description, "Jewish jazz."

The follow-up album, *The Hidden Light*, is much in the same vein, but perhaps a bit more accessible than *Between Heaven and Earth* with melodies that stick closer to the originals. Bob Weiner is still Statman's drummer, but the quartet now includes pianist Bruce Barth and bassist Scott Lee, playing a mixture of original compositions and Hasidic songs.

*Songs of the Breslever Chassidim: Today* is a low-budget, cassette-only curiosity worth seeking out if only for Statman's spirited mandolin, clarinet, and saxophone accompaniment on these contemporary Hasidic prayer tunes featuring Rabbi Yaacov Klein's vocals drenched in funky electronic keyboards. (Pp. 83–90)

## YALE STROM

*Cholent with Huckleberry* (Zmiros) (1982) Global Village 129
*Eclectic Klezz* (Zmiros) (1986) Global Village 110
*With a Little Horseradish on the Side* (Hot Pstromi)
   (1991) Global Village 158
*Wandering Jew* (Yale Strom and Klazzj) (1997) Global Village 174

Credit Yale Strom for carving his own path on these albums by his various groups. For the most part, violinist/arranger/composer Strom doesn't merely recapitulate new versions of the same standard repertoire. He discovers previously unknown melodies on his own frequent field-research expeditions to Eastern Europe and the Mediterranean and develops arrangements that are often heavily flavored with co-territorial influences. Strom also adds his own world-beat-influenced touches to the arrangements.

This formula worked best on Hot Pstromi's *With a Little Horseradish on the Side*, which may be only partially due to the presence of clarinetist/

mandolinist Andy Statman in the ensemble, although his virtuosity undoubtedly brought out the best in the other musicians. For their part, the
musicians stretch out on a selection of long, dynamic, inventive instrumentals, including the title track, a Strom composition that connects flamenco to Jewish music.

Zmiros was one of several groups founded and led by Strom, an active
folklorist, researcher, composer, and documentary filmmaker. With Zmiros,
Strom took a folksy, varied approach, mixing and matching traditional
and original melodies in a host of different styles. Hence, the aptly titled
albums: *Eclectic Klezz,* which includes Sephardic and Middle Eastern
melodies and a few vocal numbers, and *Cholent,* named after a traditional, Jewish, anything-goes-in-the-pot stew. *Cholent* is a more stately affair, featuring all Eastern European–based instrumentals performed by a
quartet. Both recordings boast selections not often heard elsewhere.

*Wandering Jew,* credited to Yale Strom and Klazzj—the successor group
to Zmiros—adds saxophone to the ensemble, and the result is a fuller exploration of Strom's acoustic, world-jazz fusion, with little apparent reference to Eastern European Jewish music.

## SULAM
*Klezmer Music from Tel Aviv* (1992) Wergo SM 1506-2

It is one of the incongruities of twentieth-century Jewish culture that
klezmer remains virtually unheard in the modern Jewish state of Israel.
Sulam, led by clarinetist Moshe "Mussa" Berlin, is the rare exception. The
group, which includes several Russian and Polish émigrés, recorded this
album live in Berlin in 1990. With flute and piano in the quintet (which
also includes violin and percussion), the arrangements are more "theatrical" than folksy, but the players clearly have a deep feeling for the music,
some of which has a Middle Eastern orientation, as might be expected.

## ALICIA SVIGALS
▌ *Fidl: Klezmer Violin* (1997) Traditional Crossroads TCRO 4286

Simply put, Jewish soul music has never sounded more soulful than it
does on *Fidl,* the definitive album of klezmer violin and perhaps the

single-most important modern reconstruction of Old World klezmer, period. Digging deep into the core repertoire, Svigals—best known for her work with the Klezmatics—provides a kind of how-to on klezmer fiddle ornamentation, while at the same time making a highly personal artistic statement about the history of the music and the violin's place in the klezmer ensemble.

Svigals has assembled an ensemble of virtuosos to accompany her on this all-acoustic effort, including fellow Klezmatics Lorin Sklamberg and Matt Darriau, Joshua Horowitz of Budowitz, Lauren Brody, Steven Greenman, and Elaine Hoffman Watts. Even so, this is Alicia's show all the way, and she channels through her violin everything that is poignant, joyous, heartbreaking, and timeless about the music. As if Svigals's performance were not already enough reason to own this CD, Walter Zev Feldman's liner notes make it equally essential.

## DAVE TARRAS

*Tanz!* (Dave Tarras and Sam Musiker) (1956) Epic
*Master of the Jewish Clarinet* (1979) Balkan Arts US 1002 (NR)
*Master of Klezmer Music Vol. 1: Original Recordings 1929–49*
   (1989) Global Village 105
▌ *Yiddish-American Klezmer Music 1925–56* (1992) Yazoo 7001
*Freilachs for Weddings* (1998) LaserLight 12 933
*Mazal Tov!* (1998) LaserLight 12 934
*Master of Klezmer Music Vol. 2: Freilach Yidelach*
   (1997) Global Village 106

Dave Tarras is virtually synonymous with the classic klezmer of the immigrant era. Unfortunately, there is yet to be gathered in one place a collection of Tarras's recordings that befit his talent and stature. The first volume of the Global Village series contains excellent representations of several periods of Tarras's career, although about half of it comes from just one session in 1939. Fortunately, this captures Tarras at the peak of his powers. *Yiddish-American Klezmer Music 1925–56* is the best broad overview of Tarras's overarching career and versatility.

*Tanz!* was never reissued and is out of print, but there seem to be plenty of copies in circulation, and it is worth searching for at libraries, used record stores, and tag sales. Not only is it a priceless document of Sam Musiker's attempt at a genuine klezmer-swing fusion, it includes some of Tarras's most mature, eloquent solos. The LaserLight disks are another story altogether—they don't even credit Dave Tarras as the band-leader, and the origin of these recordings is unknown. But they are budget priced, and when it comes down to it, you simply cannot have enough Dave Tarras. (Pp. 64–70, 73–74)

## RICHARD TEITELBAUM
*Golem* (1995) Tzadik TZ7105

This is the soundtrack to an electronic, multimedia opera based on the Yiddish folk legend of the Golem, a kind of Jewish Frankenstein monster said to have been created by Rabbi Lowe of Prague in the sixteenth century. The album employs live musicians, vocals, synthesizers, and electronically treated sounds and samples for an ominous sonic palette. Recorded live in Amsterdam in 1994, the composition veers from spoken-word passages to ululating vocals to Brian Eno–like ambient piano.

## TWELVE CORNERS KLEZMER BAND
▍ *Git Azoy (It's Good This Way)* (1999) DRK-204

This Rochester, New York–based septet has recorded a folksy mixture of classic instrumentals and Yiddish vocal numbers. With clarinet, violin, accordion, cello, guitar, banjo, and drums at their disposal, versatility is the group's stock in trade. On numbers like "Sadegurer Khosid," "Max's Bulgar," "Odessa Bulgar," and "Dem Trisker Rebns Khosid," they cook up a lively, traditional dance groove. The centerpiece of the album is an evocative, Old World–flavored medley of "Firn di Mekhutonim Aheym" and "Freylekhs fun der Khupe," featuring vivid ensemble interplay among clarinetist Rob Mendel, accordionist Zeljko Kuvizic, banjoist Pete Rushefsky, violinist Glenna Chance, drummer Sean Michael Sullivan, and cellist Roey Mendel.

## 24TH STREET KLEZMER! BAND

*Bagels & Grits* (1997) 353697.11

This nine-piece, intergenerational band from Florida plays spirited versions of familiar instrumentals and vocals, including jazzy versions of "Husid'l in D Minor" and "My Little Cousin." But for the most part, with a lineup that includes recorder and electronic keyboard, this is elementary stuff—klezmer-by-numbers.

## TZIMMES

*Sweet and Hot* (1993) TZ-1

*A Lid for Every Pot* (1995) TZ-22

*KlezMyriad* (1998) TZ-333

Based in Vancouver, Tzimmes boasts an international cast of musicians who present Jewish music with a pan-global, pan-cultural approach that includes Eastern European, Sephardic, Israeli, and contemporary music. All three of the group's albums present a diverse portrait of Jewish instrumental and vocal music through folk-like, percussive playing. As it happens, klezmer is the least well served of the various genres the group presents in its self-described, "Jewish world-beat" style. Otherwise these are lovely, well-annotated, enjoyable journeys through the variegated world of Jewish music.

## JEFF WARSCHAUER

▌ *The Singing Waltz: Klezmer Guitar and Mandolin*
(1997) Omega OCD 3027

Both on his own and in various duets and groups (with his wife, violinist Deborah Strauss, and with the Klezmer Conservatory Band), Jeff Warschauer has established a reputation as one of the leading mandolinists of the contemporary revival. In addition, Warschauer has made great strides toward integrating the acoustic guitar into the contemporary ensemble—not as a rhythm instrument, but as one approximating the various traditional lead roles of the tsimbl, clarinet, and violin.

On *The Singing Waltz*, Warschauer exhibits his stylistic innovations on solo pieces like "Sadegerer Khosid," based on a 1916 recording by tsimblist Joseph Moskowitz, and in ensemble numbers like his version of Dave Tarras's "Tants Istambul." Warschauer is joined here by contemporary luminaries Kurt Bjorling and Alan Bern of Brave Old World, Hankus Netsky of the Klezmer Conservatory Band, and David Harris of Shirim.

## WEST END KLEZMORIM

*Freylekhs 21* (1991) Global Village 153

This band of New York professional musicians led by clarinetist Harold Seletsky includes famed bluegrass banjo and mandolin player Barry Mitterhoff, along with a tuba player, drummer, accordionist, and vocalist. The group favors a very American, well-played, Yiddish theater–influenced style (dramatic vocals in Yiddish and English by Mary Feinsinger, and jazzy clarinet by Seletsky) that will likely appeal to fans of Kapelye.

## WHOLESALE KLEZMER BAND (see also Sherry Mayrent)

*Shmir Me* (1992) Oyfgekumener OYF002 (NR)

*Prayer for a Broken World* (1996) Oyfgekumener OYF004

▎ *Yidn Fun Amol: Jews of Long Ago* (1997) Oyfgekumener OYF005

The Yiddish word *heymish*—meaning homey and familiar—best sums up the Wholesale Klezmer Band. Based in western Massachusetts since 1982, the group plays a soulful brand of music with a distinctive, Old World flavor, in spite of the fact that much of its repertoire is modern or original. In part, this is a function of the group's all-acoustic instrumentation and folksy arrangements, but the group also pulls on nostalgic heartstrings with its paeans to lost values, cultural and otherwise.

In clarinetist Sherry Mayrent the group has a top-notch arranger, composer, and soloist, and Yosl Kurland is a warm Yiddish vocalist and badkhn, as well as one of only a few writers composing contemporary Yiddish song. Trombonist Brian Bender, accordionist Owen Davidson, and drummer Richie Davis fill out the group with a high degree of instrumental virtuosity.

The group's well-annotated recordings typically mix klezmer staples with new compositions, original songs, stories, and overlooked gems expressive of yidishkayt. *Prayer for a Broken World,* for example, imaginatively sequences the Holocaust lullaby "Dremlen Feyglekh" in a medley with two Naftule Brandwein tunes that evoke Jews at war. In fact, the entire recording is a "concept album" dealing with war and the longing for peace—an ethical, spiritual, and musical response to the fratricidal quarrels that have plagued the Balkans in the last decade.

As the title indicates, *Yidn Fun Amol: Jews of Long Ago* pays tribute to tradition, not merely by reconstructing it, but by perpetuating it. The album opens with "Dem Klezmers Lebn," which could easily be mistaken for a classic bulgar. In fact, it is a new composition by Sherry Mayrent. The album continues with examples of Wholesale's pulsing, Old World–style dancing and listening music. The centerpiece is "Redt Yidish (Speak Yiddish)," an original song by Yosl Kurland that traces the history of the language of Eastern European Jewry and celebrates its revival.

### YIDDISHE CUP KLEZMER BAND
*Klezmerized* (1994) Yiddishe Cup YC1001 (NR)
▌*Yiddfellas* (1999) Yiddishe Cup YC1002

This Cleveland-based group is a versatile ensemble whose five musicians play almost three times as many instruments between them, including perhaps the only recorded use of the theremin (a proto-electronic instrument) in klezmer music. On *Yiddfellas*, they specialize in a prerevival style that pays tribute to Mickey Katz ("That's Morris"), Hasidic song ("Shabbos nign") and Yiddish theater ("Rozhinkes mit Mandlen"), with plenty of Tarras- and Brandwein-influenced instrumentals and even an Old World–style, flute-tsimbl duet.

### YID VICIOUS
*Klez, Kez, Goy Mit Fez* (1998) Uvulittle UVU101

In spite of this Madison, Wisconsin–based septet's name, Yid Vicious plays a pretty straightforward brand of mostly acoustic klezmer. With two horns, clarinet, and violin, the group has myriad melodic possibilities to exploit, and on its all-instrumental selection of mostly familiar staples, each of the instrumentalists gets a turn in the spotlight.

The electric guitar is put to good use as a rhythm instrument on songs like "Khsidim Tants" and "Leben Zol Palestina." The group's version of the "Russian Sher," here titled "Devil's Sher" and featuring some serious wah-wah effects, gives new meaning to klezmer as Jewish "soul" music. They also give the much-covered "Fun Tashlikh" an innovative workout, kind of western-swing-meets-progressive-rock. In addition to the group's name, Yid Vicious boasts some of the best song titles in klezmer, including "Never Mind the Cossacks" and "Anarchy in the Ukraine." The album title, by the way, is a nonsensical rhyme, which literally means "Klez, cheese, Gentile with a fez."

## ZOHAR
*Keter* (1999) Knitting Factory KFR 236

The brainchild of downtown pianist Uri Caine and Moroccan-born khazn Aaron Bensoussan, *Keter* features a dizzying fusion of Caine's original, keyboard-trio jazz, Bensoussan's soaring, Arabic-style chants, and world-beat-infused electronica tracks programmed by DJ Olive. Ancient meets thoroughly modern on this provocative collaboration, inspired by the Kabbalah.

## JOHN ZORN (see also Mystic Fugu Orchestra)
*Kristallnacht* (1993) Tzadik TZ 7301
▌ *Bar Kokhba* (1996) Tzadik TZ7108-2
▌ *The Circle Maker* (1998) Tzadik TZ7122-2
*Filmworks VIII* 1997 (1998) Tzadik TZ7318

John Zorn's turn toward composing overtly Jewish-themed music began with *Kristallnacht,* recorded in November 1992. Latter-day klezmorim David Krakauer and Frank London lend a patina of authenticity to the album's opening track, "Shtetl (Ghetto Life)," a poignant portrayal of Jewish life in Eastern Europe harshly interrupted by the voice of Adolf Hitler and what sounds like the incitement of a mob.

What follows next is twelve minutes of ear-shattering ugliness—Zorn's sonic metaphor for Kristallnacht, the historic Night of Broken Glass, the nationwide pogrom that announced Germany's intention to destroy European Jewry. Zorn rightly makes the horror virtually unlistenable, and the album even comes with a warning from Zorn against "prolonged or repeated listenings."

The piece continues in this vein, alternating moments of pensive meditation with violent noise, performed by an ensemble including violinist Mark Feldman, guitarist Marc Ribot, and keyboardist Anthony Coleman. (Zorn himself does not play on the piece.) The English translations of the individual song titles give a clear indication of Zorn's thematic concerns: "Never Again," "Embers," "Rectification," "Looking Ahead," "Iron Fist," and "Nucleus—The New Settlement." It is a hugely ambitious, audacious piece of work, a musical representation of the Holocaust that will undoubtedly earn a place among the supreme musical statements of the twentieth century.

*Bar Kokhba* and *The Circle Maker* are both gorgeously rendered, double-CD packages featuring an array of small groups—duos, trios, and quartets, under the umbrella of the Masada Chamber Ensembles. They play jazz- and classical-style arrangements of Zorn's original Jewish compositions, ranging from Afro-Cuban jazz pieces to angular, dissonant, modern-classical string chamber music to traditional-flavored Yiddish melodies, all performed by the cream of the crop of the downtown avant-garde: Anthony Coleman, David Krakauer, Mark Feldman, Marc Ribot, John Medeski, and Dave Douglas. (Again, Zorn himself does not appear on these recordings.)

*Bar Kokhba* spreads the classical- and jazz-flavored tunes throughout both disks, so that atmospheric guitar-and-bass duets share time with European folk-flavored string trios, and delicate piano solos glide into pizzicato dances. *The Circle Maker* is divided into two discrete programs: "Issachar," featuring a string trio on one CD, and "Zevulun," expanding the string trio on the second CD into a lively, expressive sextet including guitar, drums, and percussion. Taken in total, *Bar Kokhba* and *The Circle Maker* contain some of John Zorn's most accessible, conventionally beautiful music.

Although Zorn's *Filmworks VIII 1997* recording is not part of Tzadik's Radical Jewish Culture series, it includes music performed by the Masada Chamber Ensembles for the soundtrack of "The Port of Last Resort," a documentary about Jewish refugees from Germany who escaped to Shanghai. A few of the pieces include improvisations by Min Xiao-Fen on the Chinese *pipa*.

## JOHN ZORN'S MASADA

▎ *Alef (One), Beit (Two), Gimel (Three), Dalet (Four), Hei (Five), Vav (Six), Zayin (Seven), Het (Eight), Tet (Nine)* (1994–97) DIW 888, 889, 890, 899, 900, 915, 923, 925, 933

▎ *Live in Jerusalem 1994* (1999) Tzadik TZ 7322

▎ *Live in Taipei 1995* (1999) Tzadik TZ 7323

▎ *Live in Middleheim 1999* (1999) Tzadik TZ 7326

Any group that included saxophonist John Zorn, trumpeter Dave Douglas, bassist Greg Cohen, and drummer Joey Baron would be on anyone's short list of the best jazz ensemble of the 1990s, no matter what style of music they played. All Masada's recordings are great and worth seeking out. The nine studio recordings actually stem from only five recording dates—the first four were all recorded on one long day in February 1994. *Four,* or *Dalet,* is only twenty minutes long, but all the rest are full-length CDs. They all feature the quartet playing Zorn's themes and improvising individually and collectively. In general, each recording seems to strike a balance between group improvisation, frenetic "free jazz," and more conventional, structured improvisation, where musicians take turns soloing or responding to each other's musical statements.

Masada's tunes are alternately frenzied and lyrical, brassy and prayerful. Zorn's playing is a catalog of different styles, including his trademark honks, squawks, and squeals (think of them as blasts of the *shofar,* or ram's horn) and Dave Douglas is practically his equal in the imagination he brings to his instrument.

The differences among Masada's albums are subtle. *Alef/One* is almost as jazzy as it is Jewish, and several numbers swing quite conventionally. *Beit/Two* kicks off with "Piram," one of Zorn's best-realized fusions of avant-swing in a Jewish mode, with especially smart work by Masada's dynamite rhythm section of Greg Cohen and Joey Baron. The album continues in a strongly realized Jewish mode and joins *Gimel/Three* among the best of Masada.

*Hei/Five* contains some of Masada's most "free" or "out" pieces—works that rely heavily on in-the-moment, all-group improvisation—but even these contain the kernels of Zorn's compositions at their core. *Het/Eight* presents some strongly Jewish, lyrical melodies and a pensive, Old World–style march along with the more far-out improvisations.

The live albums capture the dynamic immediacy and spontaneity of Masada in concert. *Jerusalem 1994* and *Taipei 1995* are both double-CDs. (Pp. 146–154, 160–64)

## ZMIROS (see Yale Strom)

## Compilations

### REISSUES

▌ *Klezmer Music: Early Yiddish Instrumental Music 1908–27*
  (1997) Arhoolie/Folklyric 7034

Compiler Martin Schwartz says this updated version supersedes an earlier LP- and cassette-only reissue titled *Klezmer Music: The First Recordings*. With twenty-four selections representing some of the earliest recorded examples of European and American klezmer—including many rare pieces and virtuosic solos—this is one of the finest reissues of its kind. It includes an introductory essay and detailed notes on the individual selections.

▌ *Klezmer Pioneers: European and American Recordings 1905–52*
  (1993) Rounder 1089

This essential compilation of early recordings, coproduced by Henry Sapoznik and Dick Spottswood, is particularly strong in its representation of early band arrangements and basic repertoire. The essay that accompanies the recording discusses the evolution of the large-band approach in American klezmer.

*Yikhes (Lineage): Early Klezmer Recordings 1911–39*
   (1995) Trikont US-0179
*Doyres (Generations): Traditional Klezmer Recordings 1979–94*
   (1995) Trikont US-0206
*Shteygers (Ways): New Klezmer Music 1991–94* (1995) Trikont US-0207

With these three albums, compilers Joel Rubin and Rita Ottens attempt nothing less than a recorded survey of the entire history of klezmer. It is an ambitious goal, and they come quite close to achieving it. *Yikhes,* in particular, is one of the best reissues of its kind—drawn from the collection of Martin Schwartz, but with little overlapping of Schwartz's own reissue of vintage recordings.

At eighteen tracks, *Doyres* does a good, generous job covering the main bases of the revival period. Some of the selections on *Shteygers* aren't exactly cutting-edge "new klezmer," but the album does include hard-to-find tracks by Don Byron and Elliott Sharp. The omission of Rubin's former bandmates in Brave Old World, however, makes this otherwise wonderfully annotated and inclusive series somewhat short of definitive.

*Klezmer Music 1910–42* (1996) Global Village 104

Originally produced by Henry Sapoznik and issued on the Smithsonian/ Folkways label (Folkways FSS 34021), this was a landmark effort when it was first released in 1980, one of the first reissues of vintage recorded klezmer. Beware this knockoff version, which dispenses with the original liner notes by Sapoznik, Andy Statman, and Zev Feldman, and features poor sound reproduction. Look for a planned reissue with remastered sound and new liner notes on the Living Traditions label.

*Jakie Jazz 'Em Up* (1984) Global Village 101

Includes a baker's dozen of some of the earliest klezmer recordings waxed in the United States, almost half by the Abe Schwartz and Harry Kandel orchestras. The selections are interesting, and while serious students of klezmer will want to own this and every other reissue they can get their hands on, others should proceed with caution: the recording suffers from poor surface-noise reduction compared to other, similar reissues.

# CONTEMPORARY

## International Yiddish Festival: Cracow 1990
### (1991) Edition Kunstlertreff EK 17 10 56

Featuring an international cast recorded at the second Festival of Jewish Culture in Cracow, Poland, in 1990, this album emphasizes Yiddish song, with selections by Poland's Golda Tencer, France's Ben Zimet, Germany's Manfred Lemm, and Boston's Klezmer Conservatory Band, featuring Judy Bressler on two numbers. Twenty-two tracks in all, this album makes a nice survey of the field of contemporary Yiddish vocals.

## Patterns of Jewish Life (1993) Spectrum/Wergo SM 1604-2

This two-disk collection features highlights from a 1992 Berlin concert series that was part of an overall exhibition on Jewish culture past and present. Curated by Joel Rubin, the groups represented here include Brave Old World (of which Rubin was a member at the time), the Epstein Brothers, Hasidic rock group Piamenta, and Yiddish theater stars Seymour Rexsite and Miriam Kressyn performing a selection of classic theater tunes with accompaniment by keyboardist Zalman Mlotek, a leading figure in contemporary Yiddish stage music.

The recording, which also features Sephardic, Israeli, and cantorial music, is pristine, capturing Brave Old World in a particularly poignant program of songs from the Lodz Ghetto, and the Epstein Brothers, backed by Peter Sokolow and Brave Old World's Stuart Brotman, in a rousing set of classic klezmer.

## ▌ Klezmer Music: A Marriage of Heaven and Earth (1996) Ellipsis Arts 4090

Loosely assembled around the theme of a wedding, this lovingly annotated compilation of one dozen tracks includes a 64-page booklet, with essays by Michael Alpert and Frank London and an interview with Andy Statman. These artists and their groups are represented here, as are other top contemporary klezmer groups, mostly from the mainstream of the klezmer renaissance, including the Flying Bulgar Klezmer Band, the Chicago Klezmer Ensemble, and European groups such as Di Naye

Kapelye, Budowitz, and La'om. Amply illustrated and annotated, this would make a beautiful gift for someone first getting interested in klezmer, or for provoking someone's interest.

*Klezmer 1993: New York City* (1993) Knitting Factory Works KFW 123

▌ ***The Jewish Alternative Movement: A Guide for the Perplexed***
   (1998) Knitting Factory KFR 216

*Klezmer Festival 1998: Live at the Knitting Factory* (1999)
   Knitting Factory KFR 238

*Knitting on the Roof* (1999) Knitting Factory KFW 260

Six of the nine tracks on *Klezmer 1993: New York City* are by the Klezmatics or one of the several offshoots of that group, including early versions of both Frank London's Hasidic New Wave and Matt Darriau's Paradox Trio. The other three tracks are by John Zorn's Masada, the New Klezmer Trio and, curiously enough, the Billy Tipton Memorial Quartet—a tribute band dedicated to Tipton, who was not a klezmer musician but a jazz musician who happened to be a woman who for decades passed as a man. One of the Klezmatics' tracks is an example of their ongoing collaborations with poets (which have included Allen Ginsberg and Jerome Rothenberg), this one with Alollo Trehorn on a tribute to Karl Marx. Nevertheless, *Klezmer 1993* is recommended only for avid collectors or diehard Klezmatics fans.

For those curious about the cutting edge of new Jewish music but who don't have the resources or inclination to delve too deeply into it, *The Jewish Alternative Movement: A Guide for the Perplexed* features tracks by fifteen different artists and is a good way to sample the downtown scene. The ubiquitous Klezmatics are here, along with offshoots Hasidic New Wave and Paradox Trio, but so are Radical Jewish Culture artists Uri Caine, Naftule's Dream, David Krakauer, Gary Lucas, and Anthony Coleman, as well as Forgiveness and Wally Brill.

*Klezmer Festival 1998* includes tracks by seven different performers— two each by Hasidic New Wave, Naftule's Dream, Klezmokum, Pharaoh's Daughter, and Psychedelicatessen (another group led by Frank London, this one specializing in spoken texts by the likes of Franz Kafka juxtaposed against psychedelic Jewish music), and single tracks by Paradox

Trio and Gary Lucas. All but the Lucas number were recorded live at the Knitting Factory during the "Jewsapalooza" festival in December 1998. A good sampler of some of the more offbeat efforts of the downtown Jewish scene.

*Knitting on the Roof* features a dozen new versions of songs from the Broadway musical *Fiddler on the Roof,* filtered through the sensibility of several cutting-edge visionaries from downtown's Jewish music scene (Hasidic New Wave, Naftule's Dream), and a few artists not typically associated with new Jewish music. Pop star Jill Sobule turns in a straightforward reading of "Sunrise, Sunset," but the most innovative cuts include Negativland's hip-hop fueled, sample-crazed reading of "Tevye's Dream," the Residents' electronic rendition of "Matchmaker," and Come's postmodern take on "Do You Love Me?"

### *Klezmania: Klezmer for the New Millennium* (1997) Shanachie 67007

Henry Sapoznik produced this fine introduction to neoklezmer and new Jewish music, which includes a hip-hop-fueled remix of the Klezmatics' already-funky "Khsidim Tants," a rare Don Byron track, selections by the New Orleans Klezmer Allstars, the New Klezmer Trio, and Ahava Raba, and an example of German group Aufwind's Manhattan Transfer–like a cappella klezmer. The album might be worth it for two novelties alone: "Crown Heights Affair" by hip-hop group Godchildren of Soul, which samples the Klezmatics, and a surf-guitar version of the classic Yiddish folk song, "Tum Balalaika."

### *Festival of Light* (1996) Six Degrees/Island 162-531 069-2
### *Festival of Light 2* (1999) Six Degrees 657036 1018-2

The first volume in this series of ostensibly Chanukah-themed albums works as an introduction to some of the more esoteric, spiritually oriented efforts of new Jewish music artists and others experimenting with the genre, but few of the songs have anything to do with Chanukah. Backed by an all-star band of musicians from the Klezmatics and Masada Chamber Ensembles, folk-pop hit-maker Marc Cohn kicks off the album with a soulful version of the holiday anthem, "Rock of Ages." Singer-songwriter Jane Siberry draws on the talents of many of the same musicians on her version of a doina, Don Byron, the Masada String Trio, and Wally Brill are also on hand, but folk-rockers Peter Himmelman and David Broza—the Jewish answer to Sam and Dave—carry away top honors with the funky original, "Lighting Up the World." While a bit heavy on new agey instrumentals, *Festival of Light 2* addresses the holiday more directly. It also contains a few keepers, including an original Chanukah song by pop wiseguys They Might Be Giants, and a swinging version of "Oh Chanukah" by the Frank London Big Band.

### *The Soul of Klezmer (Rêve et Passion)* (1998) Network 30.853

This two-disk box-set juxtaposes contemporary, vintage, and classic klezmer, cleverly sequenced to bring out the connections between such seemingly disparate musicians as the New Orleans Klezmer Allstars and Muzsikas, for example, or Budowitz and the Epstein Brothers. While most of the tracks are available elsewhere, a few rarities crop up, including two cuts by the Frank London/Lorin Sklamberg/Uri Caine Nigunim trio recorded live in France, a live number by Budowitz, and a previously unreleased duet by Alicia Svigals and Lauren Brody. A fine survey of the development of mainstream, instrumental klezmer in America and Europe from the early century through the renaissance.

## Sound Tracks

### *Partisans of Vilna: The Songs of World War II Jewish Resistance* (1989) Flying Fish FF 70450

A supergroup of contemporary Yiddish performers with the members of Kapelye at its core offers poignant renditions of songs originally written and performed by members of Vilna's Jewish underground during World War II. Among the vocalists are Michael Alpert, Henry Sapoznik, Adrienne Cooper, and Josh Waletzky, who directed the 1986 documentary film in which these songs were originally heard.

### *Carpati: 50 Miles, 50 Years* (1996) Global Village 173

In the Carpati region of Southwestern Ukraine before World War II, Jewish and Gypsy musicians swapped melodies and licks in each other's wedding bands. They also shared the distinction of being targets of German genocidal ambitions. The documentary film that shares this album's title profiles Zev Godinger, one of the few remaining survivors of this unique cross-cultural relationship. The soundtrack, performed by Yale Strom and his group Zmiros, alternates spoken-word accounts in Hungarian, Yiddish, and Romani, the Gypsy language, with examples of the Gypsy-Jewish crossover repertoire. (Translations provided.)

## Children's Music

One of the great things about klezmer music is its accessibility to children of all ages. Most children will respond instantly to klezmer on some level, if only as upbeat dance music. As such, most of the previously mentioned albums should be considered for kids, too. In particular, don't overlook Gary Lucas's *Busy Being Born,* which is ostensibly a children's album. Conversely, also, there are a couple of excellent recordings specifically oriented to children, which adults will enjoy, too.

### GERRY TENNY AND BETTY ALBERT SCHRECK
*Let's Sing a Yiddish Song (Lomir Zingen a Yiddish Lid)*
   (1988) Global Village 134

A kind of primer of Yiddish folk song, this recording features a baker's dozen of traditional folk songs, some in klezmer-style arrangements, others owing more to the American folk revival and nursery rhymes. The accompanying booklet includes English translations and transliterated lyrics, making this an ideal album for families wanting to increase their literacy in yidishkayt.

### YOUNG PEOPLE'S KLEZMER WORKSHOP
▌ *Oy Vey!* (1997) Backyard Partners BP001
*Oy Vey! Chanukah!* (Sruli and Lisa) (1999) Backyard Partners BP002 (NR)

There's nothing childish about the klezmer music or stories performed on *Oy Vey!* by an all-star band led by Sruli and Lisa and including David

Licht of the Klezmatics, Lauren Brody of Kapelye, and Brian Bender of the Wholesale Klezmer Band. The stories, songs, liner notes, jokes, and Yiddish lessons offered within make this an ideal introduction to klezmer.

## VARIOUS ARTISTS

▌*Di Grine Katshke: The Green Duck* (1998) Living Traditions LTD 1801

A small, superstar ensemble teams up for this novel collection of Yiddish animal songs for children; some centuries-old folk tunes, others by modern or contemporary Yiddish poets. Coproduced by vocalist Paula Teitelbaum and vocalist/keyboardist Lorin Sklamberg, other players include Frank London of the Klezmatics, Jeff Warschauer of the Klezmer Conservatory Band, and Adrienne Cooper, Lauren Brody, and Henry Sapoznik of Kapelye. The CD comes with a lovely 44-page booklet that includes transliterated and translated lyrics, papercut illustrations, and a great foundation upon which families can begin to build a basic Yiddish vocabulary.

## The Hot List

Here is a list of CDs recommended for those interested in exploring the depth and variety of klezmer and new Jewish music above and beyond the essential albums listed on page 166:

Steven Bernstein, *Diaspora Soul*

Brave Old World, *Beyond the Pale*

Don Byron, *Plays the Music of Mickey Katz*

Cayuga Klezmer Revival, *Klezmology*

Chicago Klezmer Ensemble, *Sweet Home Bukovina*

Anthony Coleman, *Sephardic Tinge*

Di Naye Kapelye, *Di Naye Kapelye*

Epstein Brothers Orchestra, *Kings of Freylekh Land: A Century of Yiddish-American Music*

Flying Bulgar Klezmer Band, *Tsirkus*

Erik Friedlander, *The Watchman*

Bob Gluck, *Stories Heard and Retold*

Ben Goldberg, *What Comes Before* (Goldberg/Schott/Sarin)

Hasidic New Wave, *Jews and the Abstract Truth; Kabalogy*

Kabalas, *Time Tunnel*

Kapelye, *Levine and His Flying Machine; On the Air: Jewish-American Radio*

Mickey Katz, *Simcha Time: Mickey Katz Plays Music for Weddings, Bar Mitzvahs, and Brisses*

King Django, *King Django's Roots and Culture*

Klezmatics, *Shvaygn=Toyt; Rhythm + Jews; The Well*

Klezmer Conservatory Band, *A Touch of Klez!; Old World Beat; Live! The Thirteenth Anniversary Album; Dancing in the Aisles*

Klezmokum, *ReJew-Venation*

The Klezmorim, *First Recordings 1976–78; Notes from Underground; Jazz-Babies of the Ukraine*

David Krakauer, *Klezmer, N.Y.*

Wolf Krakowski, *Transmigrations*

Sy Kushner Jewish Music Ensemble, *KlezSqueeze!*

La'om, *Riffkele*

Frank London, *The Shvitz; Nigunim; The Debt; Shekhina*

Gary Lucas, *Busy Being Born*

Sherry Mayrent, *Hineni*

Joseph Moskowitz, *The Art of the Cymbalom: The Music of Joseph Moskowitz, 1916–1953*

Naftule's Dream, *Search for the Golden Dreydl; Smash, Clap!*

New Klezmer Trio, *Masks and Faces; Melt Zonk Rewire*

New Orleans Klezmer Allstars, *The Big Kibosh; Fresh out the Past*

New Shtetl Band, *Jewish and Balkan Dance Music*

Paradox Trio, *Source*

Joel Rubin Jewish Music Ensemble, *Beregovski's Khasene*

Shirim, *Klezmer Nutcracker*

Shloinke, *Shloinke*

Lorin Sklamberg and Paula Teitelbaum, *Di Grine Katshke: The Green Duck*

Andy Statman, *Jewish Klezmer Music; Klezmer Suite; Songs of the Breslever Chassidim: Today* (with Yaacov Klein); *Songs of Our Fathers: Traditional Jewish Melodies* (with David Grisman); *Between Heaven and Earth: Music of the Jewish Mystics; The Hidden Light*

Twelve Corners Klezmer Band, *Git Azoy (It's Good This Way)*

Jeff Warschauer, *The Singing Waltz: Klezmer Guitar and Mandolin*

Wholesale Klezmer Band, *Yidn Fun Amol: Jews of Long Ago*

Yiddishe Cup Klezmer Band, *Yiddfellas*

Young People's Klezmer Workshop, *Oy Vey!*

John Zorn, *The Circle Maker*

John Zorn's Masada, *Alef-Tet; Live in Jerusalem 1994; Live in Taipei 1995; Live in Middleheim 1999*

Compilations, *Klezmer Music: A Marriage of Heaven and Earth; The Jewish Alternative Movement: A Guide for the Perplexed; The Soul of Klezmer (Rêve et Passion)*

## Klezmer by Style

The following stylistic groupings are not intended to pigeonhole bands into categories; the best groups dance over such distinctions and defy simple classification. This listing is simply intended as a helpful guide for the neophyte listener wading through the rich diversity of contemporary klezmer.

**Avant-klezmer:** Ambarchi/Avenaim, Anthony Coleman, Ben Goldberg, Hasidic New Wave, David Krakauer, Steve Lacy, Frank London, Masada, Mystic Fugu Orchestra, Naftule's Dream, New Klezmer Trio, Zeena Parkins, Glenn Spearman, John Zorn

**Classical-klezmer:** Erik Friedlander, Jewish Trio, David Krakauer, Kroke, Psamim, John Schott, John Zorn

**Electro-klezmer:** Wally Brill, Bob Gluck, Rea Mochiach and Alon Cohen, Zeena Parkins, Richard Teitelbaum, Zohar

**Folk-klezmer:** Di Naye Kapelye, Kaila Flexer, Freilachmakers Klezmer String Band, Golden Gate Gypsy Orchestra, La'om, Muzsikas, New Shtetl Band

**Jazz-klezmer:** Alexandria Kleztet, Austin Klezmorim, Steven Bernstein, Warren Byrd and David Chevan, Anthony Coleman, Mike Curtis Klezmer Quartet, Marty Ehrlich, Flying Bulgar Klezmer Band, Hasidic New Wave, Jewish Trio, Klezmokum, the Klezmorim, Kol Simcha, David Krakauer, Lox and Vodka, Masada, Metropolitan Klezmer, Minnesota Klezmer Band, Modern Klezmer Quartet, Naftule's Dream, New Klezmer Trio, New Orleans Klezmer Allstars, New Shtetl Band, Oomph, Original Klezmer Jazz Band, Shawn's Kugel, Shira, Andy Statman, John Zorn

**Neo-Hasidim:** Atzilut, Shlomo and Neshama Carlebach, Hasidic New Wave, Klezmatics, Frank London, Sherry Mayrent, Mystic Fugu Orchestra, RebbeSoul, Andy Statman, Wholesale Klezmer Band

**Neo-traditionalists:** Budowitz, Chicago Klezmer Ensemble, Cincinnati Klezmer Project, Joshua Horowitz, Joel Rubin, Alicia Svigals, Wholesale Klezmer Band

**Progressive-klezmer:** Alexandria Kleztet, Brave Old World, Cayuga Klezmer Revival, Flying Bulgar Klezmer Band, Kabalas, King Django, Klezamir, Klezmatics, David Krakauer, La'om, Frank London, New Orleans Klezmer Allstars, Shawn's Kugel, Shirim, Shloinke, Yid Vicious

**Revivalists:** Austin Klezmorim, Don Byron, Catskill Klezmorim, Ensemble Klezmer, Finjan Klezmer Ensemble, Di Gojim, Harry's Freilach,

Kapelye, Klezamir, Klezgoyim, Klezical Tradition, Klezmer Conservatory Band, Klezmer Plus!, the Klezmorim, Sy Kushner, La'om, Margot Leverett, Lox and Vodka, Machaya Klezmer Band, Maxwell Street Klezmer Band, Mazeltones, Metropolitan Klezmer, New Shtetl Band, New York Klezmer Ensemble, Old World Folk Band, Itzhak Perlman, Joel Rubin, Shirim, Andy Statman, Twelve Corners Klezmer Band, Jeff Warschauer, Wholesale Klezmer Band, Yid Vicious, Yiddishe Cup Klezmer Band

**Shtetl-metal:** Ambarchi/Avenaim, Hasidic New Wave, Kletka Red, Frank London, Naftule's Dream, Marc Ribot, Selfhaters (Anthony Coleman)

**Sui Generis:** Giora Feidman, Mickey Katz, Kramer, Gary Lucas

**Vintage:** Naftule Brandwein, Epstein Brothers Orchestra, I. J. Hochman, Harry Kandel, Joseph Moskowitz, Abe Schwartz, Dave Tarras

**World-beat klezmer:** Ahava Raba, Atzilut, Davka, Golden Gate Gypsy Orchestra, King Django, Klezmatics, Wolf Krakowski, Muzsikas, Nunu!, Oomph, Paradox Trio, Poza, Salomon Klezmorim, Shawn's Kugel, Yale Strom, Sulam, Tzimmes, Zohar

**Yiddishists:** Finjan Klezmer Ensemble, Kapelye, Klezical Tradition, Klezmatics, Klezmer Conservatory Band, Wolf Krakowski, Machaya Klezmer Band, Maxwell Street Klezmer Band, Mazeltones, Minnesota Klezmer Band, Odessa Express, West End Klezmorim, Wholesale Klezmer Band

## Music Retailers

With the combined resources of these three mail-order specialty houses, you should be able to track down almost any klezmer or Jewish music recording in the world.

**Tara Music,** www.jewishmusic.com, (800) 827-2400, P.O. Box 707, Owings Mills, MD 21117

**A Bisl Yidishkayt,** www.yiddishmusic.com, (781) 643-1957, P.O. Box 400331, Cambridge, MA 02140–0004

**Hatikvah Music International,** www.hatikvahmusic.com, (323) 655-7083, 436 N. Fairfax Ave., Los Angeles, CA 90036

# GLOSSARY

**badkhn:** wedding poet

**badkhones:** the wedding poet's songs and recited repertoire

**Bukovina:** region in Eastern Europe that has been part of the Ottoman, Russian, and Austro-Hungarian empires, Romania, the USSR, and Ukraine. Name means "land of beech trees." Region especially associated with Old World klezmer.

**bulgar (bulgarish, bulgareasca):** one of the most common klezmer dance tune genres, which gained popularity in Eastern Europe in the late nineteenth and early twentieth centuries and was made especially popular by Dave Tarras in America. Derived from a Bessarabian/Moldovan dance, so called because of the large Bulgarian population in Bessarabia, or East Romania. Usually a fast circle dance in 2/4. Related to the sirba.

**dobriden (good day):** greeting piece, often followed by a fast dance tune

**doina:** based on a Romanian shepherd's lament, the doina is a highly formulaic, nonmetric suite intended for listening and to showcase the improvisational abilities of the soloist, usually performed during the wedding banquet. As such it was very popular among immigrant clarinetists. The doina begins with a *forshpil,* followed by the main section, consisting of improvisations on a mode, and concluding with a moderate-to-fast dance in double time, sometimes called a *nokhshpil.* The pieces are somber in atmosphere, and the melodies, such as they are, are played over long sustained notes or chords of the tsimbl or accordion.

**fantazi:** a listening piece

**fidl:** old world violin

**forshpil:** prelude (intro to a doina, for example)

**freylekhs:** literally "happy," a generic term for common, upbeat, circle- or line-dance tunes, usually in 2/4 or 4/4, that often borrow their melodies from zmires or nigunim, and frequently performed in medleys of up to three different songs that change scale or mode

**gasn nign:** literally "street tune," a processional melody at Jewish weddings and other affairs

**Hasidim (Hasid, Hasidic, Hasidism):** members of a populist, mystical Jewish movement that was born in the forests of Poland in the mid-1700s and emphasizes ecstatic emotion over rote learning

**hekhsher:** seal of kosher approval

**heymish:** emotionally warm, familiar

**honga:** a Moldovan-derived line dance in 2/4

**hora:** Not to be confused with the popular Israeli folk dance of the same name, in klezmer hora refers to a Romanian-Jewish slow line dance performed in a "limping" or irregular 3/8 or 5/8 meter. Often found in a suite following a doina, the hora (also known as the *zhok, londre,* or *volekhl krimer tants*), was also often used as a gasn nign.

**kale:** bride

**kale baveynen:** ritual in which bride is brought to tears by the badkhn

**kale bazetsn:** ritual seating of the bride

**kale bazingen:** ritual veiling of the bride

**kapelye:** band of musicians

**khasene:** wedding

**khazn:** cantor

**khazones:** the body of liturgical melodies sung by the khazn

**khosid, khosidl (lit., "little Hasid"):** a slow-to-moderate tempo, improvised circle or line dance, with a nign-like melody and feel, in 2/4 time

**khosn:** groom

**khupe:** ritual wedding canopy

**kneytshn:** "cut-off" or "swallowed" notes—with a soblike character, usually played by fiddle or clarinet—that give klezmer its distinctive, characteristic quality. Borrowed from cantorial technique.

**kolomeyke:** fast Ukrainian dance with two strong beats at the end of each phrase

**krekhts (pl. krekhtsn):** "achy" notes, usually played by fiddle or clarinet, that give klezmer its distinctive, characteristic quality, borrowed from cantorial technique

**landsmanshaftn:** immigrant-era social organizations based on geographic origins in Old World

**mazltov:** a piece played at the table of honored guests at a wedding

**mekhutonim:** in-laws

**meshoyrer:** apprentice cantor

**mikve:** ritual bath

**mitnagdim:** rationalist strain of religious Jews, opposed to mysticism

**mitzve:** religious commandment or obligation

**muzikant:** musician, preferred term of learned musicians

**nign (pl. nigunim):** a wordless melody sung by Hasidic Jews to induce ecstatic states of consciousness. Many klezmer tunes are based on nigunim.

**rebbe:** Hasidic spiritual leader

**sekunde:** second fiddle in a kapelye, usually plays rhythm against primary fidl

**shadkhn:** Old World matchmaker

**sher (lit., "scissors" dance):** a Russian-style square dance in a moderate 2/4 tempo, popular among the immigrant generation, musically similar to the freylekhs but a bit slower. Typically, a sher lasts about twenty minutes and is actually a medley of different songs.

**shikker:** a drinker, or a drunk

**shtetl (pl. shtetlekh):** a small Jewish town in Eastern Europe

**shteyger:** mode, similar to a scale, but implying more about how a melody will be played

**shtroyfidl:** straw-fiddle, folk instrument invented by Michael Joseph Gusikow

**shul:** school; synagogue

**shviger:** mother-in-law

**simkhe:** a Jewish party centered around a life-cycle event, such as a wedding or bar mitzvah

**sirba:** a traditional Romanian dance genre related to the bulgar, popular among American Jewish immigrants, with characteristic triplets in the melody over a rhythm in 2/4 time

**skotshne:** a piece in the tempo and character of a dance tune, but played in a more elaborate style as a virtuoso piece for listening

**slivovitz:** plum brandy; a favored, Old World drink

**tish nigunim:** slow or moderate tempo melodies often associated with prayers, as well as pensive rubato pieces in a vocal style, that were traditionally played or sung at the wedding banquet or on *Shabbos* (the Jewish Sabbath)

**treyf:** not kosher; something forbidden

**tshoks:** "bent" notes with a laughlike quality, usually played by clarinet or fiddle, that give klezmer its distinctive, characteristic quality

**vulekhl:** literally "from Wallachia," a province of Romania. A dance or tune in Romanian-Jewish style such as a doina or hora.

**yeshive bokher:** religious student

**yidishkayt:** Yiddish culture in general terms

**yikhes:** Old World social status

**zhok:** a native Romanian dance, actually refers to an entire diversified genre of music and dance. See also hora.

**zmires:** table songs

## Klezmer Festivals and Workshops

There are several annual and biannual klezmer festivals that gather together various bands and performers in one place at one time. Some combine entertainment with education, including lectures, performances, master classes, and workshops. The concert business being as volatile as it is, the details of such events may change from year to year, but here are a few of the more well-established festivals and workshops with brief descriptions and contact information:

**Ashkenaz.** Toronto: Presented by David Buchbinder, the founder and leader of the Flying Bulgar Band, Ashkenaz is one of the largest festivals of its kind. Held every two years at Toronto's Harbourfront Centre, it bills itself as "A Festival of New Yiddish Culture," going beyond klezmer to embrace other Yiddish music and arts, including drama, poetry, and performance art. Typically held in late summer, in 1999 the third Ashkenaz festival boasted 175 artists from ten countries, including Eastern Europe, Sweden, Israel, and South America. Performers included Brave Old World, Aufwind, Hasidic New Wave, Marty Ehrlich, Marc Ribot, Dave Douglas, the Klezmer Conservatory Band, David Krakauer, and the Paradox Trio. The festival also features a weeklong potpourri of events including theater, dance, art exhibits, film, readings, lectures, storytelling, children's events, many of which are free. 642 King Street West, Suite 100, Toronto, Ontario M5V 1M7 (416) 973-3000 (www.ashkenaz.org)

**Jewish Culture Festival.** Cracow, Poland: In the summer of 1999 Cracow hosted the eighth annual Jewish Culture Festival, which in recent years has included a mix of concerts by Polish and international groups, including Brave Old World, Hasidic New Wave, Salomon Klezmorim, Anthony Coleman, Chicago Klezmer Ensemble, Jeff Warschauer/Deborah Strauss Duo, Di Naye Kapelye, and the Klezmatics. Also lectures and films. (www.jewishfestival.art.pl)

**Jewsapalooza.** Every year during Christmas week the Knitting Factory in downtown New York hosts a festival of traditional and cutting-edge klezmer groups. In past years performers have included Andy Statman, the Klezmatics, Hasidic New Wave, Naftule's Dream, Klezmokum, Gary Lucas, and KlezMs. Knitting Factory, 74 Leonard Street, New York, NY 10013 (212) 219-3006 (www.knittingfactory.com)

**KlezKamp.** Parksville, New York: The grand old dame of klezmer workshops—KlezKamp: The Yiddish Folk Arts Program—celebrated its fifteenth anniversary in 1999. Held every year during Christmas week at the Paramount Hotel in the Catskills region of upstate New York, KlezKamp has nurtured the klezmer revival. Originally sponsored by YIVO, the weeklong event is now run by Living Traditions, an organization presided over by KlezKamp founder Henry Sapoznik and Klezmatics vocalist Lorin Sklamberg, and is dedicated to the perpetuation of Yiddish music and culture. A family-oriented gathering, KlezKamp features music, dance, language, and culture workshops as well as a lively children's program, with nightly concerts, jam sessions, and dancing into the wee hours. Teachers typically include members of top bands including the Klezmatics, the Klezmer Conservatory Band, and Budowitz, as well as old-timers such as Sid Beckerman and Elaine Hoffman Watts, daughter of the famed klezmer percussionist Jacob Hoffman. Write for information at Living Traditions, 430 West 14th Street, Suite 409, New York, NY 10014. (212) 691-1272 (www.livingtraditions.org)

**KlezKanada.** Lantier, Quebec: Held annually at Camp B'nai Brith in Lantier, which is sixty miles north of Montreal, KlezKanada boasts an impressive array of instrumental workshops, panel discussions, and other activities. In its fourth year in 1999, the KlezKanada staff included members of Brave Old World and the Klezmer Conservatory Band, as well as such veteran klezmorim as the Epstein Brothers, Ray Musiker, and Pete Sokolow. Write to KlezKanada c/o J.E.C., 5151 Cote St. Catherine Road, Suite 200, Montreal, Quebec H3W 1M6. (514) 345-2610 (www.klezkanada.com)

**Leeds (England) Klezmer Festival.** Held annually in September at Leeds Metropolitan University, includes workshops and concert. In 1999 staff included Merlin Shepherd of Budowitz, Freylach Spielers, and the Sheffield Klezmer Band. Write to Leeds Klezmer Festival, P.O. Box 182, Leeds, 4UH, England. (www.klezmer.co.uk/klezmfest)

**Tsfat.** The annual Klezmer Festival in Tsfat, Israel, takes place over three days each August and includes performances by klezmer bands from Israel and other nations. Write to Klezmer Festival, 27 Piness Street, Neve Zedek, Tel Aviv, Israel. 972-3-517-6364 (ilansh@ibm.net)

## Klezmer on the Silver Screen

### DOCUMENTARIES

**Alle Brider** (1995, dir. by Amnon Buchbinder, Ergo Media, Inc., P.O. Box 2037, Teaneck, NJ 07666 [201-692-0404] [www.jewishvideo.com] 5 mins.) This MTV-style music video features the Flying Bulgar Klezmer Band performing its version of the popular Yiddish song, "Alle Brider." The band is seen performing at a traditional-style wedding and on an outdoor concert stage in front of an exuberant crowd. One of the only music videos of its kind, with jump-cuts and high-paced editing, to feature a klezmer band.

**In the Fiddler's House** (1995, dir. by Don Lenzer and Glenn DuBose, Angel/EMI, 304 Park Avenue South, New York, NY 10010 [212-253-3000], 55 mins.) Originally produced for public television's Great Performances series, this documentary follows world-renowned classical violinist Itzhak Perlman to Poland where, escorted by the leading musicians of the klezmer revival, he finds his Old Country musical roots. This film had unprecedented impact on bringing klezmer into the mainstream.

**Jewish Soul Music: The Art of Giora Feidman** (1980, dir. by Uri Barbash, Ergo Media, Inc., P.O. Box 2037, Teaneck, NJ 07666 [201-692-0404] [www.jewishvideo.com] 50 mins.) Originally filmed in Israel for Dutch television, this documentary catches clarinetist Giora Feidman relatively early in his career as a klezmer. Discussion includes klezmer's roots in

Hasidic melodies. While the film's sensibility and approach are dry and old-fashioned, the film includes lots of scenes of Feidman performing, catching him at a traditional wedding, in a Hasidic home in Tsfat, and with a symphony orchestra.

**A Jumpin' Night in the Garden of Eden** (1987, dir. Michal Goldman, First Run Features, 153 Waverly Place, New York, NY 10014) [1-800-229-8575], 75 mins.) This documentary profiles the klezmer revival by focusing mainly on Henry Sapoznik and Hankus Netsky, of Kapelye and the Klezmer Conservatory Band, respectively. The film includes great footage of the KCB in rehearsal and in concert, scenes from KlezKamp, and interviews with Dave Tarras and Leon Schwartz.

**The Last Klezmer: Leopold Kozlowski: His Life and His Music** (1994, dir. Yale Strom, New Yorker Films, 16 West 61st Street, New York, NY 10023 [1-800-447-0196], 84 minutes.) Although Leopold Kozlowski is a son of the Kleinman Polish/Ukrainian klezmer dynasty and a nephew of the great Naftule Brandwein, this film is not so much about klezmer as it is a portrait of Kozlowski, the Holocaust survivor. On its own terms, it is a touching profile of Kozlowski's life—from his ghetto upbringing to his Primo Levi–like experiences in the Holocaust to the postwar life he carves out for himself in Poland as a musician, teacher, and caretaker of the Yiddish music tradition. If the movie treats the term "klezmer" cavalierly, glossing over the distinctions among traditional klezmer and liturgical music, Yiddish folk and theater music ("Sunrise, Sunset" from *Fiddler on the Roof* plays a recurring role), one still comes away with a sense of the innate Jewishness of the music, and of the important and wide-ranging social role that klezmer played as a musical figure in the Old World. In the end, this is a documentary about a Polish survivor and not a film about klezmer.

**Learn to Play Klezmer Music: Improvising in the Tradition** (1997, by Andy Statman, Homespun Tapes, Box 694, Woodstock, NY 12498 [1-800-33-TAPES], 80 mins.) In the format of an instructional video by this master clarinetist of contemporary klezmer, and protégé of Dave Tarras, Andy Statman digs deep into the heart and soul of the music. By breaking down various melodies into their basic constituent parts, phrases, and rhythms, and building them back up again, Statman illustrates the ornamentation, trills, grace notes, and krekhtsn that give klezmer its distinctive, soulful quality. Along the way he also emphasizes the music's spiritual aspect. The viewer is treated to a private concert and master class by one of the true virtuosos of the genre. You needn't be a musician to benefit from Statman's insights into klezmer.

**A Tickle in the Heart** (1996, dir. Stefan Schwietert, Kino Video, 333 West 39th Street, New York, NY 10018 [www.kino.com], 84 mins.) This documentary focuses on the three Epstein Brothers, finding them in Florida and following them on trips to Berlin and to their parents' birthplace in Pinsk. We see them in mundane situations, washing their cars and cooking at home, as well as on stage performing for a lively crowd of young Germans in Berlin. The film provides context for their career and the revival of interest in klezmer both in America and Europe.

---

## FEATURE FILMS

**Yidl Mitn Fidl (Yidl with His Fiddle)** (1936, dir. Joseph Green and Jan Nowina-Przybylski, Ergo Media, Inc., P.O. Box 2037, Teaneck, NJ 07666 [201-692-0404] [www.jewishvideo.com], 92 mins.) Yiddish with English subtitles. This film is required viewing for anyone interested in klezmer. The premise is pure Hollywood, like Barbra Streisand's "Yentl": a blooming teenage girl (and klezmer fiddler) played by Yiddish star Molly Picon hides her sex to fit in in a man's world. What is especially lovely is the actual footage of pre-Holocaust shtetl life, as it was filmed in Poland, in Kazimierz, and also in Warsaw, before the Germans invaded. The film follows a kapelye traveling throughout the countryside, where the members play in courtyards and sleep in barns and scramble to make a living in a rapidly changing world. There is a great wedding scene, replete with the Old World rituals of seating and veiling the bride and reducing her to tears to the accompaniment of a badkhn and the klezmorim, as well as the wedding banquet with dancing and music. The film also includes many Yiddish-theater-style songs written by Abe Ellstein that became standards of the Yiddish repertoire.

## OTHER FILMS WITH KLEZMER MUSIC IN THE SOUND TRACK

**Camp Stories** (1996, dir. Herbert Biegel, with Elliott Gould and Jerry Stiller), music by Roy Nathanson and Jazz Passengers, soundtrack on Knitting Factory Works

**The Chosen** (1981, dir. Jeremy Kagan, with Maximilian Schell, Rod Steiger, Robby Benson), with music and appearance by Kapelye

**Deconstructing Harry** (1997, dir. Woody Allen, with Kirstie Alley, Richard Benjamin, Billy Crystal, Amy Irving), music performed by Shirim

**Enemies: A Love Story** (1989, dir. Paul Mazursky, with Ron Silver, Lena Olin), music performed by Giora Feidman

**Fast Trip, Long Drop** (1994, dir. Gregg Bordowitz), score written and performed by the Klezmatics

**The Fool and the Flying Ship** (1997), animated, with narration by Robin Williams, music by Hankus Netsky, soundtrack on Rabbit Ears

**The Jazz Singer** (1980, dir. Richard Fleischer, with Neil Diamond, Laurence Olivier), appearance by the Klezmorim

**King of the Gypsies** (1978, dir. Frank Pierson, with Sterling Hayden, Brooke Shields, Eric Roberts), music and appearances by David Grisman, Andy Statman, Matt Glaser (more Gypsy music than klezmer)

**Over the Brooklyn Bridge** (1984, dir. Menahem Golan, with Elliott Gould, Margaux Hemingway, Sid Caesar, Carol Kane, Shelley Winters), with music and appearance by Kapelye

**Schindler's List** (1993, dir. Steven Spielberg, with Liam Neeson, Ben Kingsley, Ralph Fiennes), music performed by Giora Feidman, dramatic role by Leopold Kozlowski

**A Stranger Among Us** (1992, dir. Sidney Lumet, with Melanie Griffith), music performed by Shirim

## GENERAL KLEZMER SITES

The Klezmer Shack (www.klezmershack.com): The main portal for klezmer on the Internet. Includes a listing of klezmer personnel, CDs, resources, updated news, discussion lists, and links to other sites.

Klezmer On-Line (www.klezmer.co.uk): The main, European-based klezmer portal site. Also includes an impressive database of American bands and radio programs.

## BAND WEB SITES

Alexandria Kleztet (members.aol.com/kleztet)
Aufwind  (aufwind.freepage.de)
Brave Old World (www.braveoldworld.com)
Budowitz (www.merlinms.dircon.co.uk/budowitz)
Cayuga Klezmer Revival (strad.as.arizona.edu/~sstolovy/ckr/ckr.html)
Chicago Klezmer Ensemble (members.aol.com/hupcatdisc)
Kaila Flexer (www.compassrecords.com)
Bob Gluck  (www.emf.org)
Kabalas (www.qconline.com/kabalas)
King Django (www.trescrown.com)
Klezamir (www.klezamir.com)
Klezmatics (www.aviv2.com/klezbio.html)
Klezmorim (www.klezmo.com)
Wolf Krakowski (www.kamea.com)
Kroke (www.oriente.de/e/kroke.htm)
Steve Lacy (www.imaginet.fr/~senators)
La'om (www.laom.de)
Margot Leverett (www.zianet.com/leverett/margot)
Gary Lucas (www.garylucas.com)
Sherry Mayrent (www.crocker.com/~ganeydn/wkb.html)
Metropolitan Klezmer (members.aol.com/metroklez)

Minnesota Klezmer Band (www.frozenchozen.com)
New Orleans Klezmer Allstars (www.klezmers.com)
Nunu! (www.enjarecords.com)
RebbeSoul (www.rebbesoul.com)
Shawn's Kugel (members.aol.com/shawnkugel/kugel.html)
Shloinke (www.neiu.edu/~aadams/shloinkeh.html)
Yale Strom (www.members.aol.com/stromklez)
Twelve Corners Klezmer Band (www.12cornersklezmer.com)
Tzimmes (www2.portal.ca/~jsiegel/tzimmes.html)
Wholesale Klezmer Band (www.crocker.com/~ganeydn/wkb.html)
Yiddishe Cup Klezmer Band (www.en.com/users/yiddishecup)
Yid Vicious (www.globaldialog.com/~bjacobs/home.html)

## RECORD LABEL WEB SITES

Knitting Factory Records: (www.knittingfactory.com)
Knitting Factory's Jewish Alternative Movement: (www.jewmu.com)
Tzadik Records: (www.tzadik.com)

# BIBLIOGRAPHY

## Articles

Blumenthal, Bob. "The age of Masada," *Boston Globe* (5/28/99).

Dion, Lynn. "Klezmer Music in America: Revival and Beyond," *Jewish Folklore and Ethnology Review* (6/8/86).

Feldman, Walter Zev. "Bulgareasca/Bulgarish/Bulgar," *Ethnomusicology* (Winter 1994).

————. "Rubin and Horowitz: Bessarabian Symphony [review]," *Ethnomusicology* (Fall 1996).

Gruber, Ruth Ellen. "Germany's Klezmer Craze," *New Leader* (4/7/97).

Jacobson, Marion S. "The Klezmer Club As Pilgrimage," *Jewish Folklore and Ethnology Review* (6/17/95).

Kaufman, Leslie. "Sony Builds a Mall: But Don't Call It That," *Sunday New York Times* (7/25/99).

Kirshenblatt-Gimblett, Barbara. "Sounds of Sensibility," *Judaism* (Winter 1998).

Kruth, John. "Andy Statman: From Bluegrass to Klezmer and Beyond," *Sing Out* (Fall 1986).

Loeffler, James. "Klezmania," *New Republic* (4/6/98).

Loeffler, James Benjamin. "A Gilgul fun a Nigun: Jewish Musicians in New York, 1881–1945," Harvard Judaica Research Papers No. 3 (1997).

Logan, Andy. "The Five Generations," *New Yorker* (10/29/49).

London, Frank. "An Insider's View: How We Traveled from Obscurity to the Klezmer Establishment in Twenty Years," *Judaism* (Winter 1998).

Lubet, Alex. "Maxwell Street Wedding [review]," *Ethnomusicology* (Winter 1995).

Macnie, Jim. "Agent Omnijazz: Don Byron," *Down Beat* (11/1/96).

Morris, Bob. "Yidls with Fiddles," *Village Voice* (1/23/96).

Netsky, Hankus. "Klezmer Music in an American Community: The Philadelphia Example," New England Conservatory, Boston (1998).

Netsky, Hankus. "An Overview of Klezmer Music and Its Development in the United States," *Judaism* (Winter 1998).

Pekar, Harvey. "A Brief History of Klezmer," *Pakn Treger* (Fall 1998).

Pestcoe, Shlomo. "On the Trail of Lost Roots: An Interview with Henry Sapoznik," *Sing Out* (Winter 1989).

Retica, Aaron. "David Krakauer," *The New Yorker* (10/26/98).

Rothstein, Robert A. "*Klezmer-Loshn*," *Judaism* (Winter 1998).

Sapoznik, Henry. "From Eastern Europe to East Broadway: Yiddish Music in Old World and New," *NY Folklore Quarterly* (6/10/88).

Sherrill, Stephen. "Don Byron," *New York Times Magazine* (1/6/94).

Singer, Barry. "In Yiddish Music, A Return to Roots of Torment and Joy," *Sunday New York Times* (8/16/98).

Slobin, Mark. "Learning the Lessons of Studying Jewish Music," *Judaism* (Spring 95).

————. "The Last Klezmer [review]," *Ethnomusicology* (Fall 1996).

Solomon, Alisa. "Seeking Answers in Yiddish Classics," *Sunday New York Times* (11/16/97).

Svigals, Alicia. "Why We Do This Anyway: Klezmer As Jewish Youth Subculture," *Judaism* (Winter 1998).

Yaffe, David. "Learning to Reed," *New York* (4/12/99).

## Books

Abrahams, Israel. *Jewish Life in the Middle Ages* (Philadelphia: Jewish Publication Society, 1958).

Beregovski, Moshe. *Old Jewish Folk Music: The Collections and Writings of Moshe Beregovski,* Mark Slobin, ed. (Philadelphia: University of Pennsylvania Press, 1982).

Eisenstein, Judith Kaplan. *Heritage of Music: The Music of the Jewish People* (New York: Union of American Hebrew Congregations, 1972).

Goldin, Max. *On Musical Connections between Jews and the Neighboring Peoples of Eastern and Western Europe* (Amherst: University of Massachusetts Press, 1989).

Hoffman, Eva. *Shtetl* (Boston: Houghton Mifflin, 1997).

Howe, Irving. *World of Our Fathers* (New York: Harcourt Brace Jovanovich, 1976).

Idelsohn, Abraham Z. *Jewish Music in Its Historical Development* (New York: Schocken, 1929).

Lange, Nicholas de, ed. *The Illustrated History of the Jewish People* (New York: Harcourt Brace & Company, 1997).

Lifson, David. *The Yiddish Theatre in America* (New York: Yoseloff, 1965).

Neugroschel, Joachim, trans. and ed. *The Shtetl* (New York: Perigee, 1982).

Pasachoff, Naomi, and Robert J. Littman. *Jewish History in One Hundred Nutshells* (Northvale, New Jersey: Jason Aronson, 1995).

Peretz, I. L. *The I. L. Peretz Reader* (New York: Schocken, 1990).

Roskies, Diane K., and David G. Roskies. *The Shtetl Book* (New York: Ktav, 1975).

Rubin, Joel. *Mazltov!: Jewish-American Wedding Music from the Repertoire of Dave Tarras* (Mainz, Germany: Schott, 1998).

Rubin, Ruth. *Voices of a People: The Story of Yiddish Folk Song* (New York: McGraw Hill, 1973).

Sachar, Howard Morley. *The Course of Modern Jewish History* (New York: Delta, 1977).

Sapoznik, Henry. *The Compleat Klezmer* (Cedarhurst, N.Y.: Tara, 1907).

Sendrey, Alfred. *The Music of the Jews in the Diaspora* (New York: Yoseloff, 1970).

Sendrey, Alfred, and Mildred Norton. *David's Harp: The Story of Music in Biblical Times* (New York: New American Library, 1964).

Shiloah, Amnon. *Jewish Music Traditions* (Detroit: Wayne State University Press, 1992).

Slobin, Mark. *Tenement Songs* (Urbana: University of Illinois, 1982).

Wisse, Ruth, ed. *A Shtetl and Other Yiddish Novellas* (Detroit: Wayne State University Press, 1986).

Zborowski, Mark, and Elizabeth Herzog. *Life Is with People: The Culture of the Shtetl* (New York: Schocken, 1952).

## Liner Notes

Alpert, Michael. *In the Fiddler's House* (Angel, 1995).

Alpert, Michael et al. *Klezmer Music: A Marriage of Heaven and Earth* (Ellipsis Arts, 1996).

Alpert, Michael, Joel Rubin, and Michael Schlesinger. *Dave Tarras: Master of Klezmer Music, Vol. 1* (Global Village, 1989).

Bjorling, Kurt, and Michael Schlesinger. *Abe Schwartz: Master of Klezmer Music* (Global Village, 1998).

Feldman, Walter Zev. *Alicia Svigals: Fidl* (Traditional Crossroads, 1997).

Frigyesi, Judit. *Maramaros: The Lost Jewish Music of Transylvania* (Hannibal, 1993).

Herrman, Christoph. *The Soul of Klezmer* (Network, 1998).

Horowitz, Joshua. *Budowitz: Mother Tongue* (Koch/Schwann, 1997).

Rubin, Joel. *Patterns of Jewish Life* (Spectrum/Wergo, 1993).

———. *Shteygers* (Trikont, 1995).

———. *Yikhes* (Trikont, 1995).

———. *Beregovski's Khasene* (Weltmusik, 1997).

Rubin, Joel, and Joshua Horowitz, *Bessarabian Symphony* (Spectrum/Wergo, 1994).

Rubin, Joel, and Rita Ottens. *Doyres* (Trikont, 1995).

Sapoznik, Henry. *Jakie Jazz 'Em Up* (Global Village, 1984).

———. *Klezmania* (Shanachie, 1987).

———. *Dave Tarras: Yiddish-American Klezmer Music 1925–56* (Yazoo, 1992).

———. *Naftule Brandwein: King of the Klezmer Clarinet* (Rounder, 1997).

Sapoznik, Henry, and Peter Sokolow. *Klezmer Plus!: Old Time Yiddish Dance Music* (Flying Fish, 1991).

Sapoznik, Henry, and Dick Spottswood. *Klezmer Pioneers: European and American Recordings 1905–52* (Rounder, 1993).

Schwartz, Dr. Martin. *Klezmer Music: Early Yiddish Instrumental Music 1908–27* (Arhoolie/Folklyric, 1997).

Spottswood, Dick. *The Art of the Cymbalom: The Music of Joseph Moskowitz 1916–53* (Rounder, 1996).

# Credits

## TEXT

*Bazetsnish* lyrics in chapter one excerpted from *Voices of a People* by Ruth Rubin. © 1963. Thomas Yoseloff, Publisher, New York, New York. Reprinted by permission of the publisher.

Parts of chapter four were adapted from "The Klezmatics: Revitalizing Their Roots" by Seth Rogovoy. *Sing Out!*, Volume 43, #3, Winter 1999. © 1999 *Sing Out*. Reprinted by permission of the publisher.

"Berlin 1990," lyrics by Michael Alpert; music by Michael Alpert, Alan Bern, Kurt Bjorling, Stuart Brotman. © 1994 JA/NEIN Musikverlag GmbH + Pinorrekk Musikverlag (GEMA). Recorded by Brave Old World on the album *Beyond the Pale* (Pinorrekk/Red House Records). Used by permission.

## PHOTOGRAPHS

p. 16 (Old man in crowd): Courtesy YIVO Institute for Jewish Research

p. 23 (*kapelye*, with violins): Courtesy YIVO Institute for Jewish Research

p. 33 (wedding photo): Courtesy YIVO Institute for Jewish Research

p. 34 (wedding painting): Courtesy Mishkan Le'Omanut, Museum of Art, Ein Harod

p. 58 (Abe Schwartz sheet): Courtesy The National Yiddish Book Center

p. 60 (Naftule Brandwein with band guy): Courtesy Henry Sapoznik

p. 61 (Older Brandwein): Courtesy Henry Sapoznik

p. 64 (Tarras as a boy): Courtesy Center for Traditional Music and Dance

p. 68 (Older Tarras): Photograph by Martin Koenig, courtesy Center for Traditional Music and Dance

p. 79 (The Klezmorim): Courtesy The Klezmorim

p. 84 (Andy Statman): © Lloyd Wolf

p. 92 (Kapelye): Courtesy Kapelye

p. 97 (Netsky and Bern): © Clemens Kalischer

p. 98 (KCB): Courtesy The Klezmer Conservatory Band

p. 102 (Netsky and Byron): © Clemens Kalischer

p. 111 (Brave Old World): Photograph by Katarzyna Zajda, courtesy Brave Old World

p. 115 (Klezmatics, all three photos): © Lloyd Wolf

p. 125 (Perlman): © Lloyd Wolf

p. 132 (NOKAS): © Lloyd Wolf

p. 138 (Krakowski): Photograph by Mel Freilich, courtesy Kame'a Media

p. 143 (King Django): © Dennis Renshaw

p. 147 (John Zorn): © Enid Farber

p. 157 (Krakauer): © Lloyd Wolf

p. 160 (Naftule's Dream): ©Kirstin M. Gray

# Index

Note: Page numbers in italics refer to illustrative material.

klezmer: *(continued)*
  connection between instrumental and
    vocal music, 11, 44
  definitions of, 7–9, 12
  as music for listening and reflection, 35,
    40
  musicians drawn to, 10, 13, 15, 32, 83,
    87, 125, 127–28, 134
  as party or dance music, 35, 67
*Klezmer Celebration,* 101
Klezmer Conservatory Band (KCB), 9,
    96–102, *98,* 108, 117, 124, 126, 158
  recordings, 96–97, 101–2, 193–95
*klezmer-loshn,* 54
*Klezmer Madness!,* 5
*Klezmer Music* (Brave Old World
    recording), 110–11
*Klezmer Music* (Statman recording,
    1983), 88
*Klezmer Music 1910–27: The First
    Recordings,* 49
*Klezmer Music: 1910–42,* 92
*Klezmer Pioneers: European and American
    Recordings, 1905–52,* 49
Klezmer Plus!, 104, 195
klezmer renaissance, 12–13, 74, 107–34
klezmer revival, 12, 63, 75–105, 129
  reasons for, 6–7, 75–76
*Klezmer Suite,* 88
Klezmokum, 195–96
*Klezmology,* 133
klezmorim, 9
  character of, 17–20
  freelance nature of, 27
  guilds, 23–24, 32–33
  as hereditary caste, 20, 26, 71
  inability to read music, 54, 62
  opportunities in America, 54–55
  permitted professions for Jews of
    medieval Europe, 23
  regulation of European, 24–25
  social status of, 27, 54
  *see also individual musicians*

Klezmorim, The, 76–82, *79,* 93–94, 103,
    108, 129, 153
  recordings, 77, 81–82, 196–97
*kneytshn,* 44
Knitting Factory, 2, 6, 114, 124, 162–63
  "Cyber-Seder," 162
  "Jewsapalooza" festival, 162
  Knitting Factory label, 124, 163
*kolomeyka,* 47
Kol Simcha, 198
Konitz, Lee, 153
*kozachok,* 47
Kozlowski, Leopold, 60, 198–99
Krakauer, David, 4, 11, 117, 119, 150, 155,
    *157,* 162, 199–200
Krakowski, Wolf, 135–39, *138,* 200–201
Kramer, 201
Kramtveiss, Itzikl, 58
*krekhtsn,* 44, 71
*Kristallnacht,* 162
"Kristallnacht," 149–50
Kroke, 63, 134, 201
Kronos Quartet, 148
Krupa, Gene, 73
Kushner, Sy, 95, 202
Kushner, Tony, 120
Kuzma, Nora, 133


Lacy, Steve, 153, 202
*landsmanshaftn,* 54
La'om, 202–3
*Last Klezmer, The,* 60
Lebedeff, Aaron, 72
"Leena from Palestina," 71
Leess, Howie, 104
Le Grand Klezmer, 203
*leitzim,* 40
  *see also badkhonim*
Lennon, Sean, 161
Les Miserables Brass Band, 119, 158
Letterman, David, 127
Leverett, Margot, 15, 117, 123, 203–4